"This book provides a unique blend of historical scholarship about the origins and development of Social Security and practical suggestions for how Social Security might be reformed to meet its present challenges. The scholarship is impeccable throughout. The author has a strong grasp over the materials related to the history of Social Security and utilizes a very wide range of the philosophical and ethical writing on the subject. Andy Achenbaum is the leading historian of old age, and this book only solidifies his reputation. I have no doubt that the book would be useful to students in such fields as social work, gerontology, public policy and history."

Edward Berkowitz, George Washington University

"Andrew Achenbaum is arguably the most important historian of later life in America we have ever known. With *Safeguarding Social Security for Future Generations* he offers a framework for maintaining the value and vitality of what is arguably the most important social policy innovation we've ever enacted. In the process he's done something just as important; provided a model for "pragmatic, transgenerational" understanding, cooperation, and action, one that couldn't be more timely as this country enters a period of unprecedented age diversity. Buy this book, read it carefully, and use it as a roadmap for creating a better future for all generations."

Marc Freedman, Founder, Encore.org, and author, *How to Live Forever: The Enduring Power of Connecting The Generations*

D1551769

Safeguarding Social Security for Future Generations

This book offers a unique multigenerational approach to saving Social Security. Public programs have adapted to societal aging, but fears overwhelm hopes for Social Security's future prospects. Conservatives want to privatize operations that liberals seek to expand. Younger workers are happy that Social Security protects their elders, but most do not expect benefits when needed. Achenbaum reframes conflicting perspectives and offers new models of respectful transgenerational dialogue that can mobilize pragmatic reforms.

Designed for use in gerontology, social work, and public policy courses, *Safeguarding Social Security for Future Generations* offers measured hope for leaving a legacy that safeguards the common good.

W. Andrew Achenbaum is a semiretired professor of history and gerontology in the Texas Medical Center, Houston. He served as Deputy Director of University of Michigan's Institute of Gerontology and as Professor of history, before he became founding dean of the University of Houston's College of Liberal Arts and Social Sciences. A former board chair of the National Council on Aging, he has received several teaching and public service awards and won the Gerontological Society of America's highest honor, the Kent Lectureship. Achenbaum has published six books, coedited a dozen others, and written more than 200 peer-reviewed articles at the interface of the humanities and aging.

Aging and Society

Edited by Carroll L. Estes and Assistant Editor Nicholas DiCarlo

This pioneering series of books creatively synthesizes and advances key, intersectional topics in gerontology and aging studies. Drawing from changing and emerging issues in gerontology, influential scholars combine research into human development and the life course; the roles of power, policy, and partisanship; race and ethnicity; inequality; gender and sexuality; and cultural studies to create a multi-dimensional and essential picture of modern aging.

Aging A – Z
Concepts toward Emancipatory Gerontology (2019)
Carroll L. Estes with Nicholas DiCarlo

The Privatization of Care
The Case of Nursing Homes (2020)
Pat Armstrong, Hugh Armstrong et al.

Age and the Research of Sociological Imagination
Power, Ideology, and the Life Course (2021)
Dale Dannefer

When Strangers Become Family
The Role of Civil Society in Addressing the Needs of Aging Populations (2021)
Ronald Angel and Verónica Montes-de-Oca Zavala

Safeguarding Social Security for Future Generations
Leaving a Legacy in an Aging Society
W. Andrew Achenbaum

For more information about this series, please visit: https://www.routledge.com/Aging-and-Society/book-series/AGINGSOC

Safeguarding Social Security for Future Generations

Leaving a Legacy in an Aging Society

W. Andrew Achenbaum

Routledge
Taylor & Francis Group

NEW YORK AND LONDON

Cover image: © Shutterstock

First published 2023
by Routledge
605 Third Avenue, New York, NY 10158

and by Routledge
4 Park Square, Milton Park, Abingdon, Oxon OX14 4RN

Routledge is an imprint of the Taylor & Francis Group, an informa business

© 2023 W. Andrew Achenbaum

British Library Cataloguing-in-Publication Data
A catalogue record for this book is available from the British Library

Library of Congress Cataloging-in-Publication Data
Names: Achenbaum, W. Andrew, author.
Title: Safeguarding social security for future generations :
leaving a legacy in an aging society / W. Andrew Achenbaum.
Description: Abingdon, Oxon ; New York, NY : Routledge, 2023. |
Includes bibliographical references and index.
Identifiers: LCCN 2022043986 | ISBN 9781032386355 (hardback) |
ISBN 9781032386348 (paperback) | ISBN 9781003345985 (ebook)
Subjects: LCSH: Social security–United States. |
Generations–United States.
Classification: LCC HD7125 .A33 2023 |
DDC 368.4/300973–dc23/eng/20221214
LC record available at https://lccn.loc.gov/2022043986

ISBN: 978-1-032-38635-5 (hbk)
ISBN: 978-1-032-38634-8 (pbk)
ISBN: 978-1-003-34598-5 (ebk)

DOI: 10.4324/9781003345985

Typeset in Bembo
by Newgen Publishing UK

To my wife, Barbara Lewis, and grandchildren Tabitha and Luke Harris

with love

Contents

Acknowledgments   xi

Introduction   1

PART 1
**Communication gaps across generational
perspectives**   **7**

1   Can Baby Boomers leave a meaning-filled legacy to
     Millennials?   9

2   Social-Security myths in an age of misinformation
     and big lies   24

3   Why history matters when interpreted pragmatically
     and humbly   35

4   Risks, rights, and responsibilities under Social Security   43

PART 2
**A senior historian's evolving interpretations
of Social Security**   **61**

5   The significance of the 1983 Social-Security
     amendments   65

6   Conservatives create a different historical context for
    Social Security   75

7   Will fears over a pandemic, a fractured political
    economy, and racism stir new hopes and demands for
    Social-Security reforms?   88

PART 3
**Rethinking Social Security in order to
become change agents**   **105**

8   Changing within myself to better relate to others   107

9   Negotiating solidarity, sustainability, and stewardship
    under Social Security   119

Conclusion   137

   Appendix 1   150
   Appendix 2   158
   Index   167

Acknowledgments

I owe a tremendous debt to my decades-long friend and colleague Harry "Rick" Moody. We started talking in 2008 about the sorts of legacies that we Baby Boomers might leave to our children and grand-children. After Rick and I coauthored a 2014 essay about solidarity, sustainability, and stewardship in addressing environmental issues,[1] we originally planned to write a "Legacy" book that conjoined our respective interests in social insurance and climate change. During the Covid pandemic, however, Rick and I decided to write separate texts for Routledge's audiences. Many of the nuanced and refined ideas here attest to years of phone talks, in which the two of us challenged one another and updated reference materials.

I received important ideas and feedback from friends and colleagues while writing *Safeguarding Social Security for Future Generations: Leaving a Legacy in an Aging Society*. Historian and gerontologist Tom Cole has been offering provocative questions, shrewd recommendations, encouragement, and empathy throughout this project. Toronto-based sociologist Stephen Katz supplied astute commentaries ranging from critiques on U.S. politics, ethics, and observations concerning how we senior academics were aging in disparate ways. Jon Allen, Helen Rose Ebaugh, Matt Estey, Martina Faulkner, Bob Flick, Jeremy Gordon, and John Pack helped me to dig deeper into what "measured hope," "self-conscious fear," and "inter-relational trust" mean. I profited by reliving my mentor Wilbur Cohen's Social-Security experiences and revisiting insights from social-insurance experts Nancy Altman, Robert Ball, Edward Berkowitz, Lenore Epstein Bixby, J. Douglas Brown, Theodore Marmor, Ida Merriam, Alicia Munnell, Robert Myers, and Carolyn Weaver. Members of the Institute for Spirituality and Health and the Consortium on Aging, both in Houston's Texas Medical Center, provided ongoing support, laughs, and technical assistance.

The editorial team at Routledge, especially Dean Birkencamp, kept this project on track. His associate, my invaluable resource guide Carroll Estes, recommended that I delve into websites posted by the National Academy of Social Insurance (NASI). This led in turn to exchanging ideas with its executive director, Bill Arnone and, in 2022, two Zoom conversations with the Academy's summer interns. I am grateful to Eric Kingson, a NASI charter member and co-director of Social Security Works, for alerting me to several factual errors in the text. Lewis Hodder and Jessica Phillips were part of the Routledge team who shepherded me through the publication process. I wish to thank the staff in Routledge's London office and Hemalatha Kandasamy, Sandrine Pricilla and the staff at Newgen for their careful copyediting.

Finally, I owe an enormous debt to my wife Barbara Lewis, who first and foremost shared generous love, as well as time, and space—often having to remind me about what really, really matters in late life. Along with Barbara, I dedicate *Safeguarding Social Security for Future Generations: Leaving a Legacy in an Aging Society* to my grandchildren, Tabitha and Luke. I hope and trust that they and those who follow will be beneficiaries of this program when they need it most.

Note

1   Moody, H. R. and W. A. Achenbaum. 2014. "Solidarity, Sustainability, and Stewardship: Ethics across Generations." *Interpretation*, **18**, 150–158.

Introduction

Safeguarding Social Security for Future Generations: Leaving a Legacy in an Aging Society proposes ways that Baby Boomers can transmit lessons to overlapping generations of Americans about their shared stake in a U.S. colossus. "The third act of life is about the pursuit of wisdom, self-actualization, and leaving some kind of legacy."[1] This Baby Boomer's third act might be my best act, if I offer a persuasive narrative that stimulates readers to think critically about why Social Security matters.

This book neither focuses on legacy-leaving in terms of giving away money and possessions nor encourages individuals to seek happiness in their next phases of life.[2] Instead, the book underscores why U.S. citizens across age groups need to assess the continued value of a program that for decades has provided an income floor for millions of Americans. Should we rally around efforts to sustain Social Security? Do we have time to transform contested ideas and to negotiate pragmatic solutions to preserve and expand this increasingly maligned and ignored institution, which supposedly is going bankrupt in the future? Can the Social Security program remain a building block to refurbish a polarized American democracy? Or, would we be better off right now weaning ourselves from the program? "The discussion is really about politics and values, not about affordability."[3]

Safeguarding Social Security is easier said than done. Having reached the latter stages of life, Baby Boomers are still capable of harvesting the fruits of experience, wisdom, and self-awareness—all necessary in legacy work. I, like many of my peers, appreciate fears that the program will implode before it is needed most. Grandfathers like me have a chance to persuade generations to work together to reclaim and refashion Social Security through "communal, collective" actions, which "reprise, respect, and reactivate the role of government for the

DOI: 10.4324/9781003345985-1

present and precarious future."[4] This book deals with deconstructing sound bites and forecasts that mislead audiences, especially younger ones, about the program's current status and conflicting assessments of the system's future prospects.

I want to join other generations in safeguarding Social Security. The program has never once failed to deliver monthly checks to qualified retirees, individuals with disabilities, and their eligible dependents and survivors. Social Security presently is in good health; a surplus of $10.9 billion in 2020 increased asset reserves to $2.91 trillion.[5] The program, most importantly, embodies a social compact that benefits virtually all working Americans. Fifty-two percent of U.S. workers who contribute payroll (FICA) taxes count on the program providing an income floor for their parents and grandparents.

Yet we cannot overlook countervailing data. Gallup polls indicate that less than half of those surveyed are counting on Social Security being a significant portion of their retirement portfolio. A vast majority of Americans expect significant shortfalls in the inter-generational arrangements over the next 25 years.[6] Headlines convey dire warnings that alarm Social-Security contributors and beneficiaries. Whenever commentators sensationalize forecasts of an impending fiscal crisis, new rounds of angst spread about the Social Security system leaving people empty-handed.[7]

As an historian of aging who has studied Social-Security policymaking for four decades, I know that both disinformation and expert opinions fuel crisis-thinking about the program. In their 2022 report, a *Washington Post* editorial declared, Social Security Trustees "projected a fiscal calamity on a generational scale. And yet fixing the problems are on just about no one's to-do list in Washington. That is a scandal, and Americans—particularly young Americans who stand to lose the most—should demand better."[8] This commentary raises questions by intimating a disaster-in-the-making. What happens if Social Security stops delivering benefits to nearly 60 million Americans—roughly a fifth of the U.S. population?[9] Can Social Security survive in an aging, deeply divided society grappling with major provocations here and abroad?

I invite readers of different ages—ones with dissimilar life histories, varied perspectives and distinctive experiences—to collaborate in rethinking our complementary, inter-generational commitments to safeguarding Social Security. It is important for us to assess the program's effectiveness in a disinterested manner. We must evaluate Social Security's often overlooked restorative usefulness as the United States confronts a relentless pandemic, unsettling revelations about racism, insurrections, domestic gun violence, and humiliations abroad. "We are two countries, and neither of them is going to disappear soon."[10] More than 80% of Americans believe that we are more divided now than in the 1970s.[11] Extremist media gurus warn that a fierce second Civil War will be waged not on battlefields, but among citizens in red states and blue ones.

This book argues that we can empower ourselves to be resilient agents of change. Despite four decades of lawmakers avoiding serious talk about Social Security, it is not too late to determine how the program fits into a broader context of societal virtues and mores. Nonetheless, we must acknowledge limits to Social Security's capacity to heal piercing wounds and institutional dysfunctions that currently fester in gamesmanship, falsehoods, and mistrust.

This book applies lessons of U.S. history as questions with which we can weigh Social Security's present status and future value. First, will U.S. citizens embrace hopeful and strategic steps to ensure the program's renewal? Or, second, will Americans defer action on Social Security because we remain preoccupied with hyper-partisan politics, difficult international alliances, and delays in reversing climate change? Or, third, will we diminish expectations, and choose to untether connections between Social-Security policymaking and promises and challenges associated with societal aging?

All three scenarios are possible because facets of American democracy feed one another, interacting in realms we do not fully apprehend. It so often seems beyond our control to curb worldwide inflation, defend women's rights, and end genocide. But we should not let these issues deflect or impede clear reasoning about Social Security, an institution that nowadays attracts mainly doomsday headlines predicting its undoing and demise.

I hope readers listen to this Baby Boomer historian as I draw analogies about Social Security's status in America linked to metaphors of human development and decline. When the founding fathers created a "young Republic" out of a "virgin land," half the U.S. population had not reached puberty. By 2035 there will be more Americans over age 65 than under 18.[12] Is demography a destiny that subsumes Social Security's maturation under the umbrella of societal aging? Is the United States, a nation of elders, moving toward its "grand climacteric" that tolerates sclerotic political leaders and scales down the ambitions of rising generations?

Baby Boomers can leave a transgenerational legacy about Social Security, one grounded in an historical, societal context that leaves room for critical thinking and strategic collective action across age lines. Older Americans like me want to bestow a healthful quality of life—one presumed unattainable even a few decades ago—to rising generations who will outlive us. This book contextualizes widespread concerns over the program's development, current sustainability, and future value. (See Appendix 1 to learn more about Social-Security keywords and basic operations.) This book proposes neither cutting benefits nor privatizing the system. It *does* attempt to elucidate how Social Security touches Americans' emotional lives, situating them within a troubled nation's soul. Assessing its institutional value in binding together in a polarized political economy does not rest on fiscal solutions alone. But of course Social Security's success in providing an income floor deserves serious scrutiny.

For nearly 90 years Social Security has radically reduced old-age poverty. The percentage of Americans over age 65 living in dire straits has fallen from 67% during the Great Depression to 9.3% today. In the course of Social Security's development, virtually all Americans have gained benefits because they can claim a stake in the system. With an administrative efficiency rarely matched in the private sector, Social Security allocates monthly checks to 46 million retired workers and their dependents who receive $1,400 in average monthly checks. In addition, Social Security assists three million children under the age of 18. Nine million contributors and their spouses are covered under its Disability Insurance program.

Unfortunately, too few of the program's contributors and beneficiaries understand that Social Security is an inter-generational compact based on mutual interdependence and fair play. The Federal program transfers benefits far greater than sums that individual workers paid into the system to provide an income floor that reduces poverty risks. Meanwhile, far too many Americans listen to political commentators fretting over Social Security's putatively depleted reserves. In an effort to advance communication among stakeholders, this book assesses both gloomy projections and auspicious forecasts about Social Security's sustainability.

This book also pays considerable attention to workers' bread-and-butter questions regrettably left hanging sometimes by incumbent officials and many commentators. Is the program as fair to women, minorities, and young low-income workers as it is to white-collar senior citizens? Will wage earners with crushing student debts, who are now starting out in a tight labor market, receive benefits that truly approximate Baby Boomers' current levels? Are middle-aged

Social-Security contributors of getting shortchanged in retirement because they saved too little and their private pension plans implode?

This book has three parts. The first section argues that myths and misinformation foster communications gaps that can partly be bridged by analyzing historical facts. Part 2 describes how this senior scholar has changed his perceptions and interpretations of Social Security over the decades, especially nowadays as Americans struggle under a pandemic and confront polarizing divisions over politics and values. The last section recounts how I came to listen more carefully to diverse audiences before I revamped my message to peers and overlapping age groups.

This book offers a counternarrative for rethinking the program. The book's first takeaway declares that all thoughtful Americans—policy experts, idea brokers, lawmakers, commentators, and ordinary citizens of all ages—need to reject the dichotomy between rosy forecasts and doomsday scenarios. Dualistic thinking engenders the spread of mistruths and distrust. Open-ended, reasoned, and respectful debate, in contrast, can clarify oppositional ideas and, ideally, engender fresh option.

The second takeaway in this book is that developing pragmatic, transgenerational dialogues will engender grassroots mobilizations for reconfiguring Social Security. Contributors and beneficiaries should not expect policy experts and elected officials to do all the hard work. Ideally, safeguarding Social Security for future generations empowers all of us to discover better approach to leaving a legacy in an aging society. Baby Boomers like me should not pretend to have the last word, but this grandfather has a visceral stake in helping to guide choices about Social Security that Americans have to make.

Notes

1 Samuel, Larry. 2021, February 25. "Older adults embrace 'third act' concept of retirement." *Wall Street Journal.*
2 Sharpton, Tatyana. 2021, January 30. "Rabbi Zalman Schacter-Shalomi's bold mystical journey on Judaism, and Boulder." *BLDRfly.*
3 Kingson, Eric. 2022. Quoted in Hiltzik, Michael. 2022, June 7. "Column." *L.A. Times.*
4 Estes, Carroll L. 2020. "Social insurance: Proof of concept." In *The Future of Social Insurance,* ed. Thomas N. Bethell. Washington, DC: National Academy of Social Insurance, 22.
5 Social Security Administration. August 2021. "Summary: Actuarial Status of the Social Security Trust Funds." ssa.gov/policy/trust-funds.

6 News.gallup.com/poll/1693/social.security.aspx.

7 Center for Retirement Research at Boston College. October 7, 2021. "Headlines sway perception of Social Security." https://squarewayblog. bc.eu/squared-away/headlines-sway-perception-of-social-security/.

8 Editorial Board. 2022, June 4. "Opinion: The Medicare and Social Security disaster that Washington is doing nothing to fix." *Washington Post.*

9 Office of Retirement and Disability Policy. 2021. "Fast Facts & Figures about Social Security, 2021. ssa.gov/policy/docs/ch.

10 Packer, George. 2020. "Face the brutal truth." www.theatlantic.com/ ideas/archive/2020/11/there's-no-escaping-who-we-have-become/ 616992/.

11 AP-NORC [The Associated Press-NORC Center for Public Affairs Research]. 2017. "Divided America: Perceptions of what unites and divides the country;" Politics. November 4, 2021. "We've Been on the Wrong Track Since 1972." *Daily Beast.* www.thedailybeast.com/ we've-been-on-the-wrong-track-since-1972.

12 Vespa, Jonathan. 2019. "The graying of America." Washington, D.C.: U.S. Census Bureau.

Part I

Communication gaps across generational perspectives

Safeguarding Social Security for Future Generations: Leaving a Legacy in an Aging Society entails upholding the continuation, stabilization, and healthfulness of "the reciprocal social compact between governments and promised guaranteed earned benefits to which we contribute across our lifetimes and generations."[1] Social Security, the distinctively American version of social-insurance programs around the world, covers risks through Federal Insurance Contribution Act (FICA) payroll taxes paid into the system by employees and employers. In return, millions of retirees, disabled persons, and their survivors and dependents receive monthly checks issued by the Social Security Administration. Virtually all Americans can rely on Social Security to set an income floor that mitigates risks in an aging society.[2]

Part 1 of this book sets out the conceptual framework for initiating effective transgenerational conversations about Social Security's aims, myths, and evolving developments. The four chapters in this section weave together key concepts and themes that provoke critical thinking. This will help us put the program into the context of continuities and changes in United States since Social Security's enactment in 1935.

Notes

1 Estes, Carroll L. 2020. "Social insurance: Proof of concept." In *The Future of Social Insurance*, ed. Thomas N. Bethel. Washington, DC: National Academy of Social Insurance, 23.
2 See Appendix 1 for a fuller synopsis of Social Security's keywords and operations.

DOI: 10.4324/9781003345985-2

Can Baby Boomers leave a meaning-filled legacy to Millennials?

Introduction

The challenge of balancing distinctive age groups' preferences and needs is formidable because of communication gaps between Baby Boomers and younger generations that reflect differences in life experiences. Most Americans over 65 already are receiving Social Security if they are qualified. Millennials and rising generations are mostly willing to provide an income floor for their parents and grandparents, but few younger contributors expect Social Security to be there for them if they are disabled or when retired. Millennials' perceptions of Social Security overwhelm their trusting that the program is viable.

Their fears are not chimerical. Unlike their elders, younger FICA contributors have not witnessed programmatic changes that have adapted Social Security to deal with the promises and paradoxes of societal aging.[1] That there has been no major Social-Security reforms since 1983, moreover, creates a historically constructed time lag. No wonder many Millennials, whose careers seem less fruitful than their parents', anticipate to outlive the system.

How can I, a Baby Boomer, leave a legacy that persuades audiences that it is not too late to safeguard Social Security? Do members of my generation listen to younger people and deliver fresh ideas in keywords to forge a message that makes resonates with self-interests within and across generations? After all, it is up to U.S. citizens born after 1980 to enunciate their concerns and fears so that policy analysts and lawmakers ensure that Social Security is there for them.

"Each age, it is found, must write its own books; or rather each generation for the succeeding," declared Ralph Waldo Emerson in 1837, with this caveat: "The books of an older era will not fit this."[2]

DOI: 10.4324/9781003345985-3

Emerson's essay, "The American Scholar," was first issued in a pamphlet that sold out within a month. Antebellum readers knew that creating a distinctive U.S. cultural identity required citizens to have literacy in reading and writing sufficient to intrigue and persuade overlapping generations to share ideas and to participate in nation-building.

Historical literacy trends in the United States

More than 60% of men and 33% of women in New England were literate between 1650 and 1670. Waves of New-World settlers relied on natural intelligence and rudimentary learning.[3] Benjamin Franklin, who in 1731 founded the first free-lending public Library Company of Philadelphia, opined that "if you would not be forgotten as soon as you are dead and rotten, either write something worth reading or do something worth writing."[4] DuPont de Nemours in 1800 boasted that only four in a thousand Whites could not read or write.[5]

Various associations in 19th-century America promoted transgenerational literacy. The lyceum movement spread to frontier towns; middle-class Americans gathered in Chautauqua assemblies. Public and private schools, which taught the three "r"s to antebellum youth, were by 1870 instructing nearly seven million children in elementary schools and another 80,000 in secondary schools.[6]

Literacy rates also rose over time among segments of disenfranchised Americans. Moral guides, magazines, and cookbooks catered to female audiences.[7] Although 80% of former slaves were illiterate in 1870, compared to 20% of the entire U.S. adult population,[8] the racial gap narrowed as Black writers and speakers enthralled African American communities. Waves of immigrants had to learn English or endure prejudice if they failed to assimilate.

Did changing literary benchmarks prompt the current generation gap?

U.S. literacy rates since 1930 have hovered around 70%. There were noticeable gaps, according to reports issued in the 2010s, among Hispanics, households earning less than $30,000, and individuals with low education who constituted most of America's nonreading population.[9] Children with parents who post poor literacy levels have a 72% chance of falling themselves into the lowest reading levels.[10]

Increased use of digital media has redefined what "literacy" connotes. Internet rates doubled among high-school students between 2006 and 2016; that correlated with data that teenagers were spending less time reading.[11] Those born in the United States after 1980 scored lower than 15 of 22 countries assessed for proficiency in literacy, math skills, and problem-solving.

Has the social media been widening a generational literacy gap? The evidence is mixed. Older Americans "cannot fail to notice how quickly … the young take from the media as casually as one might pick an orange from a fruit stand," opined a best-selling author over the age of 60, who noted that "cultural fluency and ease of access to the whole planet brings with it no guarantee of either talent or depth."[12] A Duke sociologist, who started a "Polarization Lab" in 2017, however, argued that "social media gives us much more to present carefully curated versions of ourselves."[13]

As America has become increasingly diverse and longer-lived, the goal of safeguarding Social Security does not necessarily have to devolve into generational warfare. We nonetheless have to break down barriers to discussions across overlapping age groups. This communication gap reflects and results from disparate socioeconomic circumstances and widening isolation and separateness across cohorts. This generational disconnect has precedents in recent U.S. history: My peers and I remember shouting matches with our parents over love and war during the 1960s. In leaving a fruitful legacy for our children and grandchildren, we elders must bear in mind that our offspring do not experience the world that we encountered. Estrangements occur whenever new historical contexts arise.

This book must listen to and address the needs of rising U.S. generations. Younger workers voice dissimilar hopes and fears concerning how Americans within and across birth cohorts can survive as novel, inchoate patterns polarize politics and values. Baby Boomers must acknowledge that misunderstandings and stereotypic differences are not driven solely by social-media jeremiads—although panic today can create subsequent bad decisions.

Laying out dimensions of transgenerational communication gaps, the rest of this chapter delves into various concepts of "age" and "generation." We shall pay attention to the role that social media plays. Besides affecting literacy rates, the internet and networks accentuate differences in the ways ideas are processed, thereby dissolving the mortar that unites Americans.[14]

Today's misunderstanding and stereotypic thinking about relations across age groups hamper attempts to leave transgenerational legacies

Mistrust and anxieties fester within and across generational lines. Baby Boomers worry that they will outlive their wits, pensions, and Medicare benefits. Millennials are apprehensive about securing and keeping jobs that will enable them to pay off college debts, buy homes, and plan ahead. The duration of Covid-19, which has killed more than a million Americans and disabled countless more, led to culture wars over vaccinations, raised urban crime rates, and increased substance-abuse deaths. All age groups risked being victims of disinformation and suffering. Political discord was further fanned by myths and rhetorical hype about abortion race and immigration.[15] Partisan differences widened over Social Security.

"When everything becomes political, that is the end of politics," observes Moshe Halbertal, a philosopher at Hebrew University in Jerusalem. "For healthy politics to flourish it needs reference points outside itself—reference points of truth and a conception of the common good."[16] Reference points are essential in safeguarding Social Security. Legacies are passed around, not just passed down. Not only do legacies transcend boundaries of time, place, and space, but their multidirectionality also fosters different ways of knowing.[17]

Some social scientists and gerontological investigators rely on measures that probe the edges of human reasoning.[18] Yet ignorance, gut feelings, and imagination, are filtered through prisms that by turns solidify intrapersonal differences and undercut the interplay between hopes and fears. To gauge whatever extent objective truth can be verified, in my opinion, inquiries must balance dystonic elements within rationality and emotionality. Exaggerated hopes can blind people to risk complacency. Acting on traumatic fears may result in reckless consequences.[19]

A plausible reference point with which to frame safeguarding Social Security would be to highlight the importance of *class*. I seriously considered that option, but chose instead to contextualize this book in terms of *generational* transformations. When situated along with individual life stories and historical events, similarities within age groups (and differences between them) affect how Baby Boomers engage in leaving legacies for our progeny. "Tumultuous times historically awaken generational awareness," posits Bobby Duffy, who directs the

Policy Institute at King's College, London. "They are connected to our desire to see our children, and their children, do better than we did."[20]

Generational frameworks help us to understand our hopes and fears about safeguarding Social Security for present and rising age groups. A generation gap has created a fault line in U.S. politics.[21] Understanding the causes and consequences of age-based divisions creates a template that underscores the impact of racial and economic inequalities, rancid politics, and Covid-related health threats. To convey legacy-leaving in terms of transgenerational discourse. this book elicits a review of concepts associated with the keyword, *generation*.[22] We can begin to reformulate our rethinking by revisiting a major article on "The Problem of Generations."

Updating Karl Mannheim's "The Problem of Generations" (1939)

Clarifying both hope-filled visions and fear-driven tensions across generational boundaries is a perplexing task. Much in Karl Mannheim's 1939 essay on "The Problem of Generations," remains salient and useful, however:

> Whether a new *generation style* emerges every year, every thirty, every hundred years, or whether it emerges rhythmically at all, depends entirely on the trigger action of the social and cultural process … It is quite impossible either to limit or to count intellectual generations (generation units) except as articulations of certain overall trends.[23]

Dialogues across generational constructs are grounded within specific historical, multidimensional, societal processes the German sociologist analyzed. They are building blocks that interconnect the locations and sources that bind generations together and situate perspective in opposition.[24]

I have updated "The Problem of Generations" to contextually frame *Safeguarding Social Security for Future Generations*. Mannheim postulated that older people constituted a demographically large and largely untapped resource for mobilizing diverse groups to redress a host of societal ills. This remains the case in a divided America today, in which young citizens often underestimate much value in elders leaving a Social-Security legacy. Baby Boomers must enter transgenerational dialogues with reconfigured messages and lessons that feed different age groups' imaginations. They must persuade and empower younger people to use ideas and talents in aligning the program to societal demands.

Mannheim's treatment of "the problem of generation," I know, has become problematic over time. Subsequent researchers posit that "generation" is a methodologically flawed, atheoretical meme. Gerontologists as well as social and bench scientists wrestle with statistical strategies for differentiating multicollinear age–period–cohort effects. Investigators rarely systematize the interplay of generational forces on U.S politics, economy and culture.[25]

Poll data indicate that economic disparities between parents and children determine U.S. age-based ideological gaps more significantly than attitudinal differences.[26] There is currently little pushback in culture wars. Few advocacy group besides Generations United focuses the media on the value of young and old working together as did Maggie Kuhn's Gray Panthers decades ago.[27]

Theoretical, methodological, and political critiques mount generational concepts in safeguarding Social Security. So do transactions in human nature. "The passage of time brings us inescapably to the realization that humans are designed to pass the torch from generation to generation," argues Marc Freedman, who for three decades has forged coalitions between older and younger persons.[28] More than Mannheim articulated in "The Problem of Generations," population aging now coalesces with the political economy and transactional bonds of an aging society's institutions and networks.[29]

Transgenerational bonds, intergenerational wounds, intragenerational fights

Deploying a transgenerational construct can clarify countervailing albeit synergistic forces of aging and diversity. In the United States, individuals in the latter stages of life enjoy comparative economic well-being. Baby Boomers' longevities give elders opportunities to have illuminating dialogues and interactive bonds with younger citizens. Millions of Millennials are poised, if not enthusiastic, to engage in transgenerational conversations that emulate dinner-table banter.[30]

Imagining fruitful talks through this lens nurtures optimism about what older and younger Americans are able to accomplish. Choosing to think and act together fulfills W. H. Auden's insight that "we're all contemporaries, facing contemporary problems."[31] It attests to what

U.S. citizens personally and collectively can do to safeguard Social Security, if we are inclined to tolerate individuated opinions and disentangle oppositional stratagems.

To forge transgenerational bonds in the context of overlapping age groups linking Social Security to uncertain pitfalls that accompany societal aging differs from perpetuating structural racism or tainted by essentialist gender roles. Nor are generational transactions necessarily as meritocratic as class markers that give citizens with high salaries and abundant wealth access to power denied to employees with lower incomes and status.

Race and ethnicity, gender and sexual identities as well as class and education status obviously intersect generational dynamics. So do factors (such as region and religion) that embody contrapuntal, underestimated, or overlooked vectors. "The *formal sociological* phenomenon can be of help in so far as we may possibly learn from what can and what cannot be attributed to the generation factor," Mannheim argued.[32] These historical, societal elements now impinge upon transgenerational bonds, intergenerational wounds, and intragenerational disagreements that will persist in future uncertainties.

Intergenerational transitions and successions are messy. Replicating neither Oedipal conflicts nor clashes between parents and youth during the 1960s, population aging reshapes generational conflicts. The number of Americans over 65 will double in decades. Millennials, the gateway to a more diverse polity, are coping with nattering circumstances that my generation mostly managed to survive: Younger, poorly educated Whites dread losing jobs and status to immigrants and minorities.[33] Incommensurate experiences compound transgenerational misunderstanding.

On many fronts, Millennials face disadvantageous circumstances compared to Baby Boomers. The percentage of respondents worried about finances, by cohort, underlies the disparities: In 2017, 34.6% of Baby Boomers compared to 52.5% of Millennials were concerned about making ends meet each month. Roughly 40% of the older cohort compared to 68% of the younger one had to pay off debts. A third of all Millennials surveyed feared losing their jobs. Home ownership at age 30 for these two subsets has fallen from 48.3% to 35.8%.[34]

In terms of safeguarding Social Security, whatever legacy Baby Boomers hope to leave Millennials must take account of differences in the two age groups' expectations and life stories. Poverty rates among seniors without Social Security was estimated to be 39%; with this income floor, the incidence fell to 9%. Child poverty stood at 16.7%

in 2022.[35] The percentage of working age households that are at risk of being unable to maintain their standards of living rose from 30% in the 1980s to over 50% in the 2010s. Confidence in receiving Social Security retirement benefits among those born before 1956 and those born between 1980 and 2000 has fallen from 66% to 25%.[36]

"Zoomers," the generation born in the late-1990s and before 2010, also will express opinions and concerns about safeguarding Social Security. Their voices increasingly will reflect experiences and expectations distinct from Millennials and different from Baby Boomers.[37] Many of them are students born in the digital era; they are more technologically savvy and dependent than older cohorts. Many identify multiracial backgrounds and fluid sexual orientations in unprecedented numbers. They come from economic strata, faith-based traditions, more markedly varied than previous generations. Surveys of Zoomers' anxieties and behavior indicate that this age group were stressed by factors (such as bullying and sexual harassment), which were exacerbated by the Covid-19 pandemic. Social Security is not on most of their long-term radar.[38]

Population aging and divergent socioeconomic circumstances enkindle stereotypic thinking in intergenerational conversations. "Boomer America never had it so good. As a result today's young Americans have never had it so bad."[39] Youth are predisposed to blame their elders for worsening income inequalities, racial unrest, and political divisions. Millennials resent older Americans still being in charge of public affairs.[40] Many in my generation fail to grasp why our survivor stories do not inspire younger cohorts to strive to attain our life satisfactions.

Misunderstandings boomerang. "A true reckoning with the consequences of Boomer policies and decisions casts a harsh light on the children of the Greatest Generation," wrote Jill Filopovic, Millennial author of *OK, Boomer* (2019). Excoriating "those Boomers who are worried about the world they're leaving their children,"[41] she notes that Baby Boomers failed to stem racial justice or climate warning, and promote gender equality, despite their self-professed idealism.

Much truth lies in such ageist complaints and stereotypic invectives. Baby Boomers *have* fumbled in passing on a better world—one that many Millennials see as crumbling. My generation, getting progressively frail while approaching death, attempt to keep dignity and pride afloat. When we feel disregarded, we cast invidious dispersions and mock the young as "snowflakes." Baby Boomers like me would like to be heard when I have something constructive to say about safeguarding Social Security as a legacy. Semi-retirement grants me extra years to think critically and speak truth with power, but I simultaneously fear and fight obsolescence. Disengagement often reduces workaholics' meaningful activities.[42]

Millennials, too, articulate unpredictable ideas and behaviors as they deal with setbacks. "Young adults once hit the road on a clearly marked path," but there are sharply diverging destinies."[43] Many youthful Republicans are more likely than their parents to support Federal welfare programs and join Black-Lives-Matter protest movements; progressives differentiate themselves ideologically from their libertarian peers. Economically, some lament accidents of birth; others resent poorly paid gig work; and "lucky" ones are ready to escape 90-hour lucrative weeks with brokerage firms. Though some Millennials returned unmarried to parental homes during the pandemic, at least a third of these adult children admit feeling estranged from a parent.[44]

Stereotypical simulacra expose collateral wounds across generational lines. Many septuagenarians are not ready to pass the torch; thirty-somethings cannot wait to take charge. Given differences in life experiences, technological competence, and intersectional rivalries in dark times, Boomers and Millennials rarely prioritize the need for consoling and healing one another.[45] It is hard to let go of competing self-interests in order to discount tensions and work together for the good of all.

Missing so far in this synopsis of generational conflicts that frustrate safeguarding Social Security are two incontrovertible truths. First, while Baby Boomers are not leaving their children a perfect world, my generation did not inherit a perfect world, either.[46] Second, "there are profound difficulties in articulating the contractual nature of intergenerational exchange, which in turn are magnified by attempts to consider the processional nature of justice over time," according to gerontologist Malcolm L. Johnson. "This is the essential conceptual element in the discourse about an intergenerational compact."[47]

The "processional nature" of intergenerational exchange is important, but it is not determinative. Trans/inter/intragenerational trajectories remain fluid because they build on historical precedents in unknown arrangements. Current potentialities and exigencies yield uncertainties and contingencies enveloped in enduring hopes and fears. So Baby Boomers and Millennials sometimes talk at cross-purposes, even as they struggle to listen carefully and to withhold judgments.[48]

Fear and hope complicate effort to communicate lessons in legacy-leaving

Unsettling interactions between fear and hope integrally shape messages of wisdom and experience that Baby Boomers wish to convey in this book. Not surprisingly, at the interstices of hope and fear lie powerful catalysts for generational miscommunication and costly inaction. Renaissance humanist Michel de Montaigne's admission—"The thing I fear most is fear"—rings true.

Baby Boomers feel threatened by domestic violence and international perils, which we have suffered throughout our lifetimes. "In the twentieth century, the idea of universality rests less on hope than on fear, less on optimism about the human capacity for good than on dread of human capacity for evil."[49] Millennials feel blindsided by these and other fears, which manifest themselves in distressing anxieties. All of us contemporaries endure impotence and trauma.[50]

Fears in due course feed distrust in elected officials' willingness and power to reform Social Security. Political maneuvering in Washington seems to displace serving ordinary citizens. Prolonging the politics of avoidance thwarts attempts to negotiate looming policy challenges, such as safeguarding Social Security. Technical language and arcane words that confuse the public. Lawmakers secure reelection by accentuating we/they cleavages that threaten, and then consolidate their base. "People are motivated by anger and fear much more so than positive emotions," declared an architect of the Reagan revolution, a reckoning honed and activated decades later by Donald Trump, Steve Bannon, and Mitch McConnell.[51]

U.S. history offers a counternarrative of hope for leaving a legacy in an aging society, however. "Hope is an embrace of the unknown and unknowable, an alternative to the certainty of both optimists and pessimists,"[52] declared Barack Obama in *Audacity of Hope* (2006). "Maybe there's no escaping our great political divide … Maybe the trivialization of politics has reached a point of new return."[53] The 44th president nevertheless expressed trust in citizens to distinguish common sense from extremists' lies, platitudes, and disinformation.

Balancing optimism and realism in hope while safeguarding Social Security will sustain its time-tested values and efficacious operations. "If the world is to be healed, it will be by ordinary people, people whose love for this life is even greater than their fear."[54] Moving forward will neither embellish hope nor mitigate coexisting fears that hurl us into this country's unknown future. U.S. citizens of all ages must muster willingness and courage to transcend parochial interests and partisan obstacles. Idea brokers and policy architects can renew institutions if they are supported by a transgenerational grassroots movement. That said, any Social-Security reforms will be hammered out and implemented only by discarding myths and falsities in an ambiguous, unfathomable future.

Another way of grasping theories of "generation" is to draw a simple analogy

Conceptualizing and contextualizing generational constructs in a worldview animated by fears and hopes may prove too daunting to convince some readers of this book. Should relying mainly on critical thinking occasion confusion and miscommunication, an intuitive metaphor may open an alternative gateway. Imagine how reconceptualizing and re-executing a transgenerational dialog in order to reform Social Security resembles crew teams competing in a race:

- The crews lined up to be successful differ in background and work histories. Some represent elite colleges, others come from nearby neighborhoods. Several scullers are seasoned professionals; many are well trained amateurs; the rest are novices. *When Social Security was launched, participation was limited to selected groups of workers who differed in age, income, and occupation.*
- Aware of these differences, race officials decided to treat all teams the same way. Rowers on 9-person crews sit port and starboard, assigned positions as either members of (1) a technical class, who keep the boat stable; (2) the powerhouse team, who are strong and fit; or (3) the stroke class which sets the timing. *Just as different-aged crew members must be treated fairly, so did New-Deal architects insist on designing even-handed criteria for potential Social-Security stakeholders.*
- Coxswains shout orders to crews navigating, time trials, and bump racing. The contest is exciting to watch; risks and uncertain outcomes lace the course. *Each race begins, proceeds, and ends in contingencies riven in fears and hopes. The process parallels challenges in launching Social Security, a system designed to determine and distribute retirement benefits justly.*
- The sport has a long history of successions—Egyptians in ancient times using oars to propel sculls were reconstructed to suit standards set by late-18th century boat clubs. The International Racing Federation (1892) instituted rules about crew members'

weight limits and designated where markers pointed to the finish line. *Similarly, Federal officials administer Social Security like coxswains, relying on normative traditions and changing operational conditions that few contributors and beneficiaries understand. Most do not know how experts operate.*

The crew-race analogy illuminates aspects of transgenerational conversations about Social-Security reforms. Coxswains are important in ensuring that scullers and sweepers proceed under criteria set by institutional rules. They are expected to ensure that crews conform to transactional patterns and parameters—all of which are subject to reconfigurations to remedy flaws and ensure fairness.

This book assumes that virtually all Baby Boomers and Millennials want to help our progeny to thrive. We earnestly try to resist temptations to demonize opponents who dare to express realistic, reasonable doubts about what the future may hold. Hopes counterbalance fears in a polarized milieu that capitalizes on divergent interpretations of common values and shared priorities. Advocates and critics of Social-Security reforms can ill afford to dismiss inconvenient headlines and contested truths, while experts, commentators, and concerned stakeholders mask in myths and misinformation how they discern system workings.

Notes

1 Pifer, Alan and Lydia Bronte. 1986. *Our Aging Society.* New York: W. W. Norton.
2 Emerson, Ralph Waldo. 1837. "The American Scholar." Quote 654871. www.goodreads.com.
3 Lockridge, Kenneth A. 1974. *Literacy in Colonial New England.* New York: W. W. Norton.
4 Quotes.net/quote/3816.
5 Reed, Lawrence W. 2020. "The myth that Americans were poorly educated before mass government schooling." Foundation for Economic Education.
6 Snyder, Tom. 1993. National Assessment of Adult Literacy. Washington, D.C.: National Center for Education Statistics.
7 Salice, Barbara. 1988. Women and illiteracy in the U.S. eric.ed.gov.
8 Snyder, National Assessment of Adult Literacy.
9 Perrin, Andrew 2019. "Who doesn't read books in America?" Pew Research Center/fact-tank.

10 Lattier, Daniel. 2016. "Did public schools really improve American literacy?" https://fee.org/articles; Editorial Team. Crisis point: The state of literacy in America.

11 American Psychological Association. 2018. "Teens today spend more time on digital media, less time reading." www.apa.org/news/press/releases/2018/08/teenagers-read-book.

12 McMurtry, Larry. 1999. *Walter Benjamin at the Dairy Queen: Reflections at sixty and beyond*. New York: Simon & Schuster, 80.

13 Heller, Nathan. 2021, July 5. "Togetherness." *The New Yorker*, 52.

14 Haidt, Jonathan. 2022, May. "After Babel." *The Atlantic*.

15 Schmidt, James. 2015. "Rendered most useful." In *Age in America*, ed. Corinne T. Field and Nicholas L. Syrett. New York: New York University Press, 148–165; Harpers Index. 2022, June, 9.

16 Quoted in Lance Ng. 2020. "The end of politics." https://medium.com@lancengym/the-end-of-politics-8b70d55604de.

17 Sasser, Jennifer. 2020, August 16. "Legacy." *Gero-Punk Ponderings*.

18 Pinker, Steven. 2021. *Rationality*. New York: Viking.

19 Hill, Samantha Rose. 2021. "When hope is a hindrance." https://aeon.com/essays/for-arendt-hope-in-dark-times-is-no-match-for-action?utm_source=atom-feed.

20 Duffy, Bobby. 2021. *The Generation Myth*. New York: Basic Books, 4.

21 Munger, Kevin. 2022. *Generation Gap*. New York: Columbia University Press.

22 Marshall, Victor W. 2010. "Generations, age groups, and cohorts: Conceptual distinctions." www.cambridge.org/core/journals/canadian-journal-on-aging.

23 Mannheim, Karl. 1939; reprinted 1972. "The problem of generations." In *Karl Mannheim: Essays*, ed. Paul Kecskemeti. New York: Routledge, 310, 315.

24 www.postkiwi.com/2005/karl-mannheim-on-generational-cohorts.

25 Dannerfer, Dale. 2021. *Age and the Reach of Sociological Imagination*. New York: Routledge, 1–19. Columbia Public Health. (no date). "Age-Period-Cohort Effect Analysis." www.publichealth.columbia.edu/research/population-health-methods/age-period-cohort-analysis; Brink, Kyle E., Zondag, Marcel M. and Jeffrey L. Crenshaw. 2015, October 2. "Generation is a culture construct." www.cambridge.org/core/journals/industrial-and-organizational-psychology/article/abs/generation-is-a-culture-construct/49B6655076ED9D7FE9.

26 Willetts, David. 2021, September 30. "Generations by Bobby Duffy-age concerns." www.ft.com/content/a35fb710-3ideas-4a72-ad71-cc80ca73642a.

27 Sanjek, Roger. 2011. *Gray Panthers*. Philadelphia: University of Pennsylvania Press.

28 Freedman, Marc. 2018. *How to Live Forever: The Enduring Power of Connecting the Generations.* New York: Public Affairs. See also, Duffy, Bobby. 2021. *Generations.* New York: Basic Books.

29 Katz, Stephen and Whitehouse, Peter J. 2017. "Legacies, generations, and ageing futures. In *Planning Later Life*, ed. Mark Sweder et al. New York: Routledge, 235–261.

30 Taylor, Paul. 2021. "Intergenerational Activism: In a Divided America, A Tonic for All Ages. Encore.org.

31 "83 Great Quotes by W. H. Auden." https://quotes.thefamouspeople.com.

32 Mannheim, "The problem of generations," 320.

33 Cramer, Reid. 2018. "To extinguish generational inequality, start by understanding diversity." *New America.*

34 National Academy of Social Insurance. 2022. Uninsured and underinsured risks in this millennium. Washington, D.C.: NASI.

35 www.povertycenter.columbia.edu.

36 National Academy of Social Insurance. 2022. Uninsured and under-insured risks.

37 Bass, Scott A. 2022. *Administratively Adrift.* New York: Cambridge University Press, 28–33.

38 Williams, Sean. 2018, September 1. "What can Generation Z expect from Social Security when they retire?" *The Motley Fool.*

39 Kotkin, Joel. 2012. "Are today's Millennials the screwed generation?" www.npr.org/2012/09/03.16039637.

40 Levy, Donne. 2020, February 27. "Historian points out this startling face about the current racial division in the Trump era." *AlterNet.*

41 Filipovic, Jill. 2019. *OK, Boomer, Let's Talk: How My Generation Got Left Behind.* New York: Simon & Schuster.

42 Moody, Harry R. 2017. "Baby Boomers: from Great Expectations to a crisis of meaning." *Generations*, **41**, 95–100.

43 Settersten, Richard and Barbara E. Ray. 2010. *Not Quite Adults.* New York: Bantam Books, ix, xi.

44 Pillemer, Karl. 2020. *Fault Lines.* New York: Avery.

45 Lee, Hermione. 2022, February 10. "Regarding the solace of others." *New York Review of Books*, 24–25.

46 Alter, Charlotte. 2020, August 23. "Memo to baby boomers, from millennials: Everything's your fault." *Houston Chronicle*, G5.

47 Johnson, Malcolm L. 2009. Procession of the generations. In *Social Insurance and Social Justice*, ed. Rogne, Leah and Estes, Carroll, et al. New York: Springer Publishing Company, 32.

48 Cooper, Richard Rand. 2021. "Reaching back to Frost." *Amherst Magazine.* Bicentennial volume, pp. 33–37.

49 Ignatieff, Michael G. 1984. *The Needs of Strangers.* New York: Viking.

50 Moody, Harry R. 2021, October 21. Personal communication.

51 The observation comes from Richard Viguerie, quoted in Wolraich, Michael. 2010. *Blowing Smoke.* New York: DaCapo Press.
52 Solnit, Rebecca. 2016. *Hope in the Dark*, 2d ed. Chicago: Haymarket Books.
53 Obama, Barack 2006. *The Audacity of Hope.* New York: Crown.
54 Macy, Joanna. 2018. "Widening circles." *Emergence Magazine.*

Chapter 2

Social-Security myths in an age of misinformation and big lies

Introduction

Despite considerable efforts, Social Security Administration (SSA) often failed to communicate effectively Social Security's aims and transactions to contributors and beneficiaries. Stakeholders for decades went to local Social-Security offices to talk with agents; nowadays, most Americans get input from social-media outlets, which often misreport facts and sensationalize the program's fiscal woes. Misinformation, disinformation and lies, rampant in communication gaps within and across overlapping generational lines, raise anxiety and feed citizens' fears.

From its enactment in the Great Depression, Social-Security officials unintentionally confused contributors and beneficiaries of all ages about the program. Misconceptions concerning Social Security's eligibility criteria, benefits structure, and sustainability die hard, leaving millions of stakeholders to wonder:[1]

> Does Social Security operate like a retirement savings account?
> Will Social Security fully fund my retirement years?
> Will I get shortchanged in return for payroll taxes contributed into the system?
> Do eligible Social Security recipients have to apply in person for benefits?
> Is 65 still Social Security's official full-retirement age?
> If I start collecting at 62, will benefits bump up when I reach full-retirement age?
> Do recipients lose Social Security benefits permanently if they continue working?

DOI: 10.4324/9781003345985-4

Will payments to my ex-spouse reduce my personal retirement benefits?

Does the Federal government raid Social Security to pay for other programs?

Do undocumented immigrants drain Social Security trust funds?

The answer to all of these questions is NO! Yet big lies and conflicting reports about Social Security persist. They incite depressing and misleading notions.

Different generations have distinctive age-specific views on Social Security

Each generation of Social-Security stakeholders voice earnest and honest concerns about the program. Americans' realistic worries and fears commingle memories and perceptions of unsettling circumstance in their lives. Distinctively varied life histories at work, in their households, and in everyday exchanges color everybody's views about Social Security. Older Americans cannot be considered a homogenous group, for instance, successfully aging in lockstep. Within their rank are vast inequalities in wealth and income. Ageism—personal insults and cultural assaults—refract their perceptions of social standing and health status.[2]

Baby Boomers wonder if the Federal government's commitment to Old Age Survivors Disability and Health Insurance (officially abbreviated as OASDHI) will cover medical expenses and caregiving assistance. If not, must senior citizens impoverish themselves in order to qualify for Medicaid, a Federal-State financed program for individuals with incomes below the poverty line? Should Congress not address these issues, will lawmakers reduce benefits? And would prolonged inaction bankrupt Social Security before our grandchildren get benefits?

Demographics come into play where I live. The number of Texans over age 65 are expected to grow from 3.9 million in 2020 to 8.3 million by 2050. More than 70% of retirees are estimated to need some form of long-term care, not covered by Medicare. A majority of the state's older citizens do not have adult children living nearby. Increasing numbers of Black and Spanish-speaking households in Texas are working; few can perform eldercare while raising children. Elderly Texans having to spend down assets to be eligible for Medicaid puts a fiscal burden on public funds in a State where lawmakers insist routinely that individuals take primary responsibility for their well-being.[3]

With increases in U.S. adult life expectancy, 65-year-old Social-Security recipients will live, on average, another ten-to-twenty extra years. How much pressure does this longevity dividend put on intergenerational transfers? Are not the program's transactions disrupted if younger (and smaller) labor pools contribute less in payroll taxes—funds needed to cover retirees' checks? Furthermore, hospital and health care expenditures (often exceeding $200,000) far outstrip cost-of-living-adjustments under Social Security. How many persons over age 75, a subgroup of older Americans increasingly suffering multiple chronic ailments and frailty, bear the burden of covering medical care? There are no crystal-ball answers or comforting solutions with which to reassure older Americans and their families. Growing older becomes a longevity gift few elders want or can afford to give to rising generations.

Younger Social-Security contributors have their own skepticism and fears to voice. While confident that their parents and grandparents can survive tough economic times, 80% doubt that they will in due course get comparable support. Forty percent of adults between 20 and 50 believe that Social Security is a Ponzi scheme. Only 20% of this age group are saving anything for "golden years." Many Millennials view retirement as a far-away stage of life in which imponderables might develop beforehand.[4]

Fears about retirement trajectories also reflect changes in plans made by older and younger Social-Security contributors as they adapt to recent booms and busts in the workplace. Most Baby Boomers, like their grandparents, underwrite retirement years on a three-legged stool—Social Security, a corporate or public pension, and private savings. Millennials and those employees newly contributing to the system, in contrast, feel that they are falling off a pogo stick. Burdened with student debt and working in gig jobs or unpaid internships, many young contributors are more preoccupied with losing in the housing market than putting money into individual retirement-savings vehicles such as IRAs or 401(k)s.

Millennials and younger cohorts have adopted distinctive approaches to deflect fretting about Social Security's fiscal health. Feeling victimized in their ill-fated job prospects, some forget that the program lifted many of their peers out of child poverty. Low-earning, physic-ally able employees postpone saving for retirement until mid-career. Should future benefits be cut by 25%, middle-aged workers calculate that payroll taxes from still-younger Federal Insurance Contributions Act (FICA) contributors would still cover most of their anticipated benefits.

A generation gap magnifies broader differences in perspectives. A Pew survey reports low interpersonal trust in Big Government.[5] Whereas Baby Boomer often rely more on friends' tips, Millennials and younger workers tap resources that lessen confidence in Federal programs like Social Security. Amidst anxieties about their current employability and fears that conditions may worsen, most youth derive little consolation when listening stories about how Baby Boomers overcame midlife crises to attain a ripe old age.

The U.S. Bureau of the Census upend generational perspectives as they alter demographic categories. More Americans who once reported to be "White" in census surveys—69% in 2000, and 58% in 2020—now are identifying themselves differently. A decade ago, 65% of children were listed as White. The 2020 census permits persons under age 18 to claim to be multiracial, Black, Hispanic, or Asian.[6] Changing bureaucratic overviews of the U.S. population's age structure in turn alters identifying who count as bona fide "Americans."

Demography and bureaucracies, in short, broaden contextual parameters for safeguarding Social Security for future generations:leaving a legacy in an aging society. They have an impact on domestic politics and policymaking at the Federal level. Doubts and anxiety over the program's current status and uncertain future permeate and perpetuate realistic fears. Millennials, having never witnessed reforms, question whether old leaders such as Mitch McConnell, Nancy Pelosi, Donald Trump, and Clarence Thomas rightly exercise their authority. Baby Boomers, who lived through much of Social Security's history, despair whether prioritizing Social Security is part of Joe Biden's promise to "restore the soul of America."

Myths about Social Security persist because misinformation competes with facts

Myths about Social Security persist for at least two reasons. Misinformation about the program's prospects diverts stakeholders' access to facts about what works and doesn't in the nation's largest social-insurance program. Reforming Social Security, many Americans suspect, is not an immediate priority in Washington compared to pocketbook issues. To this mix are the frequency and intensity of attacks and doomsday scenarios that compound and reinforce fears. Misinformation and disinformation repeated often enough assume an aura of truth. Persuaded that Social Security is going bankrupt, stakeholders accept gloomy prognosis as factual.

Does the convergence of demography and politics sufficiently explain why myths about Social Security remain so credible? Is this why naysayers seem so persuasive in presenting the program as a "success" for elders who benefit at the expense of younger workers' FICA taxes? Can Social Security's advocates quell fears that massive infusions are necessary to keep Social Security solvent? Perhaps, perhaps not.

Neither sunny optimists nor doomsdays forecast about safeguarding Social Security attract audiences with memories of how AIDS, 9/11, urban violence, climate change, Covid-19, and abortion. Ukraine captured headlines in the very period in which Social-Security news was delivered in op-eds and business writers. These developments have given Congress and the White House cover when they prefer to avoid dealing with the "third rail" of American politics. Hypothetical forecasts and gloomy diagnoses bolster Social-Security myths and lies, permitting right-wing lawmakers and millions of stakeholders to deduce that the program is doomed. George Orwell sees temptations in "believing things which we know to be untrue, and then, when we are finally proved wrong, impudently twisting facts so as to show that we were right."[7]

It does not follow, however, that it is too late to initiate constructive reforms. This book argues that measured hope can yet prevail over mounting fears. U.S. presidents and Republican and Democrat legislators, as well as Social Security's critics and supporters have been proposing various policy options about what needs to be done for decades. Virtually all of them have been rejected or tabled. If stalemates and the politics of avoidance continue, there will be no easy way to secure widespread support.

Social-Security assessment require three intervening steps to occur. First, stakeholders should reaffirm that Social Security epitomizes a transgenerational compact that entails shared burdens and collective benefits. Second, lawmakers have to set aside politics as usual, and agree that corrective action to ensure that Social Security remains a good deal. Third, Social-Security contributors and beneficiaries with different earnings records and diverse life histories must exert grassroots pressure from bottom to top.

Hope for Social-Security reforms accompany fears of Big Government's legitimation crisis

Franklin Delano Roosevelt published *Looking Forward* in March 1933, the month he was first inaugurated as the 32nd President of the United

States and two years before he signed the Social Security Act into law. The book, a compilation of Franklin Delano Roosevelt's (FDR) articles and speeches that became a *New York Times* bestseller, offered an appraisal of how banks and the Federal government's failures led to the Great Depression.[8] *Looking Forward* had a conspicuous place in the White House library, in part because Roosevelt seemed to be updating Edward Bellamy's widely read *Looking Backward* (1888). Dreaming big in his utopian novel about a young man born in an era "portentous of great changes," Bellamy's protagonist awakens in 2000 into a world with credit cards, electrified cities, and "radically different" populist politics.[9]

American journalists were not sanguine about the former New York governor's abilities and chances for success in reconstructing a U.S. political economy devastated by the Great Depression. Walter Lippmann, then the regnant political commentator, described FDR as "a pleasant man who, without any important qualifications for office, would very much like to be president."[10] Lippmann underestimated Roosevelt's tenacity in dealing with polio, fearful citizens, and a war waged on two fronts. By his 4th campaign in 1944, the haggard incumbent urged voters not to "change horses in mid-stream"; FDR won 54% of the popular voted and beat his opponent in the Electoral College by a 432–99 margin. When the President died six months later, FDR's funeral cortege was mourned by participants who had lost a father figure.

Mustering the courage to preserve FDR's New-Deal legacy is a daunting challenge, because Americans once again must decide to act in years of deep national distemper. Myths and misinformation about Social Security are fueled in a toxic environment that concurrently saps the power of democratic principles and societal commitments. We founder in intragenerational disagreements and dither in intergenerational conflicts. Transgenerational culture wars permit us to squander personal interests and disrespect collective responsibilities.

Yet diverse groups of U.S. citizens of all ages have united in the past to preserve and modify laws and institutions that bind us together. Obstacles may yet derail optimistic hope; lawmakers rarely agree on a common set of facts and fragmented media markets overwhelm a free press. Americans nonetheless have time to think critically and act boldly in evaluating Social Security, which not only provides an income floor for millions of U.S. citizens, but also complements and underscores the robustness of its democratic compact.

The past can serve as guidepost for thinking big and acting daringly in chaotic times

The lies and distrust permeating America today have been omnipresent in recent U.S. history. During President Eisenhower's second term, University of Michigan researchers began measuring people's confidence in their elected officials. Between 1958 and 1964, roughly 75% of respondents declared that government did the right thing most of the time. According to Gallup and Pew pollsters, trust in government during the Reagan administration never rose above 45%. It declined steadily, never exceeding 30% between 2007 and 2021.[11]

It is tempting to claim that Donald Trump's Big Lie about who won the 2020 election sparked anti-democratic sentiments in the United States. Pollsters indicate that 30% of Americans cling to Trump's fantasy that he or one of his designated heirs should dominate all three branches of the Federal Government in order to Make America Great Again.[12] Authors rush into print, contending that right-wing dogma in a polarized electorate and uncertain economy suppresses voter rights for millions who already consider themselves displaced, forgotten, and stressed.

Mounting loss of confidence in Big Government has shadowed Federal politics for nearly a century of U.S. history: Herbert Hoover ordered troops to disband World War I veterans pitching camp on Capitol Hill; the Supreme Court invalidated FDR's first New Deal, and Einstein condemned Truman's decision to incinerate Japan; McCarthyism destroyed careers; the press overlooked JFK's priapism and health issues; LBJ lost support over Vietnam, and Watergate investigations forced Nixon to resign; and Bill Clinton's deceptive defense of White House affairs led to impeachment hearings. Later on, neoconservative tactics to secure and maintain power in Washington were showcased by Rush Limbaugh and Fox News; George W. Bush launched wars in Iraq and Afghanistan after 9/11; then Ted Cruz, Mitch McConnell, and Tucker Carlson blamed Biden for economic downturns and illegal migrants overtaking Texas' borders.

Along with distrusting presidents and high-ranking lawmakers, Americans professed mistrust of experts, idea brokers, and institutional networks. "Education, healthcare, the law, are increasingly seen as bureaucratic and incompetent systems, consuming public funds in labyrinthine administration," observed a former archbishop of Canterbury, adding that "these alienations—well founded or not—are far more strongly marketed in the USA than in Britain, and suspicion of central government has led to reactions of an increasingly feverish and paranoid character."[13] Yet U.S. citizens are hardly unique in expressing despair and fear: Autocrats in Hungary, Russia, Turkey, North Korea, and the Americas govern nations, deploying censorship, and violent deterrents to social unrest.

Often understated in critiques of U.S. democracy are rampant disinformation and levels of ignorance evident from top to bottom. Environmental activist Robert F. Kennedy, Jr. opposes polio shots for children. A Florida osteopath and Nation of Islam acolyte are named among "the disinformation dozen" by the Center for Countering Digital Hate. Guardians of public health undercut their credibility by relying on gut feelings in offering "noble lies" to audiences, many of whom disregard scientific knowledge and common sense.[14] No wonder that respondents to surveys often ignore facts about public affairs because they find more persuasive ideas and headlines broadcasted by market-savvy media outlets.

Hannah Arendt noted that *The Origins of Totalitarianism* (1951) lie not only in Nazi and Communist propaganda, but in "people for whom the distinction between fact and fiction (i.e., the reality of experience) and the distinction between true and false (i.e., the standards of thought) no longer exist."[15] Two thirds of Americans in 2005, after all, could not name the three branches of the Federal government. Does this extent of ignorance reinforce the lack of interest in Social Security and other issues distorted by anti-rationalism and anti-intellectualism?[16] Is this why ultra-progressives are blamed for hyperbolic and disingenuous remarks, and why far-right spokespersons scrap essential facts as inconvenient evidence?

Two recent events observed by all living generations illustrate the insistent impact of untruth and deception today:

1   For four hours on January 6, 2021, Americans watched as Congress came under assault. Liberals said that the storming of the seat of government while members of the House were certifying the results of the presidential election was an impeachable offense, orchestrated by Donald Trump. Many Republican lawmakers, whose very lives were threatened, dismissed the gravity of the attack: They described the insurrectionists as people exercising 1st-amendment rights during a "normal tourist visit."

2   Throughout the Covid-19 crisis, vaccinated citizens were pitted against unvaccinated Americans, 53% of whom thought that the vaccine posed greater health risks than the disease. In the fourth

surge of hospitalizations and ICU deaths (predominantly among those who ignored or rejected basic laws of scientific causality), the governors of Texas and Florida refused to issue public-health mandates. "Double-think" provoked civil disobedience as parents refused to get their school-age children vaccinated; unmasked opponents defended their freedom to spread the virus and risk death.

These past disasters (and doubtless with more catastrophes in the offing) have exhausted the spirit of ordinary citizens across the United States. They in turn influence critical thinking about safeguarding Social Security by consolidating clusters of perspectives that pit groups against one another. Yet fears over bad things that are happening, as 19th-century philosopher Arthur Schopenhauer argued in *The World as Will and Representation* (1819), may awaken hope that humans are more than pawns in mindless charades of life in nature.

The importance of safeguarding Social Security in leaving a future legacy

Compared to press interest in global warming, partisan showcasing in a polarized Congress, and mounting deaths from a virus indifferent to human suffering, it is understandable why few Americans rarely consider how greatly cuts in Social Security will reduce retirement portfolios. Program advocates generally debate experts' policy-driven forecasts and rework statistical models. The insidious impact of racism and sexism, as well as the corrupting influence of inequalities in income and wealth are genuine threats.

Yet, should grappling with those issues invariably take precedence over imagining the extent to which safeguarding Social Security really matters? Can we envision the program as one of the few U.S. systems that serve as an institutional bulwark to American democracy? The program touches the lives of nearly the entire citizenry. If we put Social Security into the broader context of societal aging, its status and fate hardly seem comparatively peripheral. For the sake of shepherding American time-tempered values and collective engagements, we cannot afford to subscribe indefinitely to the politics of avoidance prevailing under the masks of myths and misinformation.

Safeguarding Social Security for present stakeholders and future generations invites an ironic turn in this book's narrative line: Americans have ample opportunities to revisit, reconsider, and determine whether options for Social-Security reforms merit scrutiny. We can think critically about policy initiatives already on the table:

1 Raise cost-of-living adjustments (COLAs) to keep pace with inflation.
2 Provide periodic COLA increases only to low-income or middle-class contributors.
3 Tax higher wage-earners beyond current limits to bolster FICA.
4 Eliminate the cap on payroll taxes.
5 Means-test benefits, granting them to those with too little retirement income.
6 Provide Social-Security credits to unpaid caregivers.

Conversations and negotiations will be messy and protracted. Alternative options will be introduced. Progressives will likely insist on expanding Social Security to reduce citizens' poverty risks and raise income floors. Conservatives will probably reiterate appeals to privatize current Social-Security operations, to let Americans invest retirement funds as they see fit. It remains to be seen whether lawmakers in the vital center seek to compromises by rallying around other strategies.

This book dare not predict how self-interests and incentives will determine what may or not transpire in Washington. Yet this chapter on myths in an age of misinformation entreats Social-Security policymakers and stakeholders to initiate transgenerational dialogues that rely on scrutinizing facts and evaluating options in a disinterested manner. History can prove to be an invaluable guide, as Chapter 3 argues. We can interpret and reframe Social-Security trends since the 1930s mindful of previous breakthroughs and past impasses.

Notes

1 Goss, Steve. 2020. "Social Security financing and benefits: Myths vs facts." www.ssa.gov; Markowitz, Andy. 2021. "Ten myths that refuse to die." www.aarp.org.
2 Calasanti, Toni and Neal King. 2020. "Beyond successful aging 2.0: Inequalities, ageism, and the case for normalizing old ages." *The Journals of Gerontology: Series B.*, **76**, 1817–1827.
3 Angel, Jacqueline and Jason Castillo. 2021, June 25. "Who will pay the bill for an aging Texas?" *Houston Chronicle*, A11.
4 Singh, Dhara. 2020. "2 in 5 Americans under 60 believe Social Security is a Ponzi scheme, survey finds. https://money.yahoo.com/social-security-ponzi-scheme/180625728.html; Bresiger, Gregory. 2019. "80% of

millennials are worried Social Security won't be there for them." https://fee.org/article; Barney, Lee. 2018. "Many millennials, Gen Xers don't expect to receive Social Security." *Plansponsor.*

5 Gramlich, John. 2019. "Younger Americans are less trusting of other people, and key institutions, than their elders." www.pew.research.org.

6 Frey, William H. 2021. "New 2020 census results show increased diversity countering decades-long declines in America's white and youth populations." www.brookings.edu/research.

7 Orwell, George. March 4, 2022. Quoted in *Climate Change in an Aging Society*, ed. H. R. Moody. San Francisco, CA: Self Publishing.

8 Roosevelt, Franklin Delano. 1933; reprinted 2009. *Looking Forward.* New York: Gallery Books.

9 Bellamy, Edward. 1888; reprinted 1996. *Looking Backward.* Mineola, NY: Dover Publications.

10 Leuchtenburg, William E. (no date). "Franklin D. Roosevelt: Campaigns and elections." https://millercenter.org/president/fdroosevelt/campaigns-and-elections.

11 Menand, Louis. 2021, August 16. "Legitimation crisis." *The New Yorker.*

12 Devega, Chauncey. 2021, July 14. "The power of the Big Lie." *Salon.*

13 Williams, Rowan. 2000. *Lost Icons.* New York: Morehouse, 178.

14 Stephens, Brett. 2021, July 28. "Covid disinformation comes from the top, too." *The New York Times.*

15 Arendt, Hannah. 1951. *Origins of Totalitarianism.* New York: Schocken Books.

16 Osnos, Evan. 2020, November 16. "Pulling our politics back from the brink." *The New Yorker;* see also, Jacoby, Susan. 2008. *The Age of American Unreason.* New York: Vintage.

Chapter 3

Why history matters when interpreted pragmatically and humbly

Introduction

History lessons helps all U.S. generations to rethink Social Security's priorities and reimagine the potentialities of an aging country, but they never promise happy endings. Our personal and collective storytelling of the past thus must be pragmatic, provisional, and humbling. History offers guideposts when Americans are tempted to embrace false analogies that presume nomothetic continuities in the face of unknown developments. Transgenerational conversations and mobilizations—mindful of patterns of despair and trust, and hopes and fears—may free us from historical biases and prejudices.

Safeguarding Social Security can be part of a larger long-term campaign to leave a democratic legacy upon which current and rising generations can build. As Theodore Roosevelt pronounced in his first message to Congress, delivered after William McKinley's assassination, "The fundamental role of our national life is that, on the whole and in the long run, we shall go up or down together."[1] Initiatives may take place while Americans navigate conflicting viewpoints and contested truths amidst generational successions. Interpreting past national experiences symbiotically may contextualize critical thinking about Social Security.

Paradigmatic interpretations of U.S. history vivify analogical, critical thinking

What proof exists that history can bridge conflicted viewpoints and contested truths? Will paradigmatic interpretations of U.S. history summon different age groups to collaborate in safeguarding Social Security? "One way to transcend these inherent limitations is by

DOI: 10.4324/9781003345985-5

applying the lessons of history of those who have come before," claims Jon Meacham, "and to hope that the performances of the present can light the paths of the future."[2]

Strategically conveying interpretations of U.S. history to idea brokers, lawmakers, and citizens with a stake in Social Security appears analogous to younger crews listening to aging coxswains like me, a grandfatherly author who cares about safeguarding Social Security for future generations. This tack nonetheless has limitations. Besides trying to discern "the big picture," including its blind spots, we must balance successes in providing an income floor with trachoma over Social Security's shortcomings in addressing changing individual needs. We may fail, because many U.S. citizens doubt the worth of applying history lessons.

Henry Ford resisted transfiguring interpretations of the past: "History is more or less bunk," the automaker opined. "We want to live in the present and the only history that is worth a tinker's dam is the history we make today."[3] No wonder many in the Federal government turn history into a rhetorical weapon in order to valorize American exceptionalism and denounce critical race theory. Few professional historians are public intellectuals; they are too humble and wise to claim any capacity to extrapolate future developments with ironclad surety.[4] Nuanced history stories must interpret both our estimable and shady memories as guideposts to inform rationales and shape choices we must make.

History, in my opinion, is more than an aggregate of verifiable facts, cloudy memories, and misguided prognoses. Academic historians and erudite amateurs present interpretations of Social Security's development through different versions of critical events and key figures. Since the program's evolution does not culminate in a neat story line, its interpretations are revised in competing, alternative narratives.

Readers can fairly choose among various historical analyses. In this book, I reformulate my previously held viewpoints to enhance my chances of reaching and persuading younger and older audiences. I intentionally reframe practical information, always subject to revisions given my incomplete knowledge of present realities and future uncertainties.[5] Ideas and strategies may dissolve unexpectedly and unpredictably, prompting re-presentations of how Social Security's evolution address audiences with dissimilar life histories, fears, and hopes.

Baby Boomers' updated translations of treasured principles must convince younger Americans to eschew fake news and half-truths as conduits in rethinking our shared destiny. The project may fail. The whole aim of "practical politics," asserted journalist H. L. Mencken in 1918, "is to keep the populace alarmed [and hence clamorous to be led to safety] by menacing it with an endless series of hobgoblins."[6] Fear-based misperceptions deter constructive dialog and fruitful action. Historical misunderstandings do not magically disappear. False hopes distort efforts by Americans of all ages to reimagine why Social Security matters.

Fears and hopes jostle in four critical periods in U.S. history

This book presents a counternarrative. "Hope is an embrace of the unknown and unknowable, an alternative to the certainty of both optimists and pessimists."[7] Hopes and fears *do* coexist amidst omnipresent intangibles hurling us into an unknown future, where dreaded contingencies refract our personal and collective historical identities. Yet historical reinterpretations "have their value—nothing so wonderfully expands the imaginative horizons of human potentialities fatal."[8] Let's examine four moments in U.S. history that reveal past choices between hopes and fears.

Creating a new republic: The Founding Fathers designed a federal system of checks and balances "to form a more perfect Union, establish Justice, insure domestic Tranquility, provide for the common defense, promote the general Welfare, and secure the Blessings of Liberty to ourselves and to our Prosperity."

There were limits to whom would bestow the blessings. As the Founding Fathers framed the Constitution, they stipulated in Article One who could serve in Congress: "Representatives ... shall be apportioned among the several States ... according to their respective Numbers, which shall be determined by the whole Number of free Persons ... excluding Indians, not taxed, three fifths of all other Persons." Without conceding too much to slaveholding delegates, the Constitution stipulated that the new republic would not engage in slave trade.

To get the Constitution ratified, Federalists debated Anti-Federalists. A ten-part Bill of Rights was added, which further protected the personal liberties of free men of property and standing, but was silent about the status of women, The document created a "more perfect Union" for "ourselves" than a loose confederation of independent states. Finessing who constituted "We the People" nonetheless had dire consequences.

Antebellum America: Jacksonian Americans enjoyed the blessings of democracy. Their "love of equality," Alexis de Tocqueville noted in visiting the United States during the 1830s, "should constantly increase together with equality itself, and that it should grow by what it feeds on." Rural and urban settlers relied on voluntary associations to keep self-reliance from degenerating into selfishness. Middle-class merchants, farmers, and working-class laborers valued *individualism*, which the French aristocrat characterized as "a calm and considered feeling which disposes each citizen to isolate himself from the mass of his fellows."[9] Americans maintained their forbears' concern for civic virtue, and assisted neighbors in crisis.

Tensions between advancing self-serving interests and commitments to the General Welfare grew, as cotton became king in the South and enriched Northern mill owners. Pioneers and urban dwellers in the first decades of the antebellum period chose either to ignore, sublimate, or justify the ironies, ambiguities, and faults transmitted from their Revolution-era legacy. Like the Founding Fathers, white antebellum Americans mostly chose to finesse dealing squarely with the moral, economic, and political consequences of racial injustice. While Congress sought to keep the number of slave and free states equivalent through the Missouri Compromise (1820) and the Kansas–Nebraska Act (1854), the Supreme Court's 1858 Dred Scott ruling laid bare fears that a Southern slavocracy imperiled Federalism.

The Civil War: By the 1850s, slaveholders and abolitionists were resorting to violence. "All thoughts were anxiously directed to an impending civil war," Abraham Lincoln recalled, "and the war came." Confederates rebelled against the Union, pitting brother against brother, each believing God was on their side. The 16th U.S. president in 1865 hoped to allay fears and recriminations by pledging "malice toward none, with charity for all." His plans for healing wounds and caring for widows and orphans seemed attainable. Radical Republicans passed the 13th Amendment (which abolished slavery), the 14th Amendment (which defined citizens), and the 15th Amendment (giving Black male citizens the right to vote) within three years of Lincoln's assassination.

The victorious Union "with firmness in the right" could not sustain reconstructing a war-torn nation, however. Reforms gave way to the terrorizing Ku Klux Klan, Jim Crow laws, and peonage. A majority of U.S. voters deemed Blacks to constitute an inferior race.

A gilded then progressive era: As the United States emerged as a world power, ordinary Americans were generally unmindful of the consequences of Robber Barons creating monopolies, fomenting imperialistic ambitions and being blind to their racist heritage. Citizens were also oblivious to domestic inequities pervasive in workplaces, and between Catholic neighborhoods and Protestant enclaves.

Progressives in the early 20th century, alarmed by the hazards of new fortunes amidst slums, identified societal problems enumerated through survey data and headlined in yellow journalism. Social reformers advocated the passage of laws and creation of municipal, state, and federal-level institutional bulwarks to undercut abuses of power and to counterbalance growing class-based disparities. The victories were short-lived. Teddy Roosevelt's New Nationalism faded; Republican presidents in the 1920s celebrated the "normalcy" of middle-America.

These four episodes underscore the extent to which civic discourse rises in hope and simultaneously idles in complacency or falters in fear. (See Appendix 2 for a fuller analysis.) Each generation, overwhelmed by historical prejudices and suspicions, responded differently to specific threats. Leaders and citizens acted courageously, temporized, fueled conflict, or settled for expediency.

Leaving a legacy by interpreting and revising American pragmatism

"Consider what effects, which might conceivably have practical bearings, we conceive the object of our conception to have," postulated Charles Sanders Peirce in 1878. Along with contemporaries William James and John Dewey, he articulated the philosophical and operational dimensions of American Pragmatism.[10] Facing societal challenges in a civil, evidence-based, disinterested process, these pragmatists realized, were not foolproof means for guaranteeing progress, but they were more effective than idealizing hopes and avoiding fears. Social reformers tested and rooted pragmatism into American political traditions.

The quest for reorienting the mores of American society often trumped personal self-interests and transcended partisan ideologies. "When complete agreement could not otherwise be reached," Peirce suggested facetiously, "a general massacre of all who have not thought in a certain way has proved a very effective means of settling opinion in a country."[11] To anchor knowledge, pragmatists relied credentialed experts with appropriate credential, as they urged U.S. citizens to mobilize around a "fixation of belief" resonating in common sense.

Intellectual historian James T. Kloppenberg traces pragmatic motifs from the Revolutionary-era to Barack Obama. They occurred throughout U.S. history in sequential steps. All parties, trusting objective criteria, willingly reconsider positions when necessary and resist pressure from other participants.[12]

This book uses a pragmatic template for reinterpreting the program's history by relating it to recent contours and enduring trends in our national experiences. Synergizing three paradoxical propositions drives the narrative.

First, participants must test salient values, norms, and facts that inevitably will be contested. Civic discourse must be open-ended, not dogmatic, in weighing contested arguments. "Balancing principles and effectiveness in the public sphere is hard work, an unending process of trial and error," asserts Kloppenberg. "No formulas ensure success."[13] Social-Security advocates, in assessing and reassessing the cogency of their viewpoints, must anticipate that the credibility and reliability of their facts and recommendations will be repeatedly challenged by opponents whose rallying points and lived experiences animate a different set of opinions, statistics, and proposals.

Second, idea brokers and media commentators must necessarily respect the plausibility of opposing viewpoints in order to establish a common ground for reforming Social Security. Contested truths have coexisted throughout U.S. history: Anti-Federalists challenged *The Federalist Papers*; abolitionists and women's crusaders demonized Jacksonian slaveholders as criminals and sinners; Northern Reconstruction gave way to Southern Redemption after a bloody war; Warren Harding succeeded Teddy Roosevelt, William Howard Taft, and Woodrow Wilson. Pragmatic ideals are neither doctrinal, coercive, nor iron clad.

Rational civic discourse insists on taking diverse and contradictory conflicting opinions seriously, without presuming the verisimilitude of dearly-held principles and strategies. Negotiating Social-Security compromises will fail not just when protagonists demean opponents, but when participants reluctantly or desperately settle on a centrist tipping point for the sake of consensus-making. Franklin Delano Roosevelt held firm when Alf Landon denounced the New-Deal measure. The architects of the 1983 Social-Security amendments wrestled with uncomfortable truths well into the eleventh hour. Recent stalemates attest to reified postures in a toxic environment.

Third, negotiating requires principled debate before experimentation; the process surrenders any quest for certainty in enunciating deliberative consequences. Stakeholders must be mindful that the dialog will require subsequent rounds of consensus building and reassessments. Social Security's policy elites and ordinary citizens alike must recognize that measured hope can never dispel political fear. Reforming the program is unlike racing to the finish line in regattas; the task is never complete. Yet, like coxswains and crews, idea brokers and stakeholders must cope with the contingent, unfathomable nature of future surprises and forthcoming vicissitudes.

By adhering to this three-pronged, pragmatic approach, Social-Security advocates and critics, along with contributors, and beneficiaries, must decide whether it is worth supporting the program's values and ensuring its sustainability. If Baby Boomers, Millennials, Gen-Z, and those who follow choose to reconfigure Social Security's worth in a polarized aging society, they must mollify vested self-interests and contested perspectives. In candor and trust, overlapping generation of Americans settle on if, why, and whether the program matters. History offers guidance for reinterpreting, embracing, and sharing (however provisionally) its time-tested place among competing national priorities.

This book does not conclude with leaving a legacy in an aging society that resolves debates or breaks stalemates. Instead, this book offers hope that Americans can deal with fears in promoting comity within age groups and justice across generations. By claiming that historical facts help to clarify and put present-day challenges into context, this 75-year-old grandfather appeals to skeptical younger readers and peers—many of whom, I suspect, have issues other than Social Security on their minds and agendas. This book, itself an audacious testimony to measured hope, stresses that critical thinking about Social Security prompts important questions about trends in recent U.S. history that focus on the fate and future of American democracy.

Notes

1 Roosevelt, Theodore. 1901, December 3. 1st annual message to Congress.
2 Meacham, Jon. 2018. *The Soul of America.* New York: Random House.
3 Hirst, K. Kris. 2019. "Did Henry Ford really say 'history is bunk'?" www.thoughtco.com/.
4 Staley, David J. 2007. *History and Future: Using Historical Thinking to Imaging the Future.* Lanham, MD: Lexington Books.
5 Kaag, John. 2019. *Sick Souls, Healthy Minds.* Princeton: Princeton University Press.
6 Mencken, H.L. 1918. www.goodreads.com/quotes/34754-the-whole-aim.

7 Solnit, Rebecca. 2016. *Hope in the Dark*, 2d ed. Chicago: Haymarket Books.
8 Berlin, Isaiah. (no date). Quotes and sayings. www.inspiringquotes.us/author/2809-isaiah-berlin.
9 deTocqueville, Alexis. 1835–1840. *Democracy in America*, 2 vols. Ed. Phillips Bradley. New York: Vintage.
10 Peirce, Charles Sanders. 1878. "How to make ideas clear." *Popular Science*, **12**, 286–302.
11 Peirce, Charles Sanders. 1877. "The fixation of belief," *Popular Science Monthly*, **12**, CP5, 379.
12 Kloppenberg, James T. 2011. *Reading Obama*. Princeton: Princeton University Press.
13 Ibid., xiv.

Chapter 4

Risks, rights, and responsibilities under Social Security

Introduction

I went to the 1975 American Historical Association (AHA) meeting to find a publisher for my dissertation. There, I met Paul Neuthaler, a senior editor at Basic Books. After I delivered an elevator speech, Neuthaler recommended that I do not end the book's chronology in 1940, when Ida Fuller became the first person to receive a Social-Security check. Updating the story to now, he said, would sell books. While not indifferent to money, I scoffed at the suggestion.

Neuthaler followed up by asking "Aren't you the least bit curious as to what happened after 1940?" I was stunned by the question. The editor, 40-something, was rightly proposing that I should investigate how Social Security affected images and experiences of modern old age.

One of my dissertation advisors knew Social Security's history firsthand. Wilbur J. Cohen had worked as a research assistant under Edwin Witte, his University of Wisconsin mentor, in drafting the original 1935 Social Security Act. Cohen then rose through the ranks of the Department of Health, Education and Welfare (HEW), serving as HEW secretary in 1968. I spent a lot of time with Professor Cohen, who generously shared anecdotes, private papers, personal books, Social-Security memoranda, and Congressional records. In a matter of six months, Cohen shepherded my first attempt to interpret Social Security as chapter 7 in *Old Age in the New Land* (Johns Hopkins University Press, 1978).

I owe a tremendous debt to Paul Neuthaler, who urged me to apply lived history, and to Cohen, who embodied vigilant Social-Security stewardship. Here is a vivid, personal example of two older mentors sharing practical wisdom. I listened carefully as I lay the foundation for leaving the legacy that informs this book.

DOI: 10.4324/9781003345985-6

New-Deal Initiatives

This interpretation of Social Security begins with Franklin Delano Roosevelt (FDR), who pledged to revive the United States. Almshouse populations rose 75% in the early years of a Great Depression. Insecure middle-class Americans experienced poverty risks of poverty for the first time in their lives. FDR promised throughout his 1932 presidential campaign to create "a new deal for the American people."[1] In his inaugural address on March 4, 1933, he stated that "only a foolish optimist can deny the dark realities of the moment," adding his "firm belief that the only thing we have to fear is fear itself." The president declared that "we must act quickly."[2]

President Roosevelt launched a New Deal deploying Progressive-era reformers' strategy for dealing with social problems.[3] The President (1) gauged the magnitude of the crisis; (2) relied on experts' advice and marshalled statistical data to corroborate his viewpoint; (3) created institutions to remediate the problem; and (4) tested their efficacy. "We cannot be satisfied with makeshift arrangement which will tide us over the present emergencies," declared FDR's Secretary of Labor Frances Perkins, who oversaw major welfare innovations when Roosevelt was governor of New York. "We must devise plans that will not merely alleviate the ills of today," amplifying FDR's theme, "but will prevent, as far as it is humanly possible to do so, their recurrence in the future."[4]

Roosevelt immediately declared a four-day bank holiday. Over the next 100 days, Congress enacted measures to establish the Tennessee Valley Authority and end Prohibition and, at his urging, underwrote 12 other major structural bulwarks. A conservative Supreme Court then ruled the National Industrial Act and the Agricultural Adjustment Act unconstitutional, thus overturning the First New Deal.

In response, after failing to pack the bench, FDR tried sausage-making, a mode of governance that he had learned during World War I as an undersecretary of the Navy. Roosevelt acted within the "broad Executive power to wage a war against the emergency." Repairing the U.S. political economy, opined the President, required decisive leadership to meet "an unprecedented demand and need for undelayed (sic) action [that] might call for a temporary departure from the normal balance of public procedure."[5]

Roosevelt, trying to overwhelm destabilizing fears with assurances of measured hope, evoked "the old and permanently important manifestations of the American spirit of the pioneer."[6]

To show how congruently traditional values were embodied in New-Deal initiatives, FDR used three keywords—"risks," "rights," and "responsibilities."

- RISKS referred to the paralyzing losses and collective hazards suffered during the Great Depression: "Values have been shrunk to fantastic levels ... government of all kinds is faced by serious curtailment of income; the means of exchange are frozen ... withered leaves of industrial enterprise lie on every side; farmers can find no markets ..."[7] Americans were desperate. Let us not shrink from "the grim problem of existence," Roosevelt entreated. "We are stricken by no plague of locusts ... Nature still offers her bounty and human efforts have multiplied it."[8]
- RIGHTS, enshrined in the Constitution (albeit limited to Blacks and women throughout much of U.S. history) were respected and preserved. The New Deal, FDR assured Americans, would unfold "in the warm courage of national unity; with the clear conscious of seeking old and precious ethics ... at the assurance of a rounded, permanent life."[9] Upholding individual liberties and protecting shared rights meant applying "social values more noble than mere monetary profit." Making such a choice was the rightful prerogative, as the president put it, of "the good neighbor ... who resolutely respects himself and, because he does so, respects the rights of others; the neighbor who respects his obligations and respects the sanctity of his agreements ... in the temple of our civilization."[10]
- RESPONSIBILILTIES were paired with rights in FDR's calls for action: "If I read the temper of our people correctly, we now realize, as we never realized before, our interdependence on each other; that we can not merely take but must give as well."[11] In his 1933 inaugural address, the President asked U.S. citizens to mobilize for the sake of mutual interdependence: "If we are to go forward, we ... must [be] willing to sacrifice for the good of the common discipline, because without such discipline, no leadership can be effective."[12]

Expanding the powers of his office by trial and error required adroitly specifying risks, vouchsafing rights, and demanding responsible action. This is how FDR made Social Security into the cornerstone, a major legacy, of the Second New Deal.

FDR lays the normative foundations for Social Security in the United States

In a 1934 message to Congress, President Roosevelt unveiled what he described as an American way to further "the security of the citizen and his family through social insurance":

> I am looking for a sound means which I can recommend to pro-vide against several of the great disturbing factors in life—especially those which relate to unemployment and old age ... These three great objectives—the security of the home, the security of live-lihood, and the security of social insurance ... constitute a right which belongs to every individual and every family willing to work. They are the essential fulfillment of measures already taken toward relief, recovery, and reconstruction.[13]

Unemployment and old age were indeed "disturbing factors in life." At least a quarter of the U.S. labor force was unemployed between 1929 and 1935; percentages were slightly higher among senior citizens who were out of work and luck. Hard times disrupted corporate and trade-union pensions; bank failures wiped out personal savings. For the first time in their lives, a sizable segment of the nation's middle class endured demeaning dependency. The Depression meanwhile exhausted veterans' programs, charities' assistance, and public relief.[14]

Building on the First New Deal's "relief-recovery-reform" agenda, Roosevelt and Perkins studied transatlantic "social insurance" principles.[15] Otto von Bismarck in the 1880s had inaugurated worker health insurance, worker accident insurance, and invalidity/old-age insurance under social-insurance programs; England, Denmark, and New Zealand subsequently adapted the German model. Theodore Roosevelt, running as a Progressive third-party candidate in 1912, proposed incorporating social insurance in the United States "with whatever modifications are necessary by our different ways of life and habits of thought."[16] Major U.S. newspapers posted articles entitled "Social Insurance" during the 1930s and 1940s.

Teddy Roosevelt's distant cousin did not "require the creation of new and strange values" when he assembled a Committee on Economic Security (CES) to draft social-insurance legislation. FDR forged a workable intergenerational compact to bring together government, business, and citizens.[17] He trusted Secretary of Labor Frances Perkins, who eschewed the myth of "rugged individualism." From her years as a social worker and a public servant, Perkins recognized how greatly that people had to support one another in times of need.

Secretary Perkins, the driving force who chaired CES, worked in conjunction with the U.S. Attorney General, the secretaries of the Treasury and Agriculture, and the Federal Emergency Relief Administrator. These officials were assisted by a six-member Executive Staff; an Advisory Council (headed by the president of the University of North Carolina) included corporate executives, union officials, welfare experts, academics, and the editor of *The Survey*, a leading survey journal; and a technical board aided by four actuarial consultants.

Experts, seasoned in give-and-take approaches to drafting national legislation, dominated CES. Notably absent from administrative and staff positions were persons promoting utopian schemers (such as Huey Long and Upton Sinclair) and unyielding social-insurance advocates (such as I. M. Rubinow and Abraham Epstein). CES's architects nonetheless felt threatened by the surging Townsend movement, which advocated giving a monthly $200 pension to every retired U.S. citizen over 60. Grassroots supporters might demand that the Townsend Plan be enacted before the president's team formulated an alternative. The Committee also heard from those vehemently opposed to Big-Government initiatives and Federal handouts. Their conservative voices, like the Townsend's army, constrained CES policymakers as they drafted and rejected social-insurance items.

In less than eight months the Committee on Economic Security generated several hundred staff reports, discussion papers, and statistical analyses. Publicizing updates was a necessary but secondary part of practical policymaking. Although CES initially targeted the unemployed as deserving potential recipients, the president surprised experts in November 1934 by giving priority to the needs of impoverished elders. FDR's switch was unsettling but shrewd. Relieving old-age dependency had wide appeal across the political spectrum. Idea brokers and statisticians quickly documented that at least half of all Americans over age 65 were in desperate straits. A significant number of older citizens, the Committee staff projected, would remain destitute and need some sort of relief after prosperity returned.

Experts paid less attention to educating U.S. voters, who were unaware of nuances and compromises that characterized insiders' métier. And social-insurance rhetoric was vaguely elastic. FDR sometimes pitched appeals to fellow citizens. At other times he addressed middle-class workers. Did FDR intend to help unpaid family members cooking and washing at home? Did he wish to protect Dustbowl farmers, Blacks disenfranchised and toiling in the South, and unskilled laborers? Roosevelt wanted to evaluate the differential costs of assisting selective groups of Americans, but he happily left it to staff members designated to define keywords and to refine parameters.

Key CES members worked hard and long. "I laid out a couple of bottles of something or other to cheer their lagging spirits," Frances Perkins recalled. "We stayed in session until about 2 a.m. We then voted finally, having taken our solemn oath that this was the end; we were never going to review it again."[18] Even so, CES's chair fumbled occasionally in radio addresses and congressional testimony. The Secretary of Labor was criticized by commentators who claimed that she was proposing that covered workers had to contribute what amounted to forced savings in order to get a dole. In congressional hearings, cabinet officers sometimes disagreed with Perkins' views about the range of coverage.[19]

Most of CES's old-age proposals were incorporated into the 1935 Social Security Act, however. Lawmakers concurred that "an effective program for this country involves not a choice between assistance and insurance but a combination of the two."[20] Under Title I, the old-age assistance section, Congress initially appropriated nearly $50 million "for the purpose of enabling each State to furnish financial assistance, as far as practicable … to aged, needy individuals." Almshouse residents were excluded from Title I assistance through a provision intended to shut down the dreaded institution. Age "65" was chosen as a compromise between "60" (which would cover too many) and "70" (which would cover too few). Legislative language precluded establishing other nationwide standards. Congress deleted CES references to "subsistence compatible with decency and health," rather than infringe on states' rights. Title I instead permitted states to set their own eligibility criteria and benefit levels, up to a ceiling of $15 a month that the Federal government would match. Some states gave no relief to impoverished elders.

Logistical difficulties and fiscal prudence weighed heavily in drafting old-age insurance (Title II), which was to draw from an Old-Age Reserve Account (Title VIII). Coverage was limited to employees in commercial and manufacturing sectors—roughly 60% of the labor force. Benefits were to be paid starting in 1942, funded from a 1% tax (called a "Federal Insurance Contribution Act" [FICA] to finesse constitutional scrutiny) deducted employees' wages (up to $3,000) matched by employers for the same amount. Experts deflected questions about long-term options. When would Congress raise the $3,000 ceiling? Or someday end Title I relief?

Besides attending to older Americans, the 1935 Social Security Act served other segments of the U.S. population. Title III authorized states to establish unemployment compensation plans, financed largely by taxes on employers (Title IX). Title IV allocated state aid to dependent children. Title V earmarked grants for maternal and child welfare, particularly those who were crippled or required rural public services. Funds under Title VI covered training new personnel and vocational rehabilitation. Title X gave assistance to the blind. Title VII authorized a Social Security Board (SSB) to monitor operations and cover its administrative costs. Title XI stipulated Congress's right to alter, amend, or repeal Social Security.

Upon signing Social Security into law on August 14, 1935, President Roosevelt warned Americans that "we can never insure one hundred percent of the population against one hundred percent of the hazards and vicissitudes of life."[21] Policy constraints circumscribed the social-insurance experiment. The Supreme Court might rule Social Security unconstitutional, as it had earlier New-Deal measures. Alf Landon, the Republican presidential candidate in the 1936 election, condemned the Act as "unjust, unworkable, stupidly drafted, and wastefully financed."[22] Conservatives endorsed Landon's demand to repeal Social Security.

Friendly critics also duly noted flaws. Social Security ignored age discrimination in the marketplace. Nor did the original measure tackle structural unemployment. Because Title II did not cover agricultural and domestic workers, most African Americans were denied the right to contribute payroll taxes to enable them to collect Social Security benefits. Racial disparities were understated, lest Southern white supremacists sabotage implementation. Gender inequities did not inspire remedial action: Maids, caregivers to elders being discharged from almshouses, and stay-at-home wives and mothers were not covered.

FDR and his allies took rights and responsibilities seriously—with equivocation. The word "entitlement," which appeared in the 1935 Social Security Act, referred to procedures for challenging a potential recipient's ineligibility. It did not guarantee any person's right to receive a prescribed amount of monthly assistance. Since Social Security was designed to mesh with New Deal goals of relief, recovery, reform, and reconstruction, advocates anticipated conservative challenges to Big-Government interventions. (That tack dated back to 1854, when Franklin Pierce planned to give Federal aid to the deaf.) "General welfare" in the Preamble to the Constitution generically referred to rights and responsibilities shared by Americans bound together in the commonweal. Communities, moreover, before the Depression preferred local oversight rather than Federal or State interventions to underwrite old-age support.

FDR and his New-Deal administrators invoked "risks," "rights," and "responsibilities" in ways that garnered public support while seeding misunderstandings. These keywords, hoped officials, would stir commitments to Social Security, stimulate confidence in its financing, and encourage business executives and labor officials to make workers insurance-minded. The president's colloquial style was effective. A December 1935 Gallup poll found that 89% of those surveyed endorsed the idea of providing old-age assistance for "needy" senior citizens.[23] When the Twentieth Century Fund, an independent policy-oriented research center, issued *More Security for Old Age* in 1937, the book received 188 mostly hortatory news items, 39 articles, 40 book reviews, 143 editorials, and a coast-to-coast radio program.[24]

And yet, uncertainties over contested truths loomed large in 1935. FDR, deferring to expert advice, postponed including medical assistance in the Act. Pollsters had difficulties in interpreting Americans' grasp of Social Security's aims and *modus operandi*: Respondents recognized the inadequacy of local measures for needy older people, yet their purported enthusiasm for social insurance, as established in Titles I and II, was qualified. Minor variations in the wording of pollsters' questions precluded measuring the depth and extent of support for old-age assistance; preset survey questions could not gauge familiarity with structural features of old-age insurance, particularly details about what benefits contributors could expect in return.

"Despite the numerous articles which have been written," lamented a Social-Security architect, "the two parts of the old age security program are confused and many of the essential features have been grossly misrepresented."[25] Yet distortions did not much trouble architects of the 1935 social-insurance legislation. Ensuring that Federal insiders understood Social Security's workings mattered more than informing the general public. Any initiative, reckoned program overseers in the 1930s, has flaws that inevitably surface. They recommended letting future Social-Security administrators fix things, if and when needed.

Nor did FDR and his advisors take to heart New-Dealer Thurman Arnold's prescient opinion that portraying Social Security as a faceless bureaucracy presented too negative a symbol of humanitarian spirit "We must consider institutions and the mass psychology surrounding them as living institutions, not dissimilar to human personalities," opined the Yale law professor in *The Folklore of Capitalism* (1935) and in *Symbols of Government* (1937). Arnold portrayed citizens as "never quite understanding themselves or the part they are actually playing because of the necessary illusions with which they must surround themselves to preserve their prestige and self-respect."[26]

The Social Security Administration (SSA) within three months generated 25 million numbers for individuals paying into the system. FICA contributors were issued a card printed in blue ink, which posted a nine-digit number in red letters, with spaces on which to sign their names. Cards typed up in post offices were then sent to Washington; the supply was expected to last for several generations. Social Security record-keeping thus had ties reaching back to 1775, when Ben Franklin was appointed postmaster.

Not keeping the public up-to-date about Social Security's structure and workings set the stage for consequences that undermine the system today. FDR and his policymakers felt that Americans would trust elected officials and experts to act in their best interests.[27] A communication gap between policy insiders and an ill-informed electorate ensued, bedeviling subsequent debates as experts and lawmakers effected technical adjustments to the system.

How the 1939 amendments altered Social Security

Shortly after Social Security was enacted, but before the first Title-II benefits were distributed, Congress had a window of opportunity to redesign social-insurance operations. The Supreme Court in 1937 upheld Social Security's constitutionality without ruling on the wisdom of the program's financing mechanism. Then a recession wiped out four years of U.S. recovery. Many radio and print commentators attributed the downturn to cuts in Federal spending coupled with the collection of $2 billion in FICA contributions. Conservatives along with some liberals renewed demands for new financing arrangements. The Social Security Board (SSB) reported that only a third of older Americans were financially secure. "The widespread anguish following the economic collapse," declared SSB commissioner Mary Dewson, "blew away the rosy fog which we had permitted to obscure ... unpalatable realities."[28]

SSB chair Arthur Altmeyer urged President Roosevelt in September 1937 to convene a detached advisory council of experts ... not only to offset these attacks on the Social Security Act, but really to utilize them to advance a socially desirable program, fully in accord with present fundamental principles underlying the Social Security Act and within our financial capacity.[29]

FDR, taking Altmeyer's advice, appointed employee and employer leaders, academics, consumer advocates, and public watchdogs to rework the original provisions of Title II.[30]

Franklin Roosevelt invited J. Douglas Brown to head the 1937–1938 Advisory Council. The Princeton University economist had shepherded the research team that drafted Title II in the 1935 Act. He first acted as if he were a "messenger boy" who transmitted actuarial data and statistical reports from the Council to FDR's staff, congressional insiders, and SSA employees. By 1938 Brown determined that sweeping changes were timely and appropriate.[31]

Social Security's first advisory council offered ten recommendations for liberalizing Title-II benefits, eleven proposals about financing, and countless suggestions for future action. The Council proposed paying Title-II disbursements in 1940, and increasing the contributor pool. Agricultural and domestic workers were still excluded, because experts thought there were too many administrative obstacles. So African Americans largely remained ineligible for coverage.

Most significantly, the 1937–1938 advisory board recommended shifting emphasis from employees paying into the system as individuals to characterizing Social-Security contributors as family breadwinners with potential survivors. The Council prioritized "adequacy" (a social-welfare principle) over "equity" (a private-insurance term). Without raising FICA taxes to pay for expanded coverage, Congress voted to allocate benefits on a pay-as-you-go basis—as Title II still works. The Federal government under this arrangement, the Council acknowledged, might someday have to make up any shortfalls in delivering benefits to covered recipients.[32]

By emphasizing the keyword "adequacy" to target the truly vulnerable, the Advisory Council orchestrated a bureaucratic flip that reoriented the program: "The proper test of coverage is not the special nature of a worker's employment but the universal nature of the risks he or she faces."[33] Rather than viewing SSA as an agency overseeing and mitigating workplace hazards, Brown thought Social Security was poised to serve a broader, pragmatic national purpose: "The problem of the planner of social insurance is to so relate benefits to normal earnings as to afford reasonable protection without reducing motivation in any serious degree," observed Brown, adding that "this becomes a problem in which psychology, economics, and public administration must be joined in seeking a solution."[34]

Professor Brown spoke about "a solution" to "a problem" in talks to policy technicians and top Federal officials, which magnified the American public's misunderstandings of Social Security's aims and operations. On bureaucratic grounds, his Advisory Council upheld age-based coverage as a straightforward, efficient administrative criterion; it counted "normal earnings," thus avoiding the stigma of "welfare" usually associated with means-testing. The changes enacted in the 1939 Social-Security amendments would take years for FICA contributors to recognize—precisely what the policy elite wanted to happen. Stakeholders were expected to trust that experts and watchdogs would exercise "a balanced judgment of adequacy of protection relative to funds available."[35]

Amid sharp criticism nearly 85 years later, SSA officials, Congress, and lobbyists are still struggling to explain how FICA taxes are levied and benefit levels calculated. The architects of the 1939 amendments, in balancing tradeoffs between sustaining Social-Security trust funds while expanding benefits to an expanded pool of recipients, prefigured the context in which later policy challenges took place. Because of top-to-bottom miscommunications, few Social-Security stakeholders nowadays comprehend the deftly calibrated tensions between "equity" and "adequacy." Nor do they hear or learn much about how "risks," "rights," and "responsibilities" worked, unlike Americans in the 1930s.

To put the dilemma bluntly: how persuaded are Baby Boomers and younger contributors in accepting a legacy that preserves Roosevelt's opinion that "we shall make the most orderly progress if we look upon Social Security as a development toward a goal rather than a finished product." FDR remained vague during his presidency about how his Social Security Act interacted with saving and private-insurance plans: "We shall make the most lasting progress if we recognize that Social Security can only furnish a base upon which each one of our citizens may build his individual security through his own individual efforts."[36]

To FDR, Social Security offered a rudimentary floor of protection. It was neither a dole nor a bonanza for contributors and their families. At the Teamsters Convention in September 1940, the president envisioned the next steps in extending old-age assistance and insurance:

> It is my hope that soon the United States will have a national system under which no needy man or woman within our borders will lack a minimum old-age pension that will provide adequate food, adequate clothing and adequate lodging to the end of the road ... I look forward to a system ... which, in addition to this bare minimum, will enable those who have faithfully toiled in any occupation to build up additional security for their old age which will allow them to live in comfort and happiness.[37]

Roosevelt appreciated the logistical difficulties and resistance shadowing his capacious vision. In the mix were contested viewpoints in determining when Social Security emerged.

There were in effect two plausible benchmarks with which to date when the program was actually launched. Selecting different starting dates justified divergent interpretations of risks, rights, and responsibilities under Social Security in its formative years. Conservatives could *quite* reasonably date the program's *raison d'etre*—its principles and transactions—originated in the 1935 Social Security Act. Liberals could rightly take the 1939 amendments to be the policy's *real* baseline for Social Security's emerge to be the system that operates today.

Therein, in my opinion, lies a fundamental, and enduring, source of confusion about Social Security's primary aims as well as misunderstandings concerning its basic operations. The 1939 Social-Security amendments replaced the notion of "equity" girding U.S. private pensions and in Title II of the 1935 Act. Congress rewrote the old-age insurance section in 1939 to stress "adequacy" in order to expand the rights of FICA contributors AND their families. Under the banner of mutual interdependence, American workers' payroll taxes benefited dependents and survivors who had contributed little or nothing to the program.

The shift from "equity" to "adequacy" without raising payroll taxes, however, also interjected a new risk to forecasting the system's solvency under about conceptual and programmatic changes introduced through the 1939 Social-Security amendments. As long as they received checks based on prior FICA payments, contributors permitted SSA to determine adequate floors of protection, regardless of alterations in intergenerational dynamics of income transfers. The public approved of whatever had transpired. Support for Social Security rose from 68% in 1938 to 96% in 1944.[38] The 1939 amendments were ratified before any old-age-insurance benefits were distributed. This unsettling legacy still confounds Americans.

Social-Security developments in FDR's shadow

President Roosevelt in his third term wanted to broaden Social Security's scope and effectiveness even more. The National Planning Board recommended in 1942 an audaciously comprehensive income-maintenance program. Delivering his 1944 State of the Union address as a "fireside chat," Roosevelt uttered that "in one word: security [was] the one supreme objective for the future" worldwide. "Security" meant more than relieving threats from physical harm or enemy aggression. It permeated, in FDR's mind, the economic, social, and moral rights and responsibilities to alleviate ordinary wage-earners' workplace hazards.

"Essential to peace is a decent standard of living for all individual men and women and children in all nations," pronounced FDR in his Second Bill of Rights unveiled in 1944. "Freedom from fear is eternally linked with freedom from want."[39] Pursuing this goal entailed minor risks because it was rooted deeply in the country's tradition of mutual responsibility as a practical way to promote individual rights. Roosevelt thought that he was amplifying an assertion that he had made nine years earlier: "With those taxes in there, no damn politician can ever scrap my social security program."[40] This time, however, the president did not get his way. FDR's plan for expanding social insurance was scuttled by congressional reluctance to increase the U.S. debt during World War II.

During the next several decades, Social-Security amendments fulfilled many of FDR's aims. The Federal government adhered to and refined "the politics of incrementalism," which enlarged the program's reach in a gradual, step-by-step manner. Implementing experts' recommendations into the program's 1950 amendments, for instance, Congress increased old-age insurance benefits so that, for the first time, they exceeded the average old-age assistance payments. The number of Title-II beneficiaries surpassed the number of those eligible for relief under Title I—just as policymakers had predicted roughly 20 years earlier.

In keeping with FDR's desire to raise levels of minimum security, Congress trusted that Social Security worked, and periodically liberalized old-age insurance provisions. Lawmakers extended compulsory coverage. Amendments in 1954 and 1956 provided Social-Security coverage to disabled workers. Their certifiable incapacities resulted from risks that approximated conditions, experts reasoned analogically, and permitted early-retirement criteria.

Federal lawmakers and lobbyists boldly embarked on a broad scale War on Poverty during the 1960s. They tapped abundant economic resources in a nation increasingly vaunted as a no-risk country.[41] Officials successfully widened educational opportunities for middle-class Americans and took steps to uplift the truly disadvantaged. "The challenge of the next half century," thundered President Lyndon Johnson (LBJ), "is whether we have the wisdom to use … wealth to enrich and elevate our national life, and to advance the quality of American civilization."[42] LBJ's aspirations for a Great Society surpassed FDR's New-Deal vision.

Congress passed laws to eradicate racial discrimination, to target pockets of poverty in rural and urban areas, and to revoke restrictive immigration restrictions that dated back to the 1920s. The plight of older Americans became a rallying point in an affluent Great Society. "Compassion and reason dictate that the logical extension of our Social Security system will supply the prudent, feasible, and dignified way to free the aged from the fear of financial hardship in the event of illness," declared President Lyndon Baines Johnson in 1965.[43] His campaign for underwriting hospital coverage for Social-Security beneficiaries required finesse, given President Harry S Truman's failed effort to secure national health insurance in 1948.

Academics, journalists, and labor unions made a strong case that older Americans constituted a very dependent and frail yet deserving segment of the U.S. population. Nonetheless, there remained strong opposition to governmentally funded health care. The American Medical Association warned that privileging senior citizens would undermine overall health-care delivery. Some critics questioned whether life's hazards and vicissitudes correlated neatly to chronological ages: Disabilities, chronic maladies, misdiagnoses, major workplace accidents, and traffic fatalities, noted public-health experts, threatened all ages.

Thanks to grassroots support and LBJ's landslide 1964 victory, Congress passed three major laws benefiting senior citizens in 1965. Medicare provided hospitalization and health insurance for

65-and-older Americans on Social Security. Medicaid launched a federal and state program that covered costs for indigent elders and younger people with limited income and resources. The Older Americans Act (OAA) inaugurated Federal, state, and local agencies to provide nutrition, housing, transportation, education, and social services. Great-Society policymakers hoped that OAA would mushroom into an ambitiously interlocking network of Federal partnerships and private-sector initiatives to assure well-being in late life.[44]

Broader definitions of rights in the Great Society justified initiatives to redress the needs of Americans mired in desperate circumstances. "An age attuned to the idea that a government has vast responsibilities for the material welfare and human rights of citizens," opined Harvard Law professor Archibald Cox, "can hardly share the founders' fear of strong government."[45] Allocating Federal resources for older citizens attracted less media attention than obtaining long denied minority rights. Advancing age-based capabilities and the civil-rights movement intimated ways to deal with the paradox of poverty in an affluent country.

Crucial to mounting a persuasive argument for elder rights were shifting U.S. attitudes about late life. Older Americans earlier in U.S. history were perceived as worthy albeit vulnerable citizens. During the 1960s, journalists and researchers portrayed more positive images of countless numbers of elders able to flourish and to care for their grandchildren. Stressing senior citizens' rights to freedom and autonomy, advocates depicted the income floor under Social Security as a measure that not only reduced risks of old-age poverty and dependency but also bolstered mutual responsibility and transgenerational interdependence.

Social Security, insisted an emergent gray lobby, vitally empowered older Americans to advance the commonweal.[46] Expanding social-insurance raised hopes that new generations of aging Americans could attain a ripe, productive, and comfortable old age. "The fact that today we have the capacity to abolish poverty means that we must," Social-Security commissioner Robert M. Ball declared.[47] There was in the heyday of Big Government, considerable popular support for expanding Social Security's role in lifting middle-Americans' expectations. Roughly 90% of those surveyed approved its liberalization. "Social insurance makes sense," opined Nobel laureate Paul A. Samuelson in 1967, "because we are all in the same boat."[48]

Conservatives agreed. Richard Nixon assured delegates to the 1971 White House Conference on Aging that he embraced doing more to assist older Americans. The Republican president enthusiastically endorsed what became the 1972 Social-Security amendments. Provisions consolidated Social Security's relief measures under the Supplementary Security Income program. Negotiations with Congress and Social-Security administrators raised Title-II benefits by 20%. Other compromises at the Federal level led to regularizing future payouts through automatic cost-of-living-adjustments (COLAs), which were pegged to changes in the nation's price index. In signing the 1972 amendments into law, Nixon claimed that "this landmark legislation … will end many old inequities and will provide a new uniform system of well-earned benefits for older Americans, the blind, and the disabled."[49]

Notes

1   Lepore, Jill. 2020. "In every dark hour." *The New Yorker*.
2   Roosevelt, Franklin Delano. 1933. First inaugural address. www.americanr hetoric.com/speeches/fdrfirstinaugural.html.
3   Kloppenberg, James T. 2011. *Reading Obama*. Princeton: Princeton University Press.
4   Quoted in Atlman, Nancy J. 2020. "Addressing 'unpalatable realities' laid bare by today's crises." In *The Future of Social Insurance*, ed. Thomas N. Bethell. Washington, DC: National Academy of Social Insurance, 9.
5   Roosevelt, First inaugural address.
6   Ibid.
7   Ibid.
8   Ibid.
9   Ibid.
10 Ibid.
11 Ibid.
12 Ibid.
13 Roosevelt, Franklin Delano. 1934, June 8; reprinted 1938. Objectives of the administration. *FDR Public Papers* 3, 291–292, New York: Random House.
14 Achenbaum, W. Andrew 1978. *Old age in the New Land*. Baltimore: Johns Hopkins University Press.
15 Marmor, Theodore R., Mashaw, Jerry L., and John Pakuta. 2014. *Social Insurance*. Los Angeles: Sage.
16 Roosevelt, Theodore. 1912, August. Address before the convention of the National Progressive Party. ssa.gov/history/trspeech.
17 Committee on Economic Security. 1937. *Social Security in America*. Washington, D.C.: Government Printing Office.
18 https://francesperkinscenter.org/life-new/.

19 Altman, Nancy J. 2018. *The Truth about Social Security*. Washington, D.C.: Strong Arm Press.
20 Committee on Economic Security, 189–190.
21 Roosevelt, Franklin Delano. 1935. Presidential statement upon signing the Social Security Act, August 13, 1935. *FDR Public Papers*, **4**, 44.
22 Landon, Alf. 1936, September 27. Text of Governor Landon's Milwaukee address on economic security. *The New York Times*.
23 Gallup, George. 1972. *The Gallup Poll: Public Opinion, 1936–1971*. 3 vols. New York: Random House.
24 Achenbaum, W. Andrew. 1986. *Social Security: Visions and Revisions*. New York: Cambridge University Press.
25 Schiltz, Michael E. 1970. *Public Attitudes toward Social Security, 1935–1965*. Research Report No. 33. U.S. Department of Health, Education, and Welfare: Social Security Administration.
26 Arnold, Thurman. 1935. *Symbols of Government*. New Haven: Yale University Press; Waller, S. 2005. *Thurman Arnold*. New York: New York University Press.
27 Rauch, Jonathan. 2018. "The constitution of knowledge." *National Affairs*, **17**, 3–12.
28 Dewson quoted in Altman, Nancy J. 2020. "Acknowledging 'unpalatable realities.'" *op. cit.*
29 Altmeyer, Arthur J. 1963. *The Formative Years of Social Security*. Madison: University of Wisconsin Press.
30 Pifer, Alan and Forrest Chisman. 1985. *The Report of the Committee on Economic Security, 50th Anniversary Edition*. Washington, D.C.: National Conference on Social Welfare; Berkowitz, Edward D. 1983. "The first Social Security crisis." *Prologue*, **15**, 133–149.
31 Berkowitz, Edward D. 1987. "The first advisory council and the 1939 amendments." In *Social Security at Fifty*, ed. Edward D. Berkowitz. Westport CT: Greenwood Press, 37–51.
32 *Congressional Record*. 1939, June 10, 6864
33 Brown, J. Douglas. 1977. *Essays on Social Security*. Princeton: Industrial Relations Section.
34 Brown, J. Douglas. 1957. "Social insurance." *American Economic Review*, **47**, 432–438.
35 Brown, *Essays on Social Security*.
36 Roosevelt, Franklin Delano. 1939. Letter of transmittal. www.ssa.gov/history/stool.html.
37 Roosevelt, Franklin Delano. 1940. Address to Teamster convention. www.presidency.ucsb.edu/documents/address.
38 Schiltz, *Public Attitudes*.
39 Sunstein, Cass R. 2004. "Sunstein on FDR's second bill of rights." University of Chicago Law School.
40 Schlesinger, Arthur M., Jr. 1958. *The Coming of the New Deal*. Boston: Sentry.
41 Hacker, Jacob. 2006. *The Great Risk Shift*. New York: Oxford University Press.

42 Johnson, Lyndon Baines. 1964, May 22. "The Great Society speech." Ann Arbor: University of Michigan.
43 Johnson, Lyndon Baines. 1965, July. Quoted in Michael Beschloss, "L.B.J. and Truman: The bond that forged Medicare." *New York Times*, 2015, February 28.
44 Achenbaum, W. Andrew. 1983. *Shades of Gray*. Boston: Little, Brown.
45 Cox, Archibald. 1966, November. "The Supreme Court—foreword." *Harvard Law Review*, **80**, 119.
46 Pratt, Henry J. 1976. *The Gray Lobby*. Chicago: University of Chicago Press.
47 Ball, Robert M. 1965. "Is poverty necessary?" *Social Security Bulletin*, **28**, 19–20, 24.
48 Samuelson, Paul A. 1967, February 13. "Paul A Samuelson on Social Security." *Newsweek*, 88.
49 ssagov/hist/nixstmts.html/#1972.

Part 2

A senior historian's evolving interpretations of Social Security

I have thought, taught, and written about Social Security for roughly two-thirds of my life. I have been constantly challenged to communicate meaningful and persuasive accounts about the program's history. To reach diverse audiences of all ages, I have urged gerontologists, sociologists, and social-work professors to stress my theme: "Social Security has transformed the fabric of U.S. social relationships" because it "lies at the heart of the compact between the government and the governed."[1]

My interpretations of Social Security's history have evolved as I became older and my grandchildren grow. In composing this section of this book, I want to stir younger readers' imaginations by continually raising questions that I have not yet resolved. Why do most contributors and beneficiaries still not comprehend Social Security's fundamental aims and basic operations? Who cares and bears responsibility if rising generations and those unborn end up empty-handed? What precedents in the program's evolution, grounded in recent U.S. history, prompt transgenerational ideas that might spur grassroots demands for rethinking and renegotiating Social-Security reforms?

Such questions feed a paradoxical insight: More and more Americans have counted on Social Security since Franklin Delano Roosevelt created the program in 1935, YET stakeholders' confidence in the program has eroded since reforms were enacted in the 1983 Social-Security amendments. How can a semiretired historian of aging communicate a compelling, persuasive message to peers and younger readers whose life histories, opinions, and prospects differ from mine? What rings true and makes sense to me may not grab, much less resonate, and persuade audiences diverse in age and feeling lonely and bewildered as a pandemic rages in a polarized society.

DOI: 10.4324/9781003345985-7

The first part of this book drew analogies of me as a grandfather, coxswain, and scholar struggling to find a voice to which younger people may listen. This preface offers that might resonate to younger readers. Growing up in suburban Philadelphia, I enjoyed sitting in bleachers and watching the Quaker City's equivalent of the Boston and New York marathons. Crews of high-school students, collegians, "masters" (people over age 27) and other teams came together on the last Saturday of each October to compete. Like Federal Insurance Contribution Act (FICA) contributors, they followed rules and propelled into an uncertain future.

Reluctantly, I have come to realize that aspects of this analogy— such as crews winning purses by finishing first—are inappropriate and distracting. Social Security's time frame is indefinite; its modus operandi has enlarged midcourse to serve the needs of disparate stakeholders in an aging society. Ironically, I know that parallels between competitive scullers and Social-Security stakeholders remain apt. The fast-moving Schuylkill River forces rowers to make sharp turns every few meters. Teams that veer too close to dams plunge into the deep. Similarly, Social Security's contributors have not had an easy run. Cross-currents—not just ideological or fiscal—have damned the course.

Several temporal dimensions intersect as I compose this book. By putting primary focus on readers, I have to listen as each age group makes decisions in changing times. I have to be willing to revise previous interpretations of Social Security's history, to take account of what I have learned and witnessed about the program's evolution since graduate school. At the same time, my audiences—largely college undergraduates and students pursuing advanced degrees in history, social sciences, social work, and in allied-health professions—show up several overlapping generations removed from Baby Boomers.

Another temporal dimension presents itself as I contemplate Social Security's longstanding connections to older, middle-aged, and younger U.S. citizens. Part 2 of this book must reiterate that big lies and misinformation cloud honest and pragmatic understandings of this vital institution's past record, current circumstances, and future status. This section has to weigh opinions set forth by Social Security's advocates and stewards, as well as naysayers and critics.

Situating Social Security into an historical context, I hope, predisposes readers to imagine their present and imminent stake in the program. Audiences at different stages of life histories will evaluate the program in distinctly personal ways. It remains to be seen whether transgenerational conversations and action plans fill ever-changing measured hopes amidst disillusionment and fears.

Part 2 of this book underscores parallels and divergences that encapsulate my growing older, Social Security's maturing, and how a democracy evolves. All share an uncertain future. I, too, was once a young adult; I have discarded over time erroneous ideas and outmoded assumptions about the program. Extra years have gifted me an opportunity to promote transgenerational dialogues. In the chapters that follow, I weave three dimensions of time—personal, professional, and societal—to stir imaginative, critical thinking across age groups who have a stake in safeguarding and expanding the values inherent in a Social-Security compact that works and binds us together.

Note

1   Achenbaum, W. Andrew. 2009. "Make history ground-breaking by teaching essential history: Putting Social Security in U.S. history syllabi." In *Social Insurance and Social Justice*, ed. Leah Rogne, Carroll L. Estes, et.al. New York: Springer Publishing Company, 383–398.

Chapter 5

The significance of the 1983 Social-Security amendments

Introduction

Over an advisor's desk hung a World War I poster, which read "Don't read American history—Make it!" James Montgomery Flagg designed this 1917 placard for New York City's navy recruiting station. The image showed a sailor taking a man in a business suit by the shoulder; a Liberty figure waved Stars and Stripes as the men looked toward battleships. Little did I know as an incoming doctoral student that I too would become a recruit, one conscripted to serve older experts in salvaging Social Security at a pivotal moment of U.S. history.

I had several opportunities to reconnect with Wilbur Cohen after earning my Ph.D. I remember on one visit my mentor being enraged by President Carter's 1977 decision to tighten eligibility rule under Social Security's Disability Insurance. Cohen told me that he and Arthur S. Flemming (who had served as President Eisenhower's secretary of Health, Education, and Welfare) were forming a coalition to "Save Our Security" (SOS). Eager to enlist into the cause, I helped the pair by writing policy briefs and editing press releases.

This began a new phase of my engagement in safeguarding Social Security. I was a 30-year-old untenured professor, applying historical perspectives on a popular Federal program experiencing unanticipated fiscal shortfalls. Conservative Republicans, who had no intention of governing under Franklin Roosevelt's shadow, increasingly declared that Big Government was "the problem." The shortfall provided a cover for reorienting Social Security's status and prospects when Ronald Reagan became the 40th U.S. president.

What follows is my interpretation of how Social Security's trajectory changed between 1977 and 1983. I became an eyewitness to history-in-the making. I listened to actors on the stage recount facts, fears, and

DOI: 10.4324/9781003345985-8

hopes. Their rendezvous with destiny left quite an intergenerational legacy.

A gathering storm meant no more easy votes on Social Security

The passage of the 1972 Social-Security amendment was well received by experts and voters, including a reporter respected for his mastery of the mind-boggling complexity of the Federal budget. Writing in *The New York Times*, Edwin L. Dale, Jr. was in 1973

> persuaded that Social Security at the worst is not a bad deal, and is safe, even for the young worker with 40 years of paycheck deductions ahead of him. It is not a bad deal, either, for the doctors and salesmen and other self-employed workers who tend to do the most squawking. Unless the world blows up, or the country goes bankrupt, it is highly likely that the current workers will get back from Social Security more than they paid in if they live only a few years past their retirement age, and a great deal more if they live a long life.[1]

Social Security was by the 1970s an integral part of the U.S. democratic society. The program, which absorbed an increasing share of workers' earning, was constituting ever larger percentages of Federal expenditures. Liberals, idea brokers, and Social Security Administration (SSA) officials pressed for greater coverage and increased benefits as other innovations bolstered older Americans' retirement—to the Employee Retirement Income Security Act (1974), which established vesting and funding standards for pension plans managed by private firms; and to encouraging people to create Individual Retirement Accounts (IRAs). President Gerald Ford thought these measures reinforced the three-legged stool of Social Security, pensions, and savings.

Given these precedents for expanding Social Security and increasing retirement security in the marketplace, it seems ironic that countervailing currents slowly began to undercut future growth and success. Conventional wisdom concerning Social Security and its interlocking components, warned some critics, was shortsighted. "The politically cheap expansion of programs actually tended to devalue the commitments to social policy and transform it into a predicate of economic growthmanship (sic) and mass consumerism."[2]

The opening salvo was fired by so-called "Notch babies" (FICA contributors born between 1917 and 1921), who complained that Social Security's benefit formula reduced the amount of their monthly checks. Congress fixed the error, which was caused when SSA (as required by the 1972 Social-Security amendments) transitioned to automatic cost-of-living adjustments (COLAs). Disputes flared: Since notch-baby recipients felt cheated, lawmakers insisted that SSA had generously corrected the issue. The controversy showed that the program's presumed value-neutral formulae were bureaucratic markers that unintentionally could spark claims of intragenerational inequities among Social-Security recipients.[3]

As postwar affluence gave way to stagflation during the 1970s, there were distressing threats to Social Security's transgenerational fiscal solvency. Soaring interest rates, flattening wages, and rising unemployment battered the U.S. economy. Gerald Ford expressed doubts about social-insurance financing in his 1975 State of the Union address, but election-year politics postponed any executive-branch resolution by the Republican president. Key members of Jimmy Carter's administration (1976–1980) sensed that "the optimistic expansionist philosophy that underlay Social Security planning has now changed to one of guarded hope that the best of the past can be preserved while the considerable needs of the future are addressed."[4]

Four advisory panels told President Carter that Social-Security readjustments were necessary. Experts recommended correcting the COLA formula to adjust an imbalance between contributions and payouts in Disability Insurance.[5] As he wrestled with budgetary constraints, advisors' conflicting viewpoints within the West Wing, and after Watergate resulted in a sharp decline trust in government, the president decided to tighten eligibility criteria for disabilities.

The 1977 Social-Security amendments raised FICA contributions and taxes paid by self-employed workers. This made Jimmy Carter the first president—a Democrat at that—to cut rather than to augment Social Security. Unions opposed the measure and outraged liberal Republicans and Democrats. Public confidence in the program fell, as polls documented increasing skepticism about Social Security's fiscal viability. This alarmed some observers insofar it raised related concerns about the legitimacy of Federal institutions.[6] Former secretaries of Health, Education and Welfare Arthur Flemming and Wilbur Cohen joined Social-Security stalwarts in launching "Save Our Security" (SOS), to prevent any additional programmatic cuts. "There are not going to be any more easy votes on social security," Congressman Al Ullman warned.[7]

A decades-long skein of legislative enhancements, which had expanded the program through incremental politics, was suddenly in jeopardy. In retrospect, Jimmy Carter should have tested political waters before executing unpopular policies. "Every time the press writes that Social Security has money problems," a congressman complained, "we get a ton of letters and phone calls from people who want to be reassured."[8]

The 1981 inauguration of Ronald Reagan, no friend of Social Security, presaged deeper Social-Security bloodletting. "This system is going to land on the rocks," predicted the president's Budget Director, "and by '83, you will have solvency problems coming out of your ears. You know, sometimes sheer reality has a sobering effect."[9] Edwin Dale, now chief public affair officer in Reagan's Office of Management and Budget, was acutely aware of a turn in Social-Security dynamics as the domestic economy was being battered. Distancing himself from earlier comments, Dale joined the chorus voicing concern.

Convinced that a bloated Federal government hindered U.S. economic recovery, the president proposed significant cutbacks in Social Security, including a 25% reduction in early-retirement benefits, a three-month delay in COLAs, tighter Disability Insurance eligibility criteria than Carter had effected, and eliminating "windfall" benefits for retirees with minimal covered earnings.[10] Wilbur Cohen charged that Reagan's plan was "a calamity, a tragedy, and a catastrophe." U.S. House of Representatives speaker Timothy ("Tip") O'Neill (D-Mass) denounced the president's proposal as "despicable" and "a rotten thing to do ... that robs the system of its most important feature: the confidence of the American people." Senator William Armstrong (R-Colo) called it "a masterpiece of bad timing."[11]

Although the Senate rejected the president's initiative by a 96–0 margin—its last easy vote on the program, Social Security Trustees warned that there would be inadequate funds to pay old-age benefits by July 1983. A national distemper, lingering after Nixon and Carter, was permeating political, economic, and societal fears: "Our sense of citizenship, of social warmth and a shared fate has become thin gruel," lamented influential columnist George Will.[12]

With few palatable options President Reagan decided to partner with Speaker of the House Tip O'Neill to form a bipartisan panel, The National Commission on Social Security Reform (NCSSR). This move built on Social-Security history of Federal leaders choosing seasoned experts to negotiate reforms behind closed doors. The president and House and Senate leaders each designated five members for NCSSR. Seven were ranking members of congressional committees dealing with social-security issues or aging policies. Robert Ball and Robert Myers, who for decades had been top-level Social-Security officials, were appointed. Only two NCSSR members, *bona fide* members of Washington's elite and well versed in macro-economics, had no prior involvement with the program.

NCSSR's chief assets were also liabilities: Insiders understood all too well how Capitol Hill mixed Social-Security policymaking and electoral politics. The 15 commissioners often had difficulty between differentiating (1) disinterested expertise in representing the public interest and (2) exercising self-interests as actors with partisan instincts and suspicions. For months, NCSSR appointees took a low profile in public hearings. Republicans behind the scenes curried support for Robert Myers's actuarial yardsticks projecting short-terms deficit and long-term insolvency. Democrats meanwhile circled around Robert Ball, who tried to devise compromises that would be acceptable to a conservative President and liberal Speaker of the House.[13]

In January 1983, when prospects for success seemed remote, NCSSR chairman Alan Greenspan, Senators Robert Dole and Daniel Patrick Moynihan, Robert Ball, and White House chief of staff James A. Baker III made "one more try" to break the impasse.[14] Maneuvering through backdoor negotiations, this Gang of Five formulated a bipartisan reform package, fashioning proposals with the intergenerational patina upon which Reagan and O'Neill insisted.

Claude Pepper, NCSSR's oldest member and esteemed voice of the gray lobby, declared how much had been at stake in resolving the impasse:

> Social Security is the most universal and most valued expression of our nation's conscience. It is also good business for the nation. And the agreement…represents a fair exchange of concessions by all of us in return for a restoration of national faith that this nearly half-century-old institution will be alive and well as far into the future as we can reasonably see.[15]

NCSSR voted 12–3 to send its final report to Congress. Their recommendations pleased and offended Democrats and Republicans, conservatives and liberals, alike. The commissioners increased the contributor pool by requiring Federal employees to participate; state and local workers were forbidden to terminate coverage.

NCSSR offered greater protection for disabled widow(er)s and divorced spouses. Other measures liberalized earning tests for workers who remained in the labor force beyond "normal" retirement age, and proposed (provoking liberals' protests) postponing COLAs for six months in order to cut the rate of benefit hikes. Responding both to current fiscal constraints and Baby Boomers' expected old-age needs, the Commission's package increased the Delayed Retirement Credit for each month past the eligibility age up until age 70, but NCSSR did not reach consensus about any recommendation to lift the retirement age. (The House Ways and Means committee decided to gradually lift the retirement age to 67 by 2027.)[16] Despite conservative opposition, the NCSSR package raised employee tax rates and, for the first time, taxed benefits paid to high-income individuals.

I had an opportunity in 1983 and 1984 to interview nearly all of the NCSSR commissioners, key White House participants, and dozens of their staff. In off-the-record conversations (which typically confirmed opinions these individuals were expressing in the media), I was impressed by everybody's intelligence and diligence—including those whose views differed from mine. Some contacts got personal. Robert Myers invited me home for dinners with his wife. John Heinz accepted my invitations to address university students, to whom he voiced concerns, illustrated in report cards, about how public ignorance undercut Social Security's good works. Eric Kingson, one of Robert Ball's staff, remains a friend.

Meanwhile, I supplemented person-to-person interviews by digging more thoroughly into Social Security's history. To delve more deeply into NCSSR activities and delays, I perused every pertinent article that appeared in the *Congressional Quarterly*, *The Gerontologist*, the *National Journal*, the *Social Security Bulletin*, *The New York Times*, *The Wall Street Journal*, and the *Washington Post*. To conceptualize the relevant contours of 20th-century U.S. history, I relied on a model presented by Roger Fisher and William Ury in *Getting to Yes: Negotiating Agreement without Giving In* (Penguin, 1981), to explicate the Gang of Five's negotiations. The authors recommend having respectful perspectives that focus on interests, not positions, and stressed stipulating objective criteria, counting congressional votes, and inventing options for mutual gain. Their book, it seemed to me, captured what transpired in NCSSR's eleventh hour.

The 1983 legislation was a major turning point in Social Security's history, at least as noteworthy as the 1939 and 1972 amendments. So with support from the Twentieth Century Fund, which had been interested in social-insurance policymaking since the New Deal, I made the 1983 Social-Security amendments the anchor of my historical interpretation of *Social Security: Visions and Revisions* (Cambridge, 1986). NCSSR preserved Social Security, I believed, by altering its *modus operandi*. Hewing to normative principles without eviscerating time-tested objectives, experts and lawmakers successfully defused the imminent fiscal shortfall. The 1983 amendments represented a dramatic engagement in the politics of incrementalism, to my mind, by extending a pragmatic approach in Social-Security policymaking, a construct effectively executed by Progressives and New Dealers in dealing with social problems.

Social Security: Visions and Revisions argued that Reagan, O'Neill, NCSSR, and Congress short-circuited the program's midlife crisis. Upholding individual rights and mutual responsibilities in a milieu full of risks and imponderables, they modified transactions that further advanced justice across generations. The 1983 amendments bent Social Security's trajectory to preserve and enhance Social Security's legacy. Policymakers trusted hopes over fears. "There are changes in the law," declared former HEW secretary Wilbur J. Cohen, "but none of them are fundamental changes or unreasonable in light of the situation."[17]

The times, I thought, warranted historicizing interpretations of retirement, universal coverage, gender inequities, and Federal healthcare programs through the prism of the game-changing 1983 Social-Security amendments. I derived three lessons by applying history:

1   Because it is difficult to forecast "facts" about complex, long-range issues that might upend Social Security's future, policymakers and legislators in 1983 seized on manageable, pressing "problems" that in fits and starts needed to be resolved.

2   Debates over Social Security shied away from major structural changes in operations, while reaffirming foundational principles. The Gang of Five and NCSSR pragmatically crafted technical adjustments that could be reworked in the future.

3   The executive and legislative Federal officials, who rallied around the 1983 amendments, were aware of real limitations in rectifying technical disagreements. Braced for unpredictable critiques, this bipartisan group of participants (however reluctantly) negotiated a consensus to benefit millions of stakeholders.[18]

The 1983 amendments altered the flow of incremental politics I asserted in *Social Security: Visions and Revisions*. Like NCSSR, future policymakers would not necessarily have the congressional majorities that FDR and LBJ had.

My interpretation was well received. "All serious students of Social Security, professionals and lay persons alike, should read Professor Achenbaum's monumental work," declared NCSSR executive director Robert J. Myers. "Achenbaum's book is easily the best survey of the history of social security policy that we have," opined American public historian W. Elliot Brownlee, elaborating that "Achenbaum is one of the historians of twentieth-century policy making who have something stimulating and constructive to add to discussions of contemporary policy issues." The Twentieth Century Fund seemed appreciative: "Achenbaum's intriguing historical treatment is a major contribution to understanding the system," noted the director's foreword, "his recommendations for change are also worthy of consideration."[19]

Much to my surprise and dismay, however, the Twentieth Century Fund hedged its bets by simultaneously issuing a conservative's analysis of the program. Michael J. Boskin's *Too Many Promises: The Uncertain Future of Social Security* contended that the program was on a collision course with insolvency. Social-Security advocates, according to Boskin, had excessively raised expectations about the program's way of distributing benefits. He argued that, absent major reformatting, Social Security was bound in the future to truncate employees' working careers and discourage savings.[20]

Far more influential among Washington's power elites and idea brokers than the books that Professor Boskin and I wrote was Paul Light's *Artful Work: The Politics of Social Security Reform* (McGraw-Hill College, 1985). Light interpreted the politics behind the 1983 Social-Security amendments based on his staff work for sagacious Congressman Barber Conable (R-NY). Light was an insider with easy access to NCSSR members and staffs.

Events leading up and following the passage of the 1983 Social-Security amendments, Light and I agreed, warranted the shift in social-insurance policymaking achieved through incremental politics. Like my history of Social Security, *Artful Work* offered a clear, clean, and reasonable message devoid of arcane, technical analyses of Social Security's working. What had occurred in the early 1980s and what was its significance? "Perhaps such an explanation can never emerge from the complicated history of the system," he noted.[21]

But looking back through the ebb and flow of U.S. history, we interpreted recent events differently, and derived conflicting lessons. I expected the program to continue evolving in an incremental manner. Paul Light artfully and rightly anticipated that partisan disagreements would sharpen and legislative stalemates recur throughout and after the Reagan Revolution.

Notes

1 Dale, Edwin L., Jr. 1973, January 14. "The security of Social Security: The young pay for the old." *The New York Times Magazine*, 8. 45.
2 Heclo, Hugh. 1981. "Toward the new welfare state." In *The Development of Welfare States in Europe and America*, eds. Peter Flora & Arnold J. Heidenheimer. New Brunswick, NJ: Transaction, 13–38.
3 Collins, Mitchell. 2017. "Who are the notch babies? Why does it matter?" www.medium.com
4 Ross, Stanford. 1979, July 17. "Social Security commissioner calls improvements in benefits unlikely." *New York Times*, 10.
5 Derthick, Martha. 1979. *Policymaking for Social Security.* Washington, D.C.: Brookings Institution.
6 Kingson, Eric R. 1984. "Financing Social Security." *Policy Studies Journal*, **13**, 138–139.
7 Ullman, Al. 1979, January 8. "No Social Security cuts." *The New York Times*, 12.
8 *The New York Times.* 1981, January 2. "Member of Congress and aides seeking ways to keep Social Security solvent," A11.
9 Greider, William. 1981, December. "The education of David Stockman." *Atlantic Monthly*, **248**, 43.
10 *The New York Times.* 1981, May 13. "Reagan Social Security plan explained," 1, A29.
11 Achenbaum, W. Andrew. 1986. *Social Security: Visions and Revisions.* New York: Cambridge University Press. Quotations on 78.
12 Will, George F. 1983. *Statecraft as Soulcraft,* New York: Simon & Schuster, 45. See also Morris Janowitz. 1983. *The Reconstruction of Patriotism.* Chicago: University of Chicago Press.
13 Achenbaum, *Social Security.*
14 Dole, Robert. 1983, January 3. "Reagan's faithful allies." *The New York Times*, 14; Moynihan, Daniel Patrick. 1983, January 17. "More than Social Security was at stake." *The New York Times*, 17.
15 Pepper, Claude. 1983, January 23. "A triumph of bipartisan negotiating." *The New York Times*, F2.
16 Kingson, Eric R. 1984. "Financing Social Security," *Policy Studies Journal*, **13**, 151.
17 Cohen, Wilbur J., 1983. In Achenbaum, *Social Security*, 98.

18 Achenbaum, *Social Security*, 91–97.
19 Murray Rossant. 1986. "Foreword" in Achenbaum, *Social Security*, x.
20 Boskin, Michael J. 1986. *Too Many Promises: The Uncertain Future of Social Security.* New York: Dow-Jones, Inc.
21 Light, Paul C. 1985. *Artful Work: The Politics of Social Security Reform.* New York: McGraw-Hill College.

Chapter 6

Conservatives create a different historical context for Social Security

Introduction

I wondered why did the Twentieth Century Fund published my liberal interpretation within weeks of issuing Michael Boskin's conservative rendering of the program. And why was Paul Light's *Artful Work* so well received? Had I been wrong to interpret Social-Security's history as refracted through the prism of the 1983 amendments?

To get out of my midlife funk, I reread Albert O. Hirschman's *Exit, Voice, and Loyalty*,[1] a masterpiece (alongside Fisher and Ury's *Getting to Yes*) that I had used to craft my story line. Hirschman hypothesized that people respond to institutional declines by quitting, dissenting, or redoubling. The 1981–1983 National Commission on Social Security Reform (NCSSR), I deduced, first withdrew from the public eye, then argued over partisan positions, and finally negotiated a compromise package that the Federal executive and legislative branches hoped had resolved impending and future fiscal problems. Little did I know in the late 1980s that Congress was done dealing with Social Security.

Neither Boskin, Light, nor I decided to EXIT Social Security. Instead, we raised our VOICES in distinctive keys and tempos. Boskin criticized Social Security's fiscal streams. Light's VOICE claimed that shortcomings in the 1983 amendments complemented mistaken notions enshrined by the Founding Fathers and missteps taken by later generations. Assuming that Social Security was back on course, my VOICE engendered LOYALTY to ideas that I had learned from mentors. Mine was a reasonable historical perspective, I felt; it justified my forecast that Social Security's growth would continue incrementally.

Over the next four decades, much to my dismay, conservatives crafted a different agenda for Social-Security policymaking. It took time in

DOI: 10.4324/9781003345985-9

mid-career for me to recognize and accept history-making changes in Federal, state, and local politics. I increasingly sensed that I would have to discard some of my mentors' generational legacy. To formulate an authentic approach about safeguarding Social Security required me to rethink the message I wanted to touch and persuade diverse audiences. Otherwise, I would fail in *Leaving a legacy in an aging society*, especially for younger readers with histories different from mine.

Events since 1983 undermine Social Security's handling of risks, rights, and responsibilities

Popular support for Social Security after the 1983 amendments never returned to levels of trust that had existed in the 1970s. In *Social Security: Visions and Revisions,* my 1986 interpretation of the program's history and current status, I believed that NCSSR had effected a great bipartisan compromise. The 1983 amendments ensured Social Security's immediate and long-term fiscal footing by slowing increasing Baby Boomers' retirement age, and requiring government employees to pay into the system with raised (Federal Insurance Contribution Act) FICA contributions.

The program came under steady attack, despite 50 years of embodying an intergenerational compact that was sound, fair, and worked. Another round of contextual disconnects arose between policymakers and Social-Security stakeholders. "Too rarely were Americans made aware that the much bigger problem was the unprecedented rise in income inequalities that had started around 1980."[2] Ordinary citizens doubted Social Security's continued capacity to balance individual rights and mutual responsibility. Some commentators worried that changing the program was "reopening a settled debate" about Social Security's capacity to set income floors that protected FICA contributors against risks. Reforming Social Security was increasingly mired in hyper-partisan debates over Big Government's spending.

There were several ramifications for the shift from the liberal apparatus that Franklin Delano Roosevelt (FDR) deployed to enact Social Security to conservatives' eagerness to cut back Federal institutions like Social Security. Some were relational: a new generation of Federal politicians excoriated progressive initiatives. Congressman Newt Gingrich (R-Ga)'s "Contract with America" provoked polarized divisions over democratic norms as it stoked fears that encouraged citizens to voice their distrust of experts and authority by voting New

Democrats and right-wing Republicans into office.[3] Other factors coalesced within a diversifying, recession-prone aging society. New sources of information and public opinion fostered ideological media segmentation.

Furthermore, the media broadcasted a proliferation of ageist stereotypes, which undercut images of positive, vital aging. Generational warfare, waged by conservative think tanks and foundations, threatened vested interests and established, politically influential organizations. Americans for Generational Equity (AGE), *The New Republic*, and best sellers such as Phillip Longman's *Born to Pay* caricatured older Americans as "greedy geezers." Right-wing commentators deplored the generosity of Social-Security benefits; they pitied youth struggling to pay off college debts, buy homes, and save for retirement—life events that their parents mostly took for granted, because they were usually attainable in middle-class America.

Disparities imperiled dreams of sharing earlier generations' upward mobility. World War II veterans seized opportunities for getting ahead in an affluent society; they counted on Federal officials' good-faith efforts to level the playing field and to lend support to marginalized, and mostly white poor people. Inevitably there had been postwar bumps in unemployment rates and price rises, yet they seemed less harmful than the disturbing stagflation that crippled the Carter administration and convinced President Reagan's allies and advisors that Social Security seemed on the verge of bankruptcy.

A new generation of neoconservative lawmakers began in the 1980s to propose and enact policies that fortified efforts to ensure a Reagan Revolution took hold. Ideas from recently emerged think tanks and journals fed the right-wing contention that "government is the problem." New faces in government gained populist appeal in mapping an ideological shift.[4] Those who upheld the so-called postwar "liberal consensus" lost ground. In the quest for power, moderates reacted with resentment and contempt.[5] George H. W. Bush and Bill Clinton, who presented themselves as centrists who exercised power as governors sought to reduce taxes, mayors fought urban crime, and few local officials advocated affirmative action.

> Both the Left and the Right, unwilling to brook dissent, began dismantling structures that nurture fair-minded debate...Both parties had grown hollow—hard and partisan on the outside, empty on the inside—while political debate, newly waged almost entirely online, had become frantic, desperate, and paranoid.[6]

Since the 1988 presidential election, which put George H. W. Bush into the Oval Office, Democrats won the popular vote seven out of nine times and Republicans captured the White House often enough to appoint six of the nine sitting Supreme Court justices.

Meanwhile, the media was increasingly dominated by right-wing ideologues and personalities who celebrated how power and wealth now ruled the land. "Fake news" and sensational commentaries in social-media outlets that "exacerbated the political isolation of ordinary Americans, while strengthening polarization on both the left and right, automating identity politics, and contributing, at the same time, to a distant, vague, and impotent model of political engagement."[7] Operating on a profit-oriented platform, finely tuned to fragmented markets, trolls in the social media spread disinformation. Unable to discern which "experts" were credible, audiences turned to outlets that pandered to their fears.[8]

All of this had a strong impact on Social-Security policymaking. Its advocates and critics grasped how effectively extremist journalists and pundits distorted stakeholders' views:

> The program is imperiled by intensifying partisan polarization—a problem that has been decades in the making ... President Bill Clinton and then President George W. Bush agreed on the need for reform and made it part of their governing agendas. Yet both were stymied in their efforts ... The Social Security program and those who depend on it desperately need responsible bipartisan leadership.[9]

Fiscal and ideological threats to Social Security currently are greater today than four decades ago. Broadcasts on the internet and social media often convert these potentially menacing realities into inevitable crises, which frighten many readers of this book. Having lived through no reforms since the passage of the 1983 amendments, few are aware of politically acceptable remedial fixes for the program. Instead, they have witnessed the transformation of Social Security into the third-rail of U.S. politics.

How Social Security became "the third rail" in Washington

Social Security, once a sacred calf, became a wounded cow that no longer was getting high priority in Washington. Policy elites and lobbyists rarely want to deal with Social Security's vulnerability. To my mind, the politics of avoidance that deters constructive reforms resembles antebellum Americans inching toward impending crisis over extending or abolishing slavery. Presidents since Ronald Reagan have dealt with Social Security inconsistently, which confuses stakeholders who rely on sound bites and a segmented media for information.

George H.W. Bush, taking guidance from his Council of Economic Advisors (chaired by Michael Boskin, the other Twentieth Century Fund author), created the 1988 Medicare Catastrophic Coverage Act (MCCA). Liberals were outflanked. Forty unions demanded its rescission. For the sake of fiscal austerity, one of FDR's sons, James Roosevelt who chaired the National Committee to Preserve Social Security and Medicare, started a letter campaign to oppose its implementation. MCCA was repealed the following year.

Further demands for retrenchment eviscerated support for Social Security during Bill Clinton's presidency. The 1994–1996 Social Security Advisory Council failed to reach consensus. Instead, experts issued three reports: The Maintain Benefits Plan anticipated increases in payroll taxes; the Individual Account Plan favored reducing benefits; and the Personal Security Account Plan proposed a major overhaul of the system.[10] Each approach departed significantly from the package enacted through the 1983 Social-Security amendments.

In his first term George W. Bush, more fervently conservative than Bill Clinton, advocated outpatient drug benefits under Medicare. His 2003 Medicare Prescription Drug, Improvement, and Modernization Act prompted arguments over whether (1) it was cost effective to expand Social Security, and whether (2) private health-care companies should control transactions between providers and patients.[11] Surveys taken a week after Bush signed the measure indicated that only 26% of all senior citizens approved the amendment whereas 47% opposed it. A voting bloc, once perceived as homogeneous, now divided along age, gender, region, and income lines.[12] Traditional liberal stalwarts—the AFL-CIO, Families USA, and the American Nursing Association—seized on defects; conservative groups parted from Republican lawmakers. The 2003 Act politically fragmented Social-Security coalitions.

After his reelection, President Bush made privatization of Social Security his first order of business. "Social Security has been the third rail of American politics. Grab ahold of it, and you're toast. In 2005, I did more than touch the rail. I hugged it," George W. Bush recalled after leaving office.[13] Conservative think tanks, such as the Heritage

Foundation and the Cato Institute supported Bush. American Association for Retired Persons (AARP) deployed its media savvy and considerable wealth in vehement opposition. According to Gallup pollsters, public disapproval of Bush's proposal rose from 48% to 65% between January and June 2005, sufficient enough to persuade the president to withdraw the plan.[14]

The Great Recession of 2008 then demonstrated the importance of Social Security's income floor. During this major economic downturn, Baby Boomers who suffered losses in real estate and the stock market could count on receiving monthly retirement checks. Few Americans gave thanks to the program's role as a powerful equalizing force.[15] A psychological malaise reinforced misgivings that a fiscally unstable Social-Security program would not be there for rising generations.

Barack Obama left a mixed policymaking legacy for older Americans. On the one hand, his campaign for the Patient Protection and Affordable Care Act (ACA, 2010) rewarded physicians and hospitals that treated previously uncovered low-income senior citizens. Older Americans were not ACA's main categorical target, but the measure improved the elderly's healthful well-being overall.[16] On the other hand, Obama's bipartisan National Commission on Fiscal Responsibility and Reform (2010) did not have the super-majority necessary to propose steps to reduce deficits, and to shore up Social Security's solvency. Co-chairs Erskine Bowles and Alan Simpson put together a plan, but no action was taken on the Commission's recommendations.[17] Nonetheless, the president's willingness to consider reducing the program illustrates the extent to which Democrats like Clinton and Obama were acceding to Washington's neoconservative lobbyists and lawmakers.[18] In 2013 the president proposed cutting between $200 and $300 billion from Medicare and Social Security; later on, President Obama wanted to appoint as Social-Security commissioner a Bush official, who supported privatization.

To many, Obama's indifference to Social Security paralleled his administration's desultory attention to aging issues, and possibly other policies that did not target Blacks for special attention.[19] A frustrated, disillusioned gray lobby in response persisted in efforts to change the tide. Progressive groups like "Social Security Works" championed liberalizing changes, but their values-driven strategic campaign could not decelerate the inertia sustained by the opposition politics masterminded by Mitch McConnell (R-KY) and Ted Cruz (R-TX).

Donald Trump claimed to uphold his 2016 campaign pledge not to cut Social Security, but Roger Ailes, the head of Fox News, reckoned that Trump wanted a job at NBC, not the White House.[20] The president incessantly attempted to scrap the ACA (which he derided as Obamacare); his tax reform benefitted the affluent while further piling on the national debt. Trump did little to relieve working- and middle-class Americans in the midst of a pandemic.[21] Many suspected that the Trump administration was starving Social Security under the cover provided by Covid-19.[22]

Joseph Biden during the 2020 campaign vowed to widen the Federal government's safety net from cradle to grave. Members of Congress called for expanding Social Security before Biden took office. John Larson, who chairs the House Ways and Means subcommittee on Social Security, was joined by 200 cosponsors introducing the Social Security 2100 Act. The measure would increase retirement and disability benefits, cut taxes for middle-income Americans, and keep the system solvent through the century. "Our bill," declared Congressman Larson, "would enhance and expand the nation's most successful insurance program, which touches the lives of every American."

Democratic senators Elizabeth Warren, Chuck Schumer, and ranking Finance Committee member Ron Wyden, proposed increasing by $200 monthly benefits for all veterans, Social-Security and Disability-Insurance recipients as well as beneficiaries of Supplemental Security. Congress voted to provide additional income to these groups through the end of 2021, as well as delivering direct relief to rescue the economy through the American Rescue Plan. As this book goes to press, however, Biden has not sent a Social-Security package to Capitol Hill. He has been preoccupied with the pandemic, Ukraine, and low numbers in survey polls. And without having overwhelming control of Congress, which was advantageous to FDR and LBJ, President Biden faced defeats—in large part due to Senate Minority Leader Mitch McConnell's maneuvering and Joe Manchin (D–WVa) joining Republicans to defeat funding bills.[23]

Safeguarding Social Security for Future Generations requires me to reframe the narrative

Interpreting Social Security's history by invoking "risks," "rights," and "responsibilities" was making less and less sense to me, as I watched conservatives becoming more dominant in U.S. politics after the passage of the 1983 Social-Security amendments. I wanted to keep believing—and I still do—that FDR's program remained "the brightest ornament in the federal establishment." It took me a long time to acknowledge inconvenient truth: Social Security was being targeted a program floundering in a "government gone awry."

My dilemma pit stubbornness against critical reasoning. I hesitated to substitute new keywords for "risks," "rights," and "responsibilities," which informed my *Social Security: Visions and Revisions*. I *knew* from reading scholarly and media reports that few on Capitol Hill saw Social Security as a priority after the 1983 Social-Security amendments were enacted. Yet I *resisted* discarding a heuristic framework that still served me well in teaching and writing about the program. I took comfort in deflecting elements of the reconfigured big picture.

I struggled in limbo to concoct substitute keywords for "risks," "rights," and "responsibilities." None seemed quite right. Yet looking back, I recall feeling on a gut level that I needed to reframe interpretations of Social Security's history. This were true especially since I was concurrently discerning a need to mount a reasonable and persuasive argument for Millennials and younger stakeholders, who in the main lacked much grasp of the program's development. The relative degree of their generational commitment to safeguarding Social Security would be key in assessing present and future trends. Casual conversations over dinner tables echoed media reports and my own inquiries, which further reinforced what Washington insiders told me about the low morale prevalent in Social Security's overworked staff. Agents in local offices erred in calculating clients' benefits. On top of this, older stakeholders were unwittingly divulging their Social-Security numbers to scammers. Senior citizens, according to media reports, were becoming victims of identity fraud.[24]

Anecdotal stories exposed me to more disturbing structural issues besetting the program. Technological glitches were unmasking Social Security's faceless, bureaucratic modus operandi. Computer upgrades quickly became outmoded information systems.[25] Transactions conducted through automated phone calls or over the internet were a far cry from the 1930s, when eligible workers signed up for Social-Security cards in post offices. Social Security Administration (SSA) was offering clients fewer contacts; local offices have been closed due to budgetary constraints.

Some journalists, sensationalizing reports of SSA personnel being hampered by inadequate technological and technical support, conveyed misleading depictions of Social Security's inability to meet its previously high administrative standards. Compared to the errors made by hospitals and insurance companies in billing patients, however, Social

Security was still efficiently delivering monthly checks to millions of beneficiaries.

Social Security's public face, I reluctantly admitted, *had* wrinkled with age. In media reports "social insurance" rarely seemed synonymous with Social Security; my descriptions of fixing the program in terms of "risks," "rights," and "responsibility" seemed less robust. Lawmakers, journalists, and Social-Security experts were interacting in a hostile milieu, far dissimilar to challenges that FDR faced in relieving life's modern risks and adversities. Social-Security advocates were yielding control over the policy agenda to conservative idea brokers. Congressional liberals lacked majority support to enact Social-Security reform. The gray lobby, which once had easier access to power, were presenting making their case for defending, and possibly expanding the program, on editorial pages, in sound bites and through white papers.

The politics of hope that had effectively sustained Social Security's formative years was being steadily trumped by the politics of fear. Advocates of incremental tweaks or restructuring the program to raise the transgenerational income floor had to compete with doomsday prophets and right-wing conservatives' demands to scale back benefits or retrofit Social Security into private savings accounts in order to cleanse "the deep state." Partisan bickering over pie-chart statistics and incommensurate projections too often precludes reaching any breakthrough consensus about the values and politics essential to maintaining and sustaining intergenerational transfers.

Social Security's champions faced great difficulties in allaying concerns enough to convince younger FICA contributors that Social Security will be there for them upon retirement. The disillusionment and polarization that bedevil the policy elite make Social-Security beneficiaries of all ages anxious about what they will get. Portraying the program as a New-Deal legacy that still can promote justice across generations turns off contributors, who know little—and often care less—about Social Security. Overwhelmed by the specter of gloomy economic forecasts, many fear that they will not end up being better off than their parents in a pay-as-you-go system that probably will not will yield them comparable benefits.

Yawning gaps in intragenerational fortunes truncate transgenerational dialogues. Older Social-Security beneficiaries want to protect their hard-earned monthly checks. Mounting tuition debts, gig employments, and systemic modes of inequality present risks to

Millennials and younger FICA contributors, from which survivors of the Greatest Generation and Baby Boomer parents were spared. Large pockets of the youthful electorate register a cynical distaste for politics. Millennials are indifferent or angered by partisan debates that do not prioritize their generations' needs and risks. Young Americans demand rights that embrace their age groups' diversity and disparities. The most notable shift in generational responses to Social Security comes under the rubric of mutual responsibility: Where are the incentives for rising generations of stakeholders to uphold a compact with greedy Baby Boomers?

I doubt that framing Social Security's current assets and deficits in terms of risks, rights, and responsibilities reaches the audiences that I wish to persuade. I want stakeholders, who constitute most U.S. citizens, to reevaluate the program's aims and values. It remains to be seen whether critical thinking and transgenerational conversations suffice to mobilize diverse sets of age groups to support safeguarding Social Security for future generations. Baby Boomers like me, must listen carefully to the concerns and reservations of rising generations. I hear three sets of fears that must be taken into account.

First set of fear-inducing questions: *Will Social Security be there for Millennials and younger covered workers when they retire? Why must younger workers pay heavily into a system that benefits older Americans but does not promise a favorable rate of return for them?* These questions amplify poll data indicating that roughly 80% of those for whom retirement looms in the distant future do not expect to receive Social Security.[26] This fear rests on youth whose mistrust of social institutions exceeds that of older people; 64% doubt that the federal government can solve many of America's problems that affect them.[27]

And yet, there is more volatility in younger Americans' opinions than surveys indicate. Most Social-Security contributors born between 1979 and 2000 believe that adverse views of government can be turned around—if the U.S. had honest and empathetic political leaders. Even dire actuarial projections, moreover, forecast that Millennials can count on getting twice as much from Social Security as current retirees, because FICA tax contributions compound at a faster rate than inflation. To count on Social Security, which never was intended to replace pre-retirement income fully to approximate current levels of retirement income, requires all workers to set aside money in their savings accounts, invest in corporate pension plans, and maybe to plan working part time after becoming eligible for Social-Security benefits.[28]

A second set of fear-inducing questions: *Do imminent and long-term shortages in Social Security trust fund reserves add to Federal deficits? Is the U.S. government using current F.I.C.A. contributions to reduce its staggering deficits? Are immigrants, disabled workers, and widows unfairly benefiting from contributions that should accrue to Millennials and Gen-Z?*

Conservative U.S. senators and presidents falsely assert that Social-Security entitlements are a major source of soaring federal deficits. This fear-driven argument is not sustained either by law or by Social Security's history. Ensuring Social Security's solvency simply does not increase the national debt.

By law, Social-Security surpluses must be invested in U.S. Treasury notes, which have the same credit guarantees as any other federal bond. The system's revenue and expenses, moreover, have been independent of pressures to hide budgetary shortfalls.[29] Some misinterpret recent American history, to claim that President Johnson used Social-Security surpluses to mask the costs of waging the war in Vietnam. LBJ actually put the funds "on budget" (as did his successors until 1986). Social Security never covered government shortfalls in other areas. Nor did it unduly privilege women, minorities, or immigrants.[30]

A third set of fearsome questions: *Has Covid-19 unsettled conventional wisdom about how Social Security operates? Does the pandemic justify Federal officials using the public-health crisis as a reason for scrapping Social Security? If not, has the coronavirus effected societal ruptures sufficiently to reduce the odds of younger workers getting retirement benefits?*

Addressing this third set of fearsome questions is elaborated in the next chapters of this book. Suffice it here to note that, despite increasingly levels of distrust in Big Government and social distancing from other citizens, more than three quarters of Americans claimed before the pandemic struck that they would cooperate with each other in a crisis. Although surveys report slight demographic differences by income, education, race, ethnicity, and youth, most U.S. citizens express reservoirs of trust sufficient to allay anxieties about joining together. Alexis de Tocqueville predicted this pattern almost two centuries ago: While Americans pride their individualism in going about their daily business, they willingly rally together when a major crisis threatens the commonweal.[31]

The pandemic *has* potentially serious ramifications on Social-Security financing and putative insolvency. Economists across the political canvas and SSA staff expect Social-Security shortfalls in this century. Everyone except cynics—those who want younger generations to do the hard work of dealing with women's rights, climate change and gun control—should take this as a wake-up call to prevent a collapse of the political economy that resembles conditions in the 1930s.[32] Safeguarding Social Security in this desperate context represents this Baby Boomer's attempt to preserve a universal program linking groups in America's democracy.

Biden's desire to restore "the soul of America" unfolds in a deeply divided nation. If the government does not act to stem racism, address climate warming, hear the raging anguish of witnesses to gun violence, dark fears will decidedly escalate and jeopardize the nation's democratic fibers. That said, a glimmer of hope may lie even in the worst-case scenarios: Americans, forced to disown myths of the country's exceptionalism, may then envision and implement constructive ways of promoting justice across generations. And therein lies a central argument for leaving a legacy in an aging society by safeguarding Social Security for future generations. Only the U.S. Post Office reaches more U.S. citizens than this program.

Notes

1 Hirschman, Albert O. 1970. *Exit, Voice, and Loyalty: Responses to Declines in Firms, Organizations, and States.* Cambridge, MA: Harvard University Press.
2 Vladeck, Bruce C. 2020. "Nursing home deaths: The safety net unravels." In *The Future of Social Insurance*, ed. Thomas N. Bethell. Washington, DC: National Academy of Social Insurance, 45.
3 Fenno Jr. Richard F. 2000. *Congress at the Grassroots.* Chapel Hill: University of North Carolina Press; Brattebo, Douglas M. 2012. "You're a mean one, Mr. Gingrich." *American Behavioral Scientist*, **57**, 46–69.
4 Gerstle, Gary. 2022. *The Rise and Fall of the Neoliberal Order.* New York: Oxford University Press.
5 Dickerson, John. 2022, April. "The patron saint of stuck presidencies." *Atlantic*, 80–83.
6 Lepore, Jill. 2018. *These Truths.* New York: W. W. Norton.
7 Ibid.
8 Rauch, Jonathan. 2018. "The constitution of knowledge." *National Affairs.*
9 Blahous, Charles. 2019, April 26. "We're running out of time. Social Security must be saved now." *Washington Post.*
10 Kollmann, Geoffrey. 1997. "Social Security: Recommendations of the 1994–1996 Advisory Council on Social Security." EveryCRSReport. com.
11 Public Law, 108–173. 2003.
12 Oliver, Thomas R., Lee, Philip R. and Helene L. Lipton. 2004. *A Political History of Medicare and Drug Coverage.* New York: John Wiley Online Library.

13 Bush, George W. 2011. "Decision points, by President George W. Bush: on Social Security." www.ontheissues.org.

14 Gallup.com. 2015, February 15. "Bush's Social Security ratings in the red."

15 Munnell, Alicia. 2022, June 7. "Social Security may be the most powerful equalizing force in our nation." *Market Watch,* 11654548539.

16 Edmonds, Molly. 2010. "5 ways seniors benefit from the Affordable Care Act." Howstuffworks.com.

17 Kingson, Eric R. 2022, July 11. Personal communication.

18 Andreo, Kimberly. 2019. "Simpson-Bowles commission summary." *The Balance.*

19 Clegg, Claude A. III. 2021. *The Black President: Hope and Fury in the Age of Obama.* Baltimore: Johns Hopkins University Press.

20 Peters, Jeremy W. 2022. *Insurgency.* New York: Crown.

21 Brandes, Paul. 2020, April 11. "Another victim of Covid-19: Social Security." *Market Watch.*

22 Baker, Kevin. 2020, July. "Easy chair." *Harper's Magazine,* **341,** 7–9.

23 Shapiro, Ira. 2022. "How Mitch McConnell wrecked the Senate." *The New Republic.*

24 Derthick, Martha, quoted in Berkowitz, Edward D. 1987. "The first advisory council and the 1939 amendments." In *Social Security at Fifty,* ed. Edward D. Berkowitz. Westport, CT: Greenwood Press, 61–75.

25 Social Security News. 2013. "It is a frustrating bureaucracy." Blogspot. com.

26 Smith, Kelly Anne. 2019, February 1. "Millennials expected to get twice as much from Social Security as retirees today. It may not be enough." www. bankrate.com.

27 Gramlich, John. 2019, August 8. "Young Americans are less trusting of other people—and key institutions—than their elders." Rainie, Lee and Andrew Perrin. 2019. "Key findings about Americans' declining trust in government and each other." Pew Research Fact-Tank.

28 Backman, Maurie. 2018, July 24. "Retirement planning: 3 truths younger workers need to know." *USA Today.*

29 Miller, Mark. 2018, November 1. "Social Security and the U.S. deficit: Separating fact from fiction." *Reuters.*

30 Social Security Administration. 2005. "Research note #20: The social security trust funds and the federal budget." Agency history. Proposed revisions to the special minimum benefit for low lifetime earners. www. ssa.gov/policy/docs/policy.

31 Bagnulo, Vince. 2020. "Making democracy great again…or not: Alexis de Tocqueville on why greatness in democratic society requires justice." *Perspectives on Political Science,* **49,** 181–190.

32 Parrish, Steve. 2020. "How to build social security's insecurity into your retirement plan." *Forbes.*

Chapter 7

Will fears over a pandemic, a fractured political economy, and racism stir new hopes and demands for Social-Security reforms?

Introduction

It is too early to interpret historical trends in 21st-century America. I nevertheless write about safeguarding Social Security with a simple legacy-leaving thesis: There remains time for transgenerational collaborations to ensure Social Security's fiscal viability in order to maintain the program's role as a stabilizing institutional force in the United States as an aging society. The Covid-19 pandemic has killed more than a million Americans, unsettled the political economy, and left the rest of us coming to terms about an aging population's growing diversity and income disparities. We remain unable to find a public square in which to share conflicted views about women's rights, racism, gun violence, and global warming.

While most Americans do not think much about Social Security, the program's current status and future prospects are unfolding amidst unexpected events, culture wars, and societal lags. "Journalism is now the *second* draft of history."[1] Safeguarding Social Security for my grand-children and readers who have lived through history-in-the-making calls me to reframe and contextualize transgenerational dialogues, knowing that I cannot confidently predict the future.

> Fear is an old emotion, laid down deep in the nervous system ... Men, however, have to be afraid not only of certain malignant organisms like typhoid germs, but also the concept of ill health ... But the apprehension with which so many Americans are now regarding the world is a different thing, an emotional state where every fresh headline increases their sense of impending disaster ... When it is in the air, as it is now, it can become an instrument for any demagogue or any unexpected event to play upon.[2]
>
> (Avis Dungan Carlson)

DOI: 10.4324/9781003345985-10

Avis Dungan Carlson was more than a self-described "obscure house-wife." A feature writer for *The New Republic* and *Redbook*, she was an advice columnist for *The St. Louis Post-Dispatch* as well as author of *Small World, Long Gone* (1975) and a meditation on old age, *In the Fullness of Time* (1977). If published now, her critique would offer readers perspectives into today's crises.

Carlson's piece actually appeared in the April 1939 issue of *Harper's Magazine*. During that year, Americans feared that Franklin Delano Roosevelt's (FDR) New Deal might not end the Great Depression. After the Germans invaded Poland that September, U.S. citizens dread the fateful day in which the Unites States would enter into war.

Avis Carlson (1896–1987) expressed apprehensions that still resonate across interlocking generational lines. She lived long enough to weather Baby Boomers' polio scares and epidemics (Hong Kong flu [1968], AIDS [1981–]). Carlson had empathy for Americans who worried that global terrorism or a nuclear holocaust were imminent. She anticipated the dismay of Millennials and younger ones who distrusted institutions and officials seemingly indifferent to theirs need for opportunities to succeed. Current headlines surely fortify such real fears.

The worldwide Covid-19 pandemic cripples "normal" American ways of life

Now, in the second decade of the 21st century, Americans of all ages deeply fear that Covid-19's persistent global impact has disrupted "normal" interactions in our aging society. More than a million U.S. citizens have lost their lives—one out of every 500 Americans—making us among the world's hardest hit epicenters, despite all our advances in clinical practices. Dire health-care delivery breakdowns and confusing official reports about vaccinations cause ordinary people to mistrust Big Government's leaders trying to heal wounds of disunity. Ironically, the coronavirus might yet prove to be a crisis-riven catalyst for change.

Early in his presidency, Joseph Biden proposed to transform social welfare beyond anything imagined by New Dealers or Great-Society architects. "The COVID-19 pandemic belongs to a class of newly salient risks against which America's current collection of safety-net programs provides inadequate protection."[3] Biden's poll doldrums indicate how greatly the pandemic irradiated weaknesses in the country's institutional fabric and allegiance to core values.

The first case of Covid-19 went largely unreported in December 2019, the same month that Congress passed the SECURE (Setting Every Community Up for Retirement Enhancement) Act. Expanding workers' access to multiple-employer retirement programs, SECURE allowed long-term, part-time employees to participate in 401(k) plans, but it did not restore confidence among young contributors who had to rearrange retirement savings under Social Security.[4]

Few observers made a connection then between a virus spreading beyond China and SECURE. President Trump's ill-informed, misguided responses to the coronavirus and Supreme Court nominations dominated the news. Well into the Biden presidency, Social-Security policymaking has been peripheral in the context of the enervating domestic politics of avoidance and fear. Putin's Ukrainian invasion rebuilt NATO alliances, but it hardly displaced threats of a nuclear holocaust or stormy relations with autocrats and dictators.

Crisis One: The pandemic transforms age-based relations and generational perspectives

Despite warning signs years ago from epidemiologists and public-health officials, few governments prepared for the global disruption caused by the coronavirus. U.S. citizens were urged to wear masks, wash hands, and practice social-distancing, but many ignored the scientific advice. Covid-19 consequently posed broad age-based risks in America:[5]

- Infants and toddlers fell prey to pathogens causing rashes and respiratory disorders; unvaccinated until 2022, they were prey to being infected by their parents or at pre-school. Fifteen million students under the age 12 lacked access to school lunches, their main meal of the day. The pandemic effected a "seismic hit" because public-school funding was tied to shrinking enrollments.[6]
- Anxiety, depression, as well as attempted and actual suicides spiked among adolescents. According to school officials and psychologists, girls experienced "persistent feelings of sadness and hopelessness." Their sense of loneliness often reflected their parents' sense of being unsupported by neighbors, employers and social services.[7] In local communities across the United States, teenagers were trying to escape abuse and neglect.
- Adults between 20 and 50 here and abroad initially registered low hospitalizations and death; three months after the first U.S. case

was reported, however, there were spikes in contagion among those within this age group, vividly among those who disregarded warnings and flocked to beaches and bars. Younger women were less likely to die from Covid-19 than men. LGBT+ individuals' morbidity and mortality rates were similar to the U.S. population.

- Those over age 50 (particularly individuals with a history of diabetes, hypertension, strokes, and cancer) risked serious long-term medical complications. Cases of mild cognitive impairment, early onset Alzheimer's and related diseases, as well as persistent fatigue and depression were already being reported by clinicians.

- Older Americans were hard hit, a tragedy compounded by ageism and indifference to their plight. Nursing-home residents represented more than 10% of all cases and 40% of Covid-19 deaths.[8] Elders accounted for an overwhelming share of U.S. deaths. "There's still exceptionally high risk among older adults, even those with primary vaccine series."[9]

- Enumerated separately were prisoners and immigrants in detention centers. Veterans—especially Vietnam-era survivors, the homeless, and those living in residential facilities—lost access to health care during the outbreak. An overstretched and underfunded Department of Veterans Affairs delayed disability benefits. The U.S. Postal Service slowed up delivery of prescription drugs. Lack of equipment and savvy caused many veterans to be denied relief if they did not have access to computers or were unfamiliar with e-file software.

Intergenerational ties loosened nationwide during the pandemic. Public-school teachers designed online learning environment and tried to interact with pupils lacking internet access or home computers. College officials scrambled to replace revenue streams long heavily dependent on tuitions, dormitory life, and food service. Houses of worship suspended weekly services and postponed weddings and funerals.[10] Sports events and fine-arts center canceled Quaker City races, exhibits, and performances. Disinformation, despair and anger victimized Americans of all ages, who endured isolation and loneliness communally.[11] Trump-era politics exposed a mental-health crisis. "Politics is a pervasive and largely unavoidable source of chronic stress that exacted significant health costs for large numbers of adult Americans between 2017 and 2020."[12]

Delta variants of the coronavirus that spread in 2021 and 2022 derailed President Biden's hopes for a decisive end to the pandemic.

Unvaccinated Americans, who defied basic science and common sense, were 11 times more likely to die than those who getting booster shots. Governors in Florida, Texas, South Dakota, and other hotspots refused to issue mask mandates for school children or in hospitals.[13] A culture war ensued, which turned avowed rights to make personal choices into a political nightmare that exacerbated mistrust.

Crisis Two: The pandemic disrupts political economies here and abroad

Meanwhile, in the midst of a seemingly endless and relentless pandemic, the United States plunged into economic disasters—the second of its threefold crisis. "We don't know how long that gap is" in exposing health inequalities and market flaws, declared Nobel-laureate Joseph Stiglitz, "but there will be consequences."[14] Joblessness approached Depression-level percentages. Despite surging unemployment claims, which exceeded the number of U.S. jobs created after the 2008 recession, businesses posted help-wanted signs. Relief measures dropped the nation's poverty rate to its lowest level since 1967—but not enough to offset household shortages, economic contractions, or global hunger.

The pandemic caused price spikes on goods such as used cars, airline tickets, and hotel rooms.[15] Gas prices soared. Supply chains could not keep up with consumer demands. Cars stretched for blocks as parents went to food pantries and schoolyards to get free meals for their children. ICU units in recurring waves of urban and rural hotspots lacked beds and equipment to care for the very ill.[16] There were too few nurses willing to risk working in hospitals and nursing homes.

The coronavirus disrupted infrastructures worldwide. Hospitals and social-service agencies in Italy and Spain were overwhelmed with patients. Britain posted one of the world's highest death rates. Lockdowns in Brazil and Peru (where only a third of households had running water) crumbled as illnesses and deaths exacerbated inequalities, overcrowding, and corruption. India dealt with a plague of locusts besides high morbidity.[17] Leaders in Africa, Turkey, and the former Soviet Union refused to publish vital statistics. Putin masked the economic tolls on Russians while he tried to de-Nazify Ukrainians.

Economic disparities escalated in America—the country presumed most likely to have the wherewithal to be spared global horrors. Many restaurants and small businesses that shut down did not reopen. Public and private relief packages were exhausted within days. Evictions and missed mortgage payments soared, although the stock market reached record highs. Few citizens could ignore stark disparities in income, wealth, and sensibilities: The new aristocracy—the aggregate affluence of the top 0.1%, is four times greater in size than in the 1990s— vaunted its privileges.[18] Millions fell out of America's middle class and lost hope.

The pandemic exposed transgenerational marketplace hazards hitherto hidden or overlooked.[19] Notable were changing employment patterns. Many retired sooner than expected in 2020, and then unretired two years later; roughly a third of older workers postponed quitting their jobs. Employees over age 50, displaced in lockdowns or restructuring, meanwhile were forced into early retirement. Essential workers—young people on gig shifts, who saw their hours cut; and middle aged, low-wage earners, who lost rights to health insurance— could not count on business owners and employers to help them out. The U.S. Class of 2020, saddled with huge tuition debts, encountered gloomy employment prospects; roughly a fifth of that group, lucky enough to land jobs, earned 20% less in their first year after college than members of the Class of 2019.[20]

Women bore the brunt of the economic downturn and lost jobs. Pay gaps had narrowed from 1979 (37.7%) through 1994 (23.2%) to 22.1% in 2021.[21] Gender inequities widened as the plague persisted. Female hourly workers rarely were eligible for sick leave. Among two-earner couples, wives shouldered more household chores and childrearing. Stress mounted as single mothers, especially in the sandwich generation, were forced to juggle work and home.[22]

Covid-19 disproportionately affected minority groups, who suffered higher incidents of infections and deaths. Spanish-speaking Americans, many of whom held menial and hazardous jobs, endured health risks, discrimination, poverty, and no medical insurance.[23] Disabilities and discriminations in health-care networks disadvantaged Blacks. "Obviously the African American community has suffered from racism for a very, very long period of time," claimed Dr. Anthony Fauci, the nation's leading disease expert.[24] While Black Americans had narrowed educational annual disparities, the racial income gap fell back in 2020 to 1950 levels.[25]

Some Americans were luckily spared physical risks and financial pain. White-collar employees worked at home; many health-care professionals could talk to patients on Zoom. Income inequalities rose; executives were handsomely remunerated and tax codes shielded wealth and corporations. As the net worth of the nation's five richest people (including Jeff Bezos and Bill Gates) rose by $584 billion,[26] child poverty rates rose, and aging Social-Security beneficiaries felt they were in jeopardy. Suddenly, unemployed (Federal Insurance Contribution Act) FICA contributors lost earnings credits for Title-II pensions. In the pandemic, unlike the 2008 recession, Social-Security cost-of-living adjustment (COLA) increases could not mitigate the threat of old-dependency among retirees.

Hyper-partisan politics transmogrified the context in which President Trump's loyalists accentuated flaws in the program's policy-making. Congressional Republicans took refuge under the Covid-19 crisis and tried to cut Social-Security benefits. The CARES (the Coronavirus Aid, Relief, and Economic Security) Act under section 2302 allowed self-employed individuals and employers to get credit for pushing off FICA taxes through 2020, and then paying only half back in 2021 and 2022 respectively. In August 2020, President Trump signed an executive order to curtail FICA contributions for the rest of the year; if reelected, he promised to "terminate" them. "I like the idea of payroll tax cuts … A lot of economists would agree with me."[27]

The 2020, 2021, and 2022 annual reports from Social Security Trustees registered no upticks in the program's 75-year deficit, though they projected shortfalls in the 2030s due to lost FICA contributions amid rising rates of unemployment.[28] (The 2022 Trustees report indicates that the shortfall will occur in 2034. Some independent econometric models project 2033 and others forecast the pandemic-related impact to occur in 2035.) These pronouncements distressed younger workers who distrusted Federal leaders' ability to restore confidence in the program. Public-opinion polls indicated that 55% of those surveyed disapproved of Trump's initiatives. Americans wanted to expand unemployment benefits, and they deplored raiding Social Security. "In this moment of crisis, when millions of Americans are struggling to make ends meet and fear for their retirement, we should be enhancing Social Security, not developing policies to reduce benefits."[29] Social Security delivered monthly checks during the pandemic, but its internet and local offices (which were closed for two years and slow to reopen), frustrated and inconvenienced stakeholders.[30]

The political climate in Washington grew more toxic as President Biden plead for bipartisan civility and collaborations.

> Extreme Republican tribalism vastly accelerated as the G.O.P. tribe became dominated by a base of largely white Christians, who feared that their long-held primacy in America's power structure was being eroded by rapidly changing social norms, expanded

immigration and globalization, leaving them feeling no longer 'at home' in their own country."[31]

Waning commitment to *E Pluribus Unum* made it difficult to welcome immigrant and racial minorities who were recasting notions of diversity in an aging nation.

Crisis Three: Coming to terms with historical patterns of diversity and structural racism

Concern about Social-Security shortfalls in a pandemic-fractured political economy periodically were overshadowed and displaced by a third crisis: the waning manifestations of representative democracy prompted conflicting responses to the steady diversity of the nation's population. American adults who are members of at least 43 identifiable religious and racial groups "tend to vastly overestimate the size of minority groups."[32] Muslims (1% of the U.S. population) suffered retaliations after 9/11. There have been numerous attacks since then on Jewish synagogues (2% of the total population) and robberies and injuries to Asian (6%).

The decennial censuses meanwhile changed how they count large American subgroups. Identifying persons with multiracial-ethnic origins is complicated by generational histories and current social realities. The 1860 census specified three categories—White, Black, and mulatto. A century later, individuals of non-White backgrounds were listed according to their father's race. Census takers in 1970 asked residents if their parents were Mexican, Puerto Rican, Cuban, Filipino, Central or South American, or came from other Spanish-speaking countries. In 2020, Hispanics (a term first utilized in 1976) represented 16.3% of the population. Blacks (12.2%) and the percentage of whites had fallen to 50%.[33]

Demography and bureaucratic alterations underscored a fundamental historical truth and societal reality. Few whites cared to dwell on the nation's painful legacy of brutalizing enslaved Blacks; men of property and standing organized Ku Klux Klan lynchings, redlining northern cities; the 1921 Tulsa massacre; Jim Crow laws enforcing segregation during the first half of the 20th century.[34] Some states, alarmed by and opposed to critical-race and replacement theories, mandated that the murders of Emmet Till, Malcolm X, and the Reverend Dr. Martin Luther King, Jr. be ignored. "Continued references to 'black leaders' or the 'black agenda' ... serve only to obscure the complexities of race in a vast, multicultural nation."[35]

The pandemic, which widened a racial gap in Black–white longevity by nearly three years, made clear other health-related differences.
Poorer overall medical histories and lack of access to good health care,
contended public-health experts, correlated with Blacks being more
likely to be employed in risky jobs—as bus drivers, cooks, maids, and
sanitation workers—than whites using laptops at home. Frequent,
random acts of violence appalled Americans. Videos of George
Floyd's chokehold killing on May 2020 were brutal evidence of an
American caste system engorged in prejudice and death. The murder
in Minneapolis bore witness to a soul-wrenching, racial legacy rife
with prejudice, inequalities, and slaughter committed by solitary acts,
executed by vigilantes, or resulting from confrontations with police.[36]

Media commentators documented widespread outrage over Floyd's
murder and broadcasted incidents of racial injustices, within the structural context of national unravelling. Hundreds of thousands took to the
streets, angered by on-camera sounds and sights of a human pleading
"I can't breathe." In a country deeply divided over social issues, mostly
peaceful, multiracial, multigenerational demonstrations mobilized in
at least 1,300 cities, suburbs, and rural towns. These protests count
among the largest and longest lasting in U.S. history. "Stop killing us,"
begged a 5-year-old in Tampa.[37] Concurrently, protesters around the
world came face to face with racism, past and present. "The American
Negro," Malcolm X had observed in his autobiography decades earlier,
"has no conception of their feeling of brotherhood for and with
him."[38]

Attempts to modulate violent impulses met with predictable back-
lash. Some laughed at the specter of White supremacists and neo-Nazis
engaging in face-to-face time with Blacks raised in public housing.
School boards and state legislatures heard taxpayers demanding
that police be charged with stopping the slaughter of children and
adolescents. Parents wanted their children to be taught the virtues of
an American exceptionalism, in history books, libraries, and curricula
that downplayed the historical brutalities of slavery and attacks on
minorities.

Fear-based responses to these three-crises paradoxically restore a measure of hope

The cascading convergence of a relentless pandemic, meltdowns in the
political economy, and reckoning of systemic racism might be another
turning point in U.S. history. Grassroots protests, unlike previous

mobilizations of resisters, looked and acted differently during the pandemic. "New, young black leaders with the Movement for Black Lives are now emerging, leaders unencumbered by past failures and buoyed by their connection to the ruckus in the streets."[39] Although White allies might yet again abandon Blacks, as some activists feared, hope remained that a new wave of social movements might crystallize opportunities to redress the horrors of racism engrained prominently in U.S. history. Proponents of Black Lives Matter sought to capitalize on potentially transformative, transgenerational realignments in a more racially and ethnically diverse aging society.

U.S. media outlets in fact entertained mixed reactions to the coalescing concatenation of upheavals. Alt-right commentators radicalized fears deeply dividing the polity. The multileveled (I/we/they) polarization they headlined stoked outcries from evangelical Christians and suburban housewives. Spikes in cases of gun violence across the nation symbolized a democracy at risk of honoring human dignity and disregarding time-tested national values. Other commentators, in contrast, offered messages of healing. They pinned hopes on ordinary Americans' commitment to recover and restore a functioning sense of justice.[40] Both were plausible scenarios in the context of undeniable facts. Institutional deadlocks and congressional filibusters persisted. An exhausted, polarized electorate nonetheless resisted calls to undertake a radical restructuring of what was the embodiment of an American way of life.

Leaving a legacy requires rethinking why safeguarding social security matters

Generations of Americans felt overwhelmed and despondent as did I. The pandemic restricted "normal" travel and interactions. Intraparty intrigues added a new "normalcy" to partisan maneuvering on Capitol Hill. Undercutting women's rights to abortion and marginalizing people with disabilities and fluid sexual identities paralleled the racial prejudices that seemed customarily "normative." Americans offered prayers for Blacks murdered in Buffalo and school children and teachers gunned down in a Hispanic town in Texas, but many Senators and locally elected officials wanted guns protected under the 2nd Amendment.

In comparison to these crises, shoring up Social-Security financing seemed trivial. Neither Donald Trump nor Joseph Biden during the 2020 presidential election said much about reforming the program. Republican stalwarts had expected the president to "starve the beast" during his second term.[41] Biden fired Trump's Social Security Administration commissioner, but was understandably preoccupied with climate change, global politics, congressional obstacles, and poor ratings.

Oppositional politics seemed likely, I reckoned, to sustain deadlocks and prolong inaction over how to save and safeguard Social Security. Many moderate Democrats, who wished to increase benefits, aligned with progressive senators like Elizabeth Warren and Bernie Sanders who proposed taxing the wealth of the super-rich to raise Social-Security checks.[42] On the right, partially privatizing Social Security remained a viable option, since abolishing the program had little chance of being implemented.[43] Divided over conflicting advice and distressing projections about long-term bankruptcy left Social-Security stakeholders "down, depressed or hopeless." To resist continued calls for policy reforms and grassroots pressure "amounts to a refusal on the part of lots of Americans to think in terms of the social whole—of what's best for the community, of the common good."[44] Yet surveys also reconfirmed that Americans were willing to change Social Security by combining benefit cuts and tax increases.[45]

Rather than running away from the "new normal" in fits of despair and disillusionment, I thought rethinking Social Security's role in a broader vision of leaving a legacy in an Aging Society. Perhaps younger Americans and my grandchildren would listen to a Baby Boomer like me, who values the program as an effective institution that binds Americans together as they uphold a representative democracy. There was a precedent: Frederick Jackson Turner presented to the American Historical Association at the 1893 Columbia Exposition on "The Significance of the Frontier in American History:"

> Behind institutions, behind constitutional forms and modifications, lie the vital forces that call these organs into life and shape them to meet changing conditions. The peculiarity of American institutions is, the fact that they have been compelled to adapt themselves to the changes of an expanding people to the changing involved in crossing a continent, in winning a wilderness, and in developing at each area of this progress out of the primitive economic conditions of the frontier into the complexity of city life.[46]

Turner boldly imagined a diverse, urbanizing society held together by interlocking institutions and intersectional policies and norms. Presciently envisioning a nation "compelled to adapt" with the closing of America's physical frontiers, the 32-year-old was beckoning prag-matic, self-reliant, confident citizens—his peers and elders—to settle hitherto unexplored domains.

Frederick Jackson Turner referred to Americans once creating outposts in the West and now facing the challenges posed in an urban, industrial social order. His comparative approach to history prompts us to probe together one more set of cross-sectional constructs and longitudinal dimensions associated with societal aging. How do the interlocking crises of the 2020s compare to the promises and dislocations that occurred in the 1960s? Building a time line for recent U.S. history affords a context (however provisional) to imagine pathways of hope and fear, intermingling freedom and frustration ahead.

How similar and different were the 1960s and 2020s?

Let's unpack societal parallels in the two time periods:

Demographically, younger generations outnumber older ones in both decades. Extremes in age, gender, religion, class, and region (among other historical vectors) create intra-group divisions and intersectional affiliations.

Politically, powerful segments of the population, vocal majorities, and silenced minorities in competing voices struggle to increase (or at least maintain) their stake in the status quo. Presidents Nixon and Trump, cavalierly dismissing advice from Washington-based commentators and lawmakers, advocate law-and-order measures that pit us-vs-them fears.

Economically, a healthy economy existed in the 1960s and 2020s, shadowed by ominous parallels. Our power elite celebrated America's global military superiority while many U.S. cycled in and out of poverty. Households worked hard to retain middle-class comforts as their children and grandchildren struggled to lift themselves by their bootstraps.

Socially, older Americans had survived economic downturns, protracted wars, and nuclear threats. Younger generations in both decades questioned how willing Big Government was responsive to invest time and resources to rebuild faith and repair wounds. Disillusionment rose.

Contextual differences between the 1960s and 2020s remind us that conflicts both impede and facilitate consensus-building:

> *Demographically*, the clash of generations in 1968 are usually delineated along binary lines—Black/Caucasian, male/female, old/young, and white collar/blue collar. Multigenerational coalitions in the early years of the 2020s intersect race and ethnicity, gender and sexual orientation.[47] Baby Boomers—who painfully remember riots in Detroit and Newark and 65,000 peers dead in Vietnam—are aghast that a million Americans succumbed to variants of Covid-19. Millennials and youth live in the shadow of 9/11 and fights over abortion and LGBTQ rights.

> *Politically*, organized groups and identifiable leaders—Dr. King's Southern Christian Leadership Council and the Black Panther party guided by Bobby Seale and Huey Newton—were in the vanguard of the 1960s civil-rights movements. There are few coxswains grabbing headlines today. Grassroots protests are mobilized by anonymous African-American teenagers and grandmothers, with ranks swelled by multiracial and pansexual demonstrators. No new transgenerational lobbies or internet coalitions emerged as idea brokers or movers and shakers.

> *Economically*, Americans were enjoying gains through hard work, union negotiations, and a Federal government willing to lift boats in the 1960s. Income inequalities and wealth concentration reached unprecedented levels, giving the ultra-rich access to power and influence. The pandemic and structural disparities exposed suffering and marginalization.

> *Socially*, Walter Cronkite, George Will, and other respected media commentators kept Americans abreast of news during the 1960s. Now, to grow niches and riches, media gurus as apposite as Tucker Carlson and Rachel Maddow segment markets with talk shows and sound bites. "Bowling alone" metaphorically underscores loneliness and desperation.[48]

Cultural indicators reveal further generational similarities and differences between the 1960s and 2020s. Unrest in both decades empowered younger age groups to demand profound societal reordering. Baby Boomers in the Great Society could not fulfill their aspirations amid assassinations at home and wars abroad. Crisis after crisis—Watergate, AIDS, 9/11, the 2008 recession, withdrawals from Iraq and Afghanistan, as well as Trump, the pandemic, and the January 6, 2021 assault —shattered citizens' sense of well-being, safety, and security. Gallup polls in 2016 reported that national pride reached a historical low point. Since then, rancorous debates in the halls of Congress have not culminated in bipartisan support over immigration, gun control, abortion, or cybersecurity. Dinner-table fights, sometime ending in domestic violence, have undercut commitments to renew and coalesce around functional, democratic institutions.

Safeguarding Social Security for Future Generations: Leaving a Legacy in an Aging Society also hangs in the balance. Uneasy and unsettling demo-graphic, political, economic, social, and moral tensions deflect critical thinking and delay decisions about reforming Social Security. Yet the present moment might prove a possible turning point that parallels the lessons of history that Frederick Jackson Turner adumbrated. If we choose to act, transgenerational conversations can engender measured hope and fragile trust to prevail over dread in the midst of crisis. We have resources at our disposal to end the politics of avoidance and mobilize grassroots support to reassess Social-Security development and future.

The challenge today is to persuade Social-Security stakeholders of all ages to reconfigure our understanding of our distinctive yet shared histories. We must dare to be change-agents willing to fulfill Turner's vision of renewable America. We must face challenges as daunting as those FDR faced in launching Social Security in the Great Depression. *Safeguarding Social Security for Future Generation: Leaving a Legacy in an Aging Society* entails generating transgenerational conversations to mobilize efforts to preserve and expand the income floor provided by the program. This in turn will help to heal structural wounds exacerbated in a pandemic, and mired in racial injustice, and broad-gauged economic disparities. "We are going to be faced with a national rebuilding project at a scale that never existed in our lifetimes."[49]

Embarking into a new frontier will not eliminate messy, frustrating Social-Security negotiations, which might yield only partial success. The hazards of defeatism and despair, associated with the politics of fear, will not vanish in efforts to reframe the politics of hope. Whatever transformative changes take place, the process begins with my own metanoia.

Notes

1 Harkin, James. 2019. "Journalism is now the *second* draft of history." *Columbia Journalism Review*, 28, pp. 6–12.

2 Carlson, Avis D. 1939; reprinted 2020. "The jitters." *Harper's Magazine*, **37**.

3 Aaron, Henry. 2020. "The social safety net: the gaps that COVID-19 spotlights." In *The Future of Social Insurance*, ed. Thomas M. Bethel. Washington, D.C.: National Academy of Social Insurance, 5; Moon, Marilyn. 2020. What will we learn from the coronavirus crisis?, *op. cit.*, 31.

4 SECURE Act. 2019, December 20. *Pentagra legislative update*; Hopkins, Jamie. 2019. "Congress set to pass SECURE Act at the last minute, impacting retirement and increasing taxes." *Forbes*.

5 Scott, Dylan. 2020. "The Covid-19 risks for different age groups, explained." *Vox*.

6 Hubler, Sean. 2022, May 18. "More than a million students lost in two years." *The New York Times*.

7 Heller, Zoe. 2022, April 8. "Down with love?" *The New Yorker*, 56; Talking Points. 2022, April 15. "Teens: An epidemic of hopelessness." *The Week*, 17.

8 Gullette, Margaret Morganworth. 2021, January 5. "American eldercide." www.dissentmagazine.org/online; Myers, Justin and Ricardo Alonso-Zaldivar. 2020, June 21. "Nursing home residents represent a quarter of U.S. deaths." Waltham, MA: Associated Press.

9 Stokes, Andrew. 2022, June 1. "Older Americans died at high rate in omicron wave." *The New York Times*.

10 Harper's Index. 2020, July. *Harper's Magazine*, **341**, 11.

11 Iglesias, Gabino. 2021, July 21. "Loneliness is a communal experience in 'Seek You.'" www.npr.org/.

12 Goldberg, Michelle. 2022, January 22. "The mental health toll of Trump era politics." *The New York Times*, 8.

13 Kolinovsky, Sarah. (2021, September 7). Biden to lay out new strategy against delta variant of COVID-19. https://abcnews.go.com/Politics/biden-lay-strategy-delta-variant-covid-19/story?id=79872980; Mandavilli, Apoorva and Roni Caryn Rabin. 2021, September 11. "Unvaccinaated 11 times as likely to die of Covid." *The New York Times*, 1.

14 Silver, Caleb. 2021, October 27. "Stiglitz: Pandemic exposed health inequality and flaws of market economy." www.investopedia.com.

15 Krugman, Paul. 2021, September 10. "Opinion." *The New York Times*.

16 Cohen, Elliot D. 2011, May 22. "The fear of losing control." *Psychology Today*. Casselman, Ben and Jeanna Smialek. 2021, September 15. "Poverty rate drops to a record low." *The New York Times*, 1.

17 Taj, Mitra and Anatoly Kurmanaev. 2020. "Peru's virus strategy crumbled once illness hit." *New York Times Digest*; Gettleman, Jeffrey and Suhasini Raj. 2020. "Already reeling, India is facing plague of locusts." *New York Times Digest*.

18 Stewart, Matthew. 2022. *The 9.9 Percent*. New York: Simon & Schuster.

19 Lohr, Steve. 2022, January 17. "Millions have lost a step into the middle class, researchers say." *The New York Times.*
20 Harper's Index. July 2020.
21 Economic Policy Institute. 2022, March 25. "The persistent gender wage gap."
22 Singh, Dhara. 2020. "Almost a third of Americans say they may never retire because of coronavirus pandemic." *Yahoo. Money*; The Week. 2019, June. "Recessions: A big setback for women in the workforce," 33.
23 Nazaryan, Alexander. 2020. "People of color account for majority of coronavirus infections, new CDC study says." *Yahoo*; Kristof, Nicholas. 2020, June 28. "Learning from Hispanic Americas." *New York Times.*
24 Connelly, Griffin. 2020. "Coronavirus: Dr. Fauci says racism contributed to black Americans being disproportionately impacted by Covid-19." *The Independent.*
25 Porter, Eduardo. 2021, June 28. "Black Americans close education gap, but pay gap persists." *The New York Times*, 5.
26 Reich, Robert. 2020. *The System: Who Rigged It. How We Fix It.* New York: Knopf. Tomlinson, Chris. 2020. "Wanted: CEO to fight income inequality by cutting executive pay." TEXASINC.
27 Johnson, Jake. 2020. "Truthout." *Common Dreams.* Larson, Alex. 2020, August 17. "Tell Congress." Social Security Works, email.
28 Munnell, Alicia H. 2020, May 6. "Opinion: Social Security report shows uptick in 75-year deficit, no change in trust fund depletion data." *Market Watch*; Brandes, Paul. 2020, April 11. "Another victim of Covid-19: Social Security," *Market Watch*; Hacker, Jacob and Paul Pierson. 2020. *Let Them Eat Tweets.* New York: Liveright.
29 Konish, Laurie. 2020. "Americans take a dim view of raiding their Social Security to cover pandemic expenses, poll finds." www.cnbc.com; Sarin, Natasha. 2020. "Tapping Social Security would be a big mistake." *Bloomberg.*
30 Altman, Nancy. 2022, April 2. "Long but important." Social Security Works.
31 Friedman, Thomas L. 2021, September 15. "Have we reshaped Middle East politics or started to mimic it?" *The New York Times*, 8.
32 Orth, Taylor. 2022, March 15. "From millionaires to Muslims, small subgroups of the population seem much larger to many Americans." https://today.yougov.com/topics/politics/articles-reports.
33 Ibid.; Jensen, Eric et al., 2021, August 4. "Measuring racial and ethnic diversity in the 2020 census." Washington, DC: United States Census Bureau.
34 Wilkerson, Isabel. 2020. *Caste.* New York: Random House.
35 Arsenault, Raymond. 2010, December 29. "The great unraveling." *The New York Times.*
36 Wilkerson, *Caste*; Anderson, Carol. 2021. *The Second: Race and Guns in a Fatally Unequal America.* New York: Bloomsbury.

37 "Malcolm X Quotes." 2021, January 21. History.com Editors.
38 Jackson, Russell A. 2020, September 30. "Emerging leaders 2020." www.iaonline.theiia.org.
39 Taylor, Keeanga-Yamahtta. 2020, June 14. "The end of black politics." *New York Times*; Younge, Gary. 2020. "What Black America means to Europe." *The New York Review of Books.*
40 Frum, David. 2020. *Trumpalypse.* New York: Harper; Robinson, Marilynne. 2020, "What kind of country do we want?" *New York Review of Books*; Gessen, Masha. 2020. *Surviving Autocracy.* New York: Riverhead.
41 Zeballos-Roig. 2020, March 6. "Trump says he's willing to cut entitlements to shrink the $23 trillion national debt." *Business insider*; Ghilarducci, Teresa. 2020. "Trump's second term plan for Social Security: Starve the beast." *Forbes*; Werschkul, Misha. 2020, March 27. "New federal bill to mitigate COVID-19's economic impact." www.budetandpolicy.org.
42 Zeballos-Roig, Joseph. 2022, June 9. "Insider." *Yahoo/news.*
43 Speights, Keith. 2020. "This presidential candidate's plan." www.fool.com/investing/2020/06/28.
44 O'Toole, Finian. 2020, July 23. "Unpresidented." *The New York Review of Books.*
45 Konish, Lorie. 2022, June 8. "Here are changes Americans are willing to make to fix Social Security, survey finds." *Navigating Uncertainty.*
46 Turner, Frederick Jackson. 1893. "The significance of the frontier in American history." http://xroads.virginia.edu-hyper/turner.
47 Joseph, Peniel E. 2020. "Protests in MLK's assassination and George Floyd's murder show what hasn't—and has—changed since 1968." *Washingto Post.*
48 Putnam, Robert D. 2020. *Bowling Alone: The Collapse and Revival of American Community.* New York: Simon & Schuster.
49 Yang, Andrew. 2020, May 17. "A new new deal." www.nwaonline.com.

Part 3

Rethinking Social Security in order to become change agents

I knew virtually nothing about psychology before I took a course in college. There I was introduced to works that Karl Jung, whose archetypes and shadows I at first found as opaque as the writings of Sigmund Freud, Ivan Pavlov, and B. F. Skinner. My head was more attuned to the political ferment and sexual freedom underway in the 1960s than being in touch with the yearnings of the heart and stirrings of the soul.

Twenty-one in 1968, I was participating in civil-rights demonstrations and joining protests against the war in Vietnam, but I mostly managed to respect and uphold my parents' ideals and decorum. Their generation dominated postwar America's upwardly mobile vital center; like many Baby Boomers I pivoted to the left. My classmates and I subscribed to Bob Dylan's belief that "the times they are a-changin'." My generation was ready to take charge in any age-based power struggles in which our "best and the brightest" elders resisted.

I went through another metamorphosis in later years as I became an elder of the tribe. While I tenaciously held on to the legacy left by older mentors, I came more self-consciously aware of my need to connect thoughts, feelings, and deeds. I dared to trust that they would re-present an integrating authenticity. This meant I had to slow down and listen to people younger than me while I wrote this book. I rethought insights and reframed the book's narrative to reach transgenerational audiences. In the process, I somehow reinvented myself as I began to reinterpret Social Security's history differently than I had before, when I was in the prime of life.

In 2022, I am semiretired and remarried. I am probably more committed to fight against racism and sexism and to promote greater equality—political and societal, as well as economic—than I was in

DOI: 10.4324/9781003345985-11

1968. But the times have changed, and so have I, as I feel a reinvigorated call to help to prepare rising generations to grapple with the challenges of societal aging, one of which is thinking through the values, norms, and political context for safeguarding Social Security.

Younger Americans differ from me and my Baby-Boomer generation not only in age, but in life histories and expectations that are engulfed in a pandemic, huge variations in wealth and income, and the historical impact of racial, ethnic, and gender-based disparities. Generation gaps come into play. Millennials and Gen Z do not trust institutions and elites that voice hyper-partisanship and pit the interests of groups against one another. And today's youth do not count much on Social Security, in part because of ignorance or lies about its operations, and in part because they have other things to do and think about.

In these unsettled times, elders have nothing to lose by giving up genuine and false gravitas—masks that served us earlier in life. We are given the chance to open up possibilities in the legacies we hope to leave. In my case, it means coming up with new approaches, and to adopt different keywords and to adapt different perspectives on what it might entail to persuade younger persons that Social Security matters as a viable transgenerational program. It protects our personal self-interests now and rightfully in the future by bringing diverse groups of stakeholders together as they face risks unlike many Baby Boomers had to accept.

Chapter 8

Changing within myself to better relate to others

Introduction

For most of my first six decades, I had mixed success in compart-mentalizing my professional and personal spheres.[1] Inflamed academic ambitions were fulfilled; my first wife and I raised two wonderfully creative daughters before we divorced. Not yet aligning how I thought with what I felt, I spent much of my third quarter of my life recognizing shadows and seeking guideposts.[2]

This book moves me into unfamiliar territory. I am no longer aiming to write a best seller that impresses scholars or policy analysts. I see myself as a grandfatherly Baby Boomer, wise and compassionate enough to spark the imaginations of readers, mostly younger than I, to consider how and why Social Security is a vital institution that many in my audience think will never fit their needs and feel is not worth refurbishing.

Re-forming Social Security before it was too late to act is this book's major takeaway theme, but I had reframe, reconfigure, and re-present how I communicated my message. My narrative had to pique readers' minds and feelings in order to persuade audiences that their stake in the program's future is greater than mine. I wanted to put Social Security into accessible historical and societal contexts. Americans are trapped in an existential dis-ease. Our democracy is not functioning well enough to unite overlapping and diverse generations. All U.S. age groups are wrestling with contested truths commingled with incessant decisions concerning how they adapt to unsettling circumstances.

Just as I needed to self-consciously link feelings and thinking in writing about safeguarding Social Security, so too readers must equip themselves before leaving a legacy in an aging society. This chapter describes my own self-conscious transformation as a pragmatic

DOI: 10.4324/9781003345985-12

paradigm invites readers to dare to do the same. Only then can generations unite to be mindful, heartfelt agents of "being the change."

The step-by-step process of convincing Americans to decide how much they want to retrofit Social Security to serve current and unfolding societal contexts begins with history; we look once more at some similarities and differences between the 1960s and 2020s. But the historiographical prelude in this chapter prompts psychological impulses that beckons us to intentionally look within ourselves to be more consciously aware of Social Security's legacy and prospects.

A historical lagniappe prepares us to delve into conscious self-awareness

We are well aware that history does not repeat itself. Twists, flips, and critical turns illuminate and blind our grasp of continuities and changes over time. This lagniappe affords a historical platform (however provisional) for taking stock of our thoughts and feelings as we continue to assess Social Security. This section offers a striking longitudinal comparison of Americans' diminishing trust and mounting skepticism of elected officials and government-funded technocrats that affect transgenerational conversations about Social Security:

- About 75% of those surveyed in 1958 responded that Washington was doing the right thing "most of the time." Public trust in government began to erode during the 1960s and 1970s, though confidence briefly returned in the 1980s (almost to 1950s-levels). Dishonest officials, disdain of basic science, public-health experts, and experiential knowledge, heightened cynicism across age and class lines. Since the 2008 recession, the percentage of Americans declaring that they always or mostly trust government has not surpassed 30%.[3]
- During the same period, however, polls have shown that Americans regardless of party affiliation and demographic characteristics have strongly supported Social Security. The National Academy of Social Insurance (NASI), for instance, released in 2013 a major research study on "Strengthening Social Security: What do Americans want." The report indicated that a significant majority of stakeholders were willing to pay more to preserve and expand benefits. NASI documented that 85% of those surveyed thought that it was more important than ever to ensure that retirees had a

decent income; 83% raising Federal Insurance Contribution Act (FICA) taxes.[4]

NASI analysts drew an important conclusion: "At a time when Americans seem deeply divided about the right size and role of government, it is striking that Americans across political and generational lines agree on specific policies to pay for and improve Social Security benefits."[5]

This book boldly extends what NASI asserted. Americans are inclined to preserving the program's solvency and sustaining its fiscal integrity. In fact, stakeholders are subconsciously predisposed to believe that Social Security serves as an economic stabilizer in communities in addition to its direct value to millions of beneficiaries.[6] Seizing on the idea that such transgenerational support can be a catalyst for renewing trust and confidence in Big Government presumes more than an ideological, historical, or rhetorical flip in discussing Social Security anew. The process of Americans reaffirming Social Security's collective value starts *within* individuals of all ages.

Individuals must change before synergizing transgenerational reforms

Individual transformations, I am more and more convinced, should precede purposeful generational deciding to act together purposefully in a society that some think is falling apart.[7] Why are some Americans motivated to critically rethink "problems" such as Social-Security financing, while other stakeholders resist synergizing transgenerational conversations and grassroots coalitions? Engaging in being political agents varies from individual to individual, from identifiable subgroups to multicolored segments of the population. Small, immediate steps must occur to foster a context in which Social Security's imminent shortfalls and long-term prospects can be faced by U.S. citizens. Success is neither quick nor easy, nor inevitable.

Appeals to disinterested thinking and transformative actions prove disconcerting to Americans who desperately want cherished ideas and valued institutions to remain bulwarks in the moment's tattered unraveling. In the depth of uncertainty, insecurity, and fear, some resort to temporizing until a semblance of "normalcy" returns. Other citizens discern that Social Security can change, simply by tweaking structural edifices and component parts. Still others deem it prudent to temporize about deteriorating conditions, and let future leaders deal with problems down the road under pressure to rectify longstanding overlooked flaws.

Psychologists and social scientists hypothesize that moving sequentially through a series of micro- and macro-stages is an indispensable catalyst for mediating differences of opinion and negotiating options for remedying programs like Social Security. The first step is enabling the program's would-be reformers to assess what makes them fearful and anxious about becoming and being agents of change. Trans-theoretical models can map the incremental manner in which nonlinear, multileveled progressions arise from inchoate suspicions to pragmatic action.

Safeguarding Social Security as a legacy left for current stakeholders and future generations becomes attainable under two conditions. On the one hand, a critical mass in Americans perceive a window of opportunity for reconsidering and rectifying the program's systemic and putative problems. On the other hand, stakeholders with hesitant minds and ambivalent feelings must be willing to commit to assessing workable solutions. Experts and ordinary U.S. citizens negotiate divergent ways of framing issues—a step that they have long avoided to do, but still have time to plumb common ground to reconcile in truth and clarity.[8]

The first stage of "Be the Change" ends if and when Social Security's advocates and critics discard their prejudices and demonizing enough to listen with open minds to contrary opinions and discomforting options. Then comes the second transformative phase: Policymakers, administrators, and stakeholders position themselves to assess and monitor whatever practical logistics are to be set into motion. Assuming efforts to participate in constructive negotiations do not recapitulate bitter stalemates, technicians and strategists can attend by trial and error to systemic slips and potential risks. Meanwhile, Social-Security officials, media producers, and oppositional information outlets should convey in clear and comprehensible terms the rationale behind refurbishing operations. In the future, when new sets of anomalies necessitate recalibrations, the pattern repeats.

I detail my own conscious-raising transformation, which mostly followed this sequence of practical steps. For decades I harbored fleeting doubts and dismissed my questions about Social Security's viability. I could not convince myself to let go of a legacy left by the generation who launched Social Security and shepherded its success during the program' formative years. My own research, after all, validated what Wilbur Cohen and some of his associates had taught me about Social-Security policymaking in Washington. I persisted as their disciple as I interpreted *Social Security: Visions and Revisions* through the prism of the 1983 amendments. Interviews with distinguished program administrators, admirable lawmakers, senior White House officials, and junior members of the National Commission on Social Security Reform bolstered my train of thought.

In retrospect, I realize that framing *Social Security: Visions and Revisions* in terms of "risks," "rights," and "responsibilities" could neither encapsulate nor illuminate what has occurred since the 1980s as new, powerful generation of Federal actors were opposed, ideologically and fiscally, to expanding the program. I had to recast my message with new keywords and reinterpretations. Trans-theoretical models proved indispensable.

I deduced from clinical studies and academic paradigms that mutual respect and epistemic trust has to undergird policymakers' communicative feedback in an environment rife with distress and duress.[9] When participants speak to one another respectfully, cooperative listeners are likely to be more receptive to wrestling with contested truths. If speakers sense that their perspectives are understood, individuals at the negotiating table can entertain dissenting opinions.[10] This facilitates collective dialogues about strategies for effecting change.

The more I read and thought about it, I listened to my gut urging me to translate heightened self-consciousness into new modes of transgenerational discourse. Ideally, the tack alerts group members to the moral and pragmatic dimensions of their dialogue. Conversely, for participants to deny or dismiss lingering contrary viewpoints rekindles resentfulness and obstructs conversations.[11] Negotiations then are likely to set parameters that situate how participants consider Social-Security reforms. To broaden the construct for critically thinking about mobilizing various generational, however, requires more than interior and interpersonal adaptations.

For transformations to reconstitute a broader for dealing with Social Security, technocrats and policymakers need to reassess the legacy they want to prioritize. This task includes owning up to mistakes—such as not fully disclosing to stakeholders what they need to know the program's aims and transactions. Despite efforts to share basic information to ordinary Americans, this strategic step has rarely occurred. As Social Security's transgenerational compact developed, FICA contributors too often were saddled with ignorance and misinformation. "It ain't what you don't know that's gets you in trouble," an

American humorist quipped. "It's what you know for sure that that just ain't so."[12]

Experts can ill afford to obfuscate details about Social Security's *modus operandi* to covered workers and beneficiaries. Idea brokers must communicate "facts," and media commentators must be held accountable when they spread disinformation. Only then can straightforward conversations between insiders and outsiders prove efficacious. Since U.S. citizens usually respond positively to honest messaging, the latter stages of transforming individuals' minds and bodies can permit collective attitudinal shifts to fuel grassroots support:

1   While Baby Boomers and Millennials reassess personal strengths and character flaws within themselves, they concurrently should reevaluate whether they are impeding or inducing intergenerational conversations. Participants of all age groups must fully recognize that each generation speaks, invariably, in distinctive voices. "I/you/we" perceptions must be modulated, leavened to share insights, humility, and empathy.
2   Participants must candidly acknowledge that transgenerational interactions about making policy changes—such as revamping Social-Security financing—are unlikely to dispel anxiety and fear. Disparate opinions will be disruptive, but negotiators must come to trust one another.[13] Constructive resolutions of unsettled issues are best accomplished in a political climate conducive to risk-taking.

To sustain "the micro-macro flip" requires reinforcement from social movements, like those that were change-makers during the pandemic. The three-fold crises in 2020 and 2021 generated grassroots responses unlike those when my generation was young in the 1960s.

Then, Baby Boomers like me put trust in following the directions of organizations such as the American Civil Liberties Union and the Student Nonviolent Coordinating Committee. By the end of the 1960s, the silent majority had cut short the Second Reconstruction we felt we were destined to effect. As we grew older, many Baby Boomers morphed into obstructionists. Others defended venerable institutions. Still others, shocked by tragic events in the 21st century, questioned nationalistic fervor as their resentments rose. That left enough radicals and progressives to rally around new types of 21st-century social movements. No more than 3.5% of the total U.S. population needs to be actively engaged in local communities.[14]

Two grassroots protests exemplify the emerging pattern.

- The Occupy Wall Street movement began in 2011 as a nonviolent protest; it revived previous groups of Americans' mobilizations inspired with civil disobedience—this time protesting economic inequalities (the 99% versus the 1%) that underscored the lack of "real" American democracy. Picketers in downtown Manhattan aided victims of Hurricane Sandy and joined Lakota Sioux in blocking pipelines, before splintering a few years later.[15]
- Black Lives Matter, founded in 2013, advocated civil disobedience against racially motivated violence, too often evidenced time after time in police brutality in cities and suburbs.

Occupy Wall Street and Black Lives Matter were orchestrated by charismatic albeit relatively unknown organizers. Teenagers and first-term congresswomen are demanding a Green New Deal that reduces economic inequities. Generating bottom-to-top headlines, multicultural and multiracial protesters embodied the strength and resources youth possess in a diverse aging society.

Meanwhile, those who seek lessons from history as they revitalize Social Security should not summarily dismiss how grassroots movements can falter and fail, if insufficiently nurtured and left uncoordinated. The consequences of invalidating *Roe v. Wade* cannot yet be verified, but some champions are identifying mistakes: "The pro-choice movement has had to contend with plenty of bad luck and bad actors."[16] Grassroots advocates have been on the defensive, playing disconnected catch-up ball. The Supreme Court upholds draconian laws passed in several states, clearly designed to terminate women's rights to abortion. Planned Parenthood deserves much credit for providing sexual and reproductive health care, but critics claim that it did not fight hard enough to protect clinics that assist vulnerable women and mothers-to-be.

Solidarity, sustainability, and stewardship are today's transformative keywords

Mindful of the potentialities and risks inherent in grassroots initiatives to reform Social Security, I propose that local activists and advocates can deploy new keywords—solidarity, sustainability, and stewardship—to replace risks, rights, and responsibilities. Here is the case for safeguarding the program can be elaborated: Americans must made that they are sustaining the program as stewards who advance generational solidarity that bolsters the common good of a democratic polity as it envelops a variety of self-interests within and across age groups.

How might transformative perspectives and 21st-century social movements reconfigure intergenerational relations that might eventuate in significant Social-Security reforms? Let's start with Baby Boomers, who have endured several forms of ageism during the pandemic.[17] Heightening older people's sense of differentness were recurring insults from younger generations' playbook, which overstate the extent to which retirees on average are inured from risks that simultaneously threatened debt-ridden, unemployed younger people bracing for dim economic futures.[18] Even with Social Security and Medicare, millions of older American households dread how quickly preexisting chronic conditions wipe out lifetime savings. The troubles endured by frail elders approaching death, despite what middle-age commentators declare, are not invariably bound to be short-term.[19] The longevity revolution in an aging society may disproportionately benefit healthy children and their well-educated parents.

Millennials and younger generations, who often project their own yearnings for "present-mindedness" onto older Americans are bound to boomerang.[20] Baby Boomers are not a homogenous group that subscribes to fixed age cut-offs as they drift into solitude and disengagement. My generation's fears of loss and decline in the 21st century in many ways parallels the journey of younger individuals with fears about current setbacks and future shocks. We elderly backbenchers will eventually cede power, wealth, and status to younger people in the wings. And in the course of generational successions, so will they.

It surely would facilitate meaningful intergenerational conversations, moreover, if Baby Boomers were to share what it was like for us once to be as young in the 1960s as Millennials, Gen-Xers, and Gen Z are today. Like them, we deemed ourselves immortal, destined to love blissfully and work forever. Baby Boomers 50 years ago claimed our right to denounce authority figures whom we mistrusted. We, too, came of age celebrating youth and denying decrepitude. Paul McCartney in 1964 voiced my age group's worries in lyrics: "Will you still need me, will you still feed me, when I'm 64."[21] Identifying and empathizing with younger listeners' desire to be change-makers themselves might overturn distortions and biases. In fact, they may permit Baby Boomers to impart advice and warnings in Social-Security policymaking.

Bridging transgenerational ties through sharing positive memories of youth and the prime of life, alas, entails risks of its own. Vietnam, stagflation, Reagan, and AIDS recall negative recollections among Baby Boomers, which are ancient history to younger age groups. Yet both generations delude ourselves if we dismiss starting global wars after 9/11 was not "the first step down a very dark and dangerous alley."[22]

George W. Bush, who launched wars in Iraq and Afghanistan after that horrific terrorist attack, invoked "the nation I know" while expressing "mixed feelings" in an address at the Flight 93 National Memorial at Shanksville, Pennsylvania on September 11, 2021. "There is little cultural overlap between violent extremists abroad and violent extremists at home," the 43rd president intoned, referencing the insurrectionist attack on the Capitol earlier that year. "But in their disdain for pluralism, in their disregard for human life, in their determination to defile national symbols—they are children of the same foul spirit, and it is our continuing duty to confront them."[23]

Baby-Boomer Bush may be rereading history in a self-serving way, but he deserves credit for maturely appealing to national unity. He did not opine that belief systems clash, distancing Americans within and across age groups, as well as orchestrating global capitalism and tolerating a delusional and disillusioned polity.[24] Yet scenarios that set generational boundaries must simultaneously face up to deeply engrained racial structures and economic disparities in our aging society.

Ibram Kendi, a 38-year old professor and activist, reminds us that "education, love, and exemplary black people will not deliver America out of racism."[25] This does not jibe with younger and older U.S. citizens like to claim that they are "explorers of the unknown, the ministers of a mystery that cannot be fathomed," voiced in a language that pierces "the heart of life, in tune with its poignancy, expressing the inexpressible."[26] Rising generations of youth did not grow up expecting that they would replicate Baby Boomer's fortuitous life histories, but they too may leave a legacy that resembles my generation's bequest. "The actual foundation of racism is not ignorance and hate, but self-interest," adds Millennial Ibram Kendi, which intersects age, gender, and class.[27]

Transgenerational conversations about Social Security cannot take place in a bubble. They must recognize that all age groups are heirs to suffering historically existential crises, deeper than we care to admit. And despite widening income gaps, we all have witnessed gains. Americans in 2020s have 50% more income at their disposal than did average citizens in 1969; air travel and televisions are cheaper, and prices fall for high-end cell phones. The time has come for all age groups to realize that Americans need each other to survive and to thrive together.[28] This is why Social Security matters.

As I ruminate about current events while transforming into an agent of change, I finally am finally equipped to recast my critical thinking, strong feelings, and commitment to *Safeguarding Social Security for Future Generations: Leaving a Legacy in an Aging Society: Safeguarding Social Security for Future Generations.* I introduce new keywords—solidarity, sustainability, and stewardship to replace the three "R"s—risks, rights, and responsibilities—I used earlier in the book. The new set elaborates, I hope, more persuasive reasons why present and rising generations of Social-Security stewards must restore and revive in trust and solidarity to decide whether sustaining a popular and effective program bolsters an American democracy.

* Solidarity speaks to our contemporary need to address risks unimaginable in the Great Depression. To mobilize grassroots support, interest groups must take account of gloomy prognoses that undercut collective will. Stakeholders, convinced that it is not too late to act, must responsibly defend their right for Federal assistance.
* Sustaining Social Security is a pragmatic and reasonable tack that embodies U.S. citizens' enduring commitments to shared values and sound finances. Honoring rights, not entitlements under the program, must be further bolstered by evidence-based assurances that the system's Trust Fund reserves are verifiably sufficient in the proximate and foreseeable future.
* Wage-earning FICA contributors and their beneficiaries must be convinced that they are Social Security's stewards. SSA must do more than shield employers, employees, and their families from workplace hazards and medical catastrophes. Stewardship summons Americans to make changes within themselves and within Social Security. The ultimate aim of transformational conversations and transgenerational mobilization is to reframe principles and update operations that worked in the past. For Social Security to survive and thrive, it must effectively serve current stakeholders and protect new generations.

Interactions replaced by this new, straightforward set of keywords speak directly to my peers, Millennials and Gen-Xers as well as my grandchildren by extending notions of risks, rights, and responsibilities.

Safeguarding Social Security for Future Generations: Leaving a Legacy in an Aging Society invokes a richer measure of solidarity to encompass an increasingly diverse nation. Fruitful conversations about Social Security's solvency problems may short-circuit sterile debates about the program's sustainability. Younger and older FICA contributors, assured of getting substantive returns on their investment, will mobilize as stewards committed to adapting a successful program that binds people together in trust and hope.

Transformative self-awareness empowers Baby Boomers like me to represent a pragmatic vision for Social Security's vital role in an aging society. I dare to communicate perspectives to overlapping generations with distinctive life experiences and ideas about the program's solidarity, sustainability, and stewardship as Social Security historically evolves in a broad institutional, time-sensitive societal context. Among the legacy gifts I and others in my generation can bestow is an interpretive narrative that stokes measured hope alongside enduring fears as we imagine and chart fresh possibilities for reform.

Notes

1 Achenbaum, W. Andrew. 2008. "Facing up to Janus." *Journal of Aging Studies*, **22**, 184–188.
2 Achenbaum, W. Andrew. 2021. "Combining spiritual aging and geropsychological development." *Journal of Gerontopsychology and Geriatric Psychiatry*, **34**, 101–107.
3 Pew Research Center. 2021. Public trust in government: 1958–2021. www.pewresearch.org/politics/2021/05/17/public-trust-in-government-1958-2021/.
4 National Academy of Social Insurance. 2021. "Public opinions on Social Security." www.nasi.org/education/public-opinions-on-social-security/.
5 Ibid.
6 Quinby, Laura D., Silicano, Robert L. and Gal Wettstein. 2021. Working Paper. Center for Retirement Research at Boston College. https://crr.bc.edu/working-papers/does-social-security-serve-as-an-economic-stabilizer/.
7 Rohr, Richard. 2020. "Wisdom in times of crisis." Albuquerque, NM: Center for Action and Contemplation.
8 Prochaska, J.O., DiClemente, C. C. and J. C. Norcross. 1992. "In search of how people change." *American Psychologist* **47**, 1102–1114; Noar, S. M., Benac, C. N. and M. S. Harris. 2007. "Does tailoring matter? Meta-analysis of tailored print health behavioral change interventions." *Psychological Bulletin* **4**, 673–693; Tomasello, Michael. 2014. *A Natural History of Human Thinking*. Cambridge, MA: Harvard University Press; Kripal, Jeffrey J. 2019. *The Flip*. New York: Bellevue Literary Press.

9 Milligan, Susan. 2014. "The divided states of America." www.usnews.com; Benjamin, Jessica. (2020). "Beyond doer and done-to." https://depthcou nseling.org.
10 Bateman, A. and Peter Fonagy. 2019. *Handbook of Mentalizing in Mental Health Practice*. Washington, D.C.: American Psychiatric Publishing.
11 Fitzgerald, Patrick. 1988. "Gratitude and justice." *Ethics*, **109**, 119–153.
12 Quote investigator. 2018, November 18. https://quoteinvestigator.com/ 2018/11/18/know-trouble/.
13 Allen, Jon G. 2021. *Trusting in Psychotherapy*. Washington, DC: American Psychiatric Association; Rorty, Richard. 1998. *Achieving Our Country*. Cambridge, MA: Harvard University Press.
14 Chenowith, Erica. 2021. *Civil Resistance*. New York: Oxford University Press.
15 Levitin, Michael. 2021. *Generation Occupy: Reawakening American Democracy*. Counterpoint Press.
16 Kelley, Lauren. 2021, December 1. "Opinion today." *The New York Times*.
17 Ayalon, Lisl et al. 2020. "Aging in times of the covid-19 pandemic: Avoiding ageism and fostering intergenerational solidarity." *The Journals of Gerontology*, **B**, 75.
18 Squaredawayblog. 2020. "Lost wealth today vs the great depression." Boston College: Center for Retirement Research.
19 Butler, Robert N. 2007. *The Longevity Revolution*. New York: Public Affairs.
20 Good Therapy. (no date). Control. www.goodtherapy.org; Cohen, Elliott D. 2010. "The fear of losing control. Find a therapist."
21 Achenbaum, W. Andrew. 2012. "How boomers turned conventional wisdom on its head." Westport, CT: Medlife, Mature Market Institute; Achenbaum, W. Andrew, Bern-Klug, Mercedes and Erlene Rosowsky. 2017. "The summer of youth." *Generations*, vol. 41, pp. 3–18.
22 Von Drehle, David. 2021, September 11. "Opinion: 20 years later, Americans kid themselves if they think the war born of 9/11 is over." *Washington Post*.
23 Rubin, Jennifer. 2021, September 11. "Opinion: Yes the Jan. 6 insurrectionists were terrorists. George W. Bush just indicted them." *Washington Post*.
24 Brooks, David. 2018. "Liberal parents, radical kids." *The New York Times*.
25 Dionne, E. J., Jr. 2020. *Code Red*. New York: St. Martin's Press; O'Neal, Lannae. 2017. "Ibram Kendi." https://theundefeated.com/features.
26 Middleton, William. 2018. *Double Vision*. New York: Knopf.
27 O'Neal, "Ibram Kendi."
28 North, Michael B. 2017. "Millennials and baby boomers are taught to hate each other—but they need each other to survive." https://qz.com/940 686; Hill, Sam. 2020. "Ok, millennial: Boomers are the great generation in history." *Newsweek*.

Chapter 9

Negotiating solidarity, sustainability, and stewardship under Social Security

Introduction

"Sometimes it is profitable to listen to the advice of older heads," observed 83-year-old George McGovern in *Social Security and the Golden Age* (2005). The decorated World War II pilot and former senator from South Dakota adamantly opposed George W. Bush's efforts in 2005 to privatize Social Security. Senator McGovern intended the book, subtitled "an essay on the new American demographic," to spark a transgenerational dialogue: "The closer I have moved into association with my grandchildren, the more I have learned from them, and from time to time, I detect ways in which I have informed them."[1]

McGovern's thoughts about the program's vital importance to Americans still ring true: "The 'better angels of our nature' reside with a strong Social Security and a working union of young and old Americans seeking to build this golden age."[2] Now, another grandfather listens, and through a new set of keywords reframes safeguarding Social Security for future generation, leaving a legacy to contemporaries and my own grandchildren.

Did Social Security's age-based criteria undermine advancing transgenerational transactions?

We focused previously on the "risks" that American workers and their families endured during the Great Depression. Because hazards were widespread and fearsome over the life course, Franklin Delano Roosevelt (FDR) and his policy experts selected "age" as a surrogate for identifying and categorizing Americans who risked economic insecurity and late-life dependency. This age-specific strategy justified

DOI: 10.4324/9781003345985-13

reasonable constraints on program costs and coverage, since Social-Security coverage was not universal in 1935. This decision also limited commitments to "solidarity," however by precluding a more fluid, transgenerational process for determining eligibility and delivering benefits.

New Dealers did not invoke any philosophical or ideological rationale for age-based eligibility criteria under the 1935 Act. Historical precedents and favorable actuarial projections were readily available. Roughly half of U.S. state-initiated and corporate-administered plans set retirement at age 70; most of the rest, including the 1934 federal Railroad Retirement System, adopted age 65. The 65-year-old cut-off, according to Committee on Economic Security actuaries, exceeded estimates of life expectancy for gainfully employed Americans: 21-year-old men on average lived to around 53, women survived to roughly age 60.[3]

Implementing the 1935 Social Security Act affected other retirement programs' eligibility criteria. In anticipation of Title I, which funded Federal-State old-age assistance, many jurisdictions in 1936 and 1937 created or amended provisions for indigent elders. New York, for instance, substituted "assistance" for each reference to "relief" in its law; legislators lowered eligibility from 70 to 65.[4] Statewide inequities nonetheless emerged.[5] Arizona, Georgia, Kansas, and North and South Carolina, Tennessee, and Virginia elected not to establish programs to relieve old-age dependency. Other jurisdictions maintained poorhouses, thereby denying institutional residents monthly support under the Act.

Congressional deliberations over the 1939 Social-Security amendments provided a chance to replace age-based criteria with a transgenerational emphasis. Titles I, IV (aid to families with dependent children), and X (relief to the blind) in the original measure, observed Rep. John McCormack (D-Mass), had allocated relief to families:

> Safeguarding the family against economic hazards is one of the major purposes of modern social legislation. Old-age legislation, contributory and noncontributory, unemployment compensation, mothers' aid, and general relief by several States and then political subdivision, aid to the blind and incapacitated, all have an important bearing on preserving the family life.[6]

Extending old-age-insurance benefits to Federal Insurance Contribution Act (FICA) contributors' dependents and survivors, experts solidified New-Deal notions of rights and mutual responsibilities. Pollsters indicated that more and more ordinary Americans evinced greater solidarity in support of the program.

Incremental improvements to Social Security subsequently modified the 65-year-old baseline. Congress added disability-insurance provisions in the 1950s to aid eligible FICA workers whose impairments forced early retirement after age 40. Broadening Social-Security coverage this way was "eminently fair... It seemed humane. It didn't cost much. It paralleled a common provision in private health insurance."[7] By the same logic, the House of Representatives in 1955 voted to lower women's retirement age from 65 to 62. The 1961 Social-Security amendments permitted men to receive partial Title-II benefits at age 62.[8]

Similarly, Congress provided hospital benefits under Medicare tied to Social Security's age-based eligibility criteria. The 1965 legislation benefited only those receiving old-age retirement insurance under Title II. State-administered Medicaid, also enacted in 1965, was analogous to Title I. Medicaid provided anti-poverty health coverage to low-income adults, children, pregnant women, the very old, and disabled people.

The Social Security Administration (SSA) informed the public about these changes. The agency periodically disseminated evidence that documented the advantages of the U.S. brand of social insurance throughout an average American's life. Eschewing a transgenerational theme, officials stressed that stakeholders qualified for enhanced protection against age-specific risks. Assistant Social-Security commissioner Ida C. Merriam in 1968 calculated the benefits enjoyed by the 2.27 million Americans born in 1935, 97% of whom were still living. "Improvements have contributed to the success of the social security program in keeping out of poverty today an estimated 10 million individuals whose income without their social security benefits would be below the poverty line" [and] "by the year 2000 surviving members will be old enough to qualify for full retirement and health insurance benefits."[9]

Today, virtually all U.S. citizens are covered under Social Security. Exceptions are workers who have not accrued 40 credits (roughly ten years of covered employment), and those who never made FICA contributions (including self-employed tax evaders). Also uncovered are immigrants (undocumented and those coming from countries excluded from prorated benefits under bilateral U.S. partnerships), and retired workers who live in foreign countries (such as Belarus, Cuba,

North Korea, or Ukraine). Additionally disqualified were spouses divorced before ten years of marriage unless they paid enough as FICA workers.[10]

Intragenerational disparities and transgenerational reservations riddle age-based criteria affecting "solidarity" under Social Security, however. In giving precedence to "adequacy" or "equity" under the 1939 amendments, Wilbur J. Cohen was told at the time, "the only result may be that the present younger workers are taxed for the increased benefits to the older people without any assurance whatsoever that they will get similar benefits when they are old."[11] Might this proviso be construed to validate Millennials' fears that Social-Security checks, generous to "greedy geezers," would not be there for them?

To remedy this putative bias, stakeholders can imagine and lawmakers can activate program reforms that are transparently fair, just, equitable, and sufficient. In the midst of a pandemic crisis, Americans can expand an adequate floor of protection to all U.S. citizens. Appeals to "solidarity" make sense: Reorienting Social Security as a vehicle that not only averts age-based "risks," but illuminates a bolder vision around which stakeholders can mobilize.

Invoking "solidarity in the face of risks" to solidify support for Social Security

Social Security since 1935 has served millions of individuals from diverse backgrounds with distinctive work histories. This social-insurance goal resonates deeply in the American grain. "E Pluribus Unum," translated as "from the many forms One," committed We the People to birth a democratic Republic.

"What then is the American, this new man?" asked Hector St. John de Crevecoeur in *Letters to an American Farmer* (1782). The new nation amalgamated "*individuals of all nations are melted into a new race of men.*"[12] Later observers elaborated on this novel accretion of unity melded through diversity. Civic engagement, declared Alexis de Tocqueville in *Democracy in America* (1840), inculcated *l'individualisme*, giving white males a stake in governance while freeing them to go about their business in solitary ways.[13] James Bryce in *The American Commonwealth* (1888) underlined "the amazing solvent power which American institutions, habits, and ideas exercise upon newcomers of all races … quickly dissolving and assimilating the foreign bodies that are poured into her mass."[14] Israel Zangwill in 1908 characterized the country as "the great melting pot." Gunnar Myrdal's study of U.S. race relations during World War II, was guardedly optimistic that America could become "a more perfect union ... continuously struggling for its soul."[15]

Yet a dystonic strain has separated "us" from "them" throughout the course of American history. Neither Crevecoeur nor de Tocqueville refer much to Black slaves in chains. Bryce omitted references to the Ku Klux Klan, and Zangwill overlooked anti-Semitism's racist undertones. Myrdal was pivotal in documenting racial discrimination and violence.

Racism was not the only stain on the body politic. Nativism besmirched the American Dream. Protestants burned convents in Philadelphia, the city of Brotherly Love, in the 1840s. Californians brutalized Asians who worked on railroads. Generations of Latin American children face border walls and deportation. Women did not get to vote until 1920, and still endure glass ceilings and sexual harassment in unequal power relationships. Current wealth disparities exceed those in de Tocqueville's America. And a seemingly casual question— "How old are you?"—sounds ageist to persons over 40 or 60.[16]

FDR during the Great Depression envisioned Federal resources bringing citizens together in solidarity. He did not require "the creation of new and strange values," in asserting that "It's rather the finding of the way once more to known, but to some degree forgotten, ideals and values." FDR hoped that "the objectives are as permanent as human nature. Among our objectives I place the security of the men, women, and children of our Nation first".[17]

Others followed suit, claiming that Social Security connected age groups together as they endured present risks and faced future hardships. "As with any framework, the stability of the entire structure depends on the contributions of each part," declared Social-Security commissioner Robert M. Ball, a major negotiator in the 1983 compromise. "Social Security compels all of us to contribute to our own future security."[18] Nancy Altman and Eric Kingson went on from serving as National Commission on Social Security Reform (NCSSR) staff to found Social Security Works. To them,

> Uncertainties—easily estimated for groups, but impossible to determine for individuals—require an insurance solution... Social Security is a trust based on broadly shared civic and religiously based principles: concerns for our parents, for our neighbors, for our children, and for the legacy we will leave those who follow.[19]

Social Security represented a workable New-Deal compact, but Americans today still have to surmount age-relevant challenges to historically deep racial, gender, and income inequities. We might attain a broader definition of "solidarity" if we think out of the box.

Breaking out of the three boxes of life to promote adult education by capitalizing on solidarity under Social Security

Our national experiences document how censuses, bureaucracies (such as Social Security), and ordinary people categorically use chronological age to mark generational shifts, track life histories, and segment social structures.[20] "Age," for instance, has organized levels of education: from preschool, children, and youth pass from one grade to another until they finish high school or vocational education; then, many enroll in institutions of higher learning to acquire certificates and degrees. This age–graded structure has epigenetic qualities: Having earned education credentials (the first box of life); men and women then "work" (the second box); and those who reach late life travel, visit family, and enjoy "leisure" (the third box).[21]

The U.S. educational system also opened pathways for adults to fulfill desires for enrichment, self-improvement, and career advancement. The 3,000 sites where Ralph Waldo Emerson and Susan B. Anthony lectured in antebellum lyceum movement gave way to the Chautauqua Institution's satellites in 12,000 communities, John Dewey's problem-based learning, Martin Knowles' self-directed learning, and Jack Mezirow's transformative learning. Corporate-based training programs enriched the theory and practice of "andragogy," as did Elderhostel, vocational education, and formal and informal modes of adult learning.[22]

This alternative branch in U.S. education mushroomed in postwar America. According to the National Center for Educational Statistics, 12.5 million students are under age 25 but 7.4 million are older. Roughly 11% of U.S. male veterans between the ages of 35 and 54 are enrolled in colleges. Nearly 80% of full-time students attending public two-year colleges are 25 or younger; a majority of students in private community colleges are adult learners taking courses in marketing, business, or nursing.[23] When companies and unions do not cover tuitions, older students freight the bill as they continue working and caregiving.

Reforming Social Security can further break down the three boxes of life, permitting stakeholders to rearrange education, work, and leisure. Encompassing a solidarity consonant with its transgenerational features, the program could provide a financial resource to help young and middle-aged stakeholders upgrade skills when they feel burdened with tuition debts and caregiving responsibilities. To deter job burnout and promote work satisfaction, workers getting retirement pensions might be permitted to borrow against their future benefits in order to pay for retraining to enhance their value or open up new opportunities.

Are Americans willing to rethink how Social Security might fulfill a broader societal objective, one embodying a fully intergenerational system? Can we envision the program girding a concept solidarity flexible enough to share transactional resources among age groups? Yes, theoretically: all Americans have a stake in the program. Highlighting a transgenerational motif to capitalize on measures of mutual interdependence would bind "We the People" closer together in a shared past and a common future. But is such a goal sustainable?

Salvaging Social Security's sustainability

A majority of Americans endorse Social-Security aims, but there was no guarantee that strong support would last indefinitely. Concerns about the program's fiscal sustainability bothered critical thinkers at the outset. Fanning anxieties was Alf Landon's 1936 campaign barb that Social Security was a "cruel hoax ... unjust, unworkable, stupidly drafted and wastefully financed."[24] FDR won in a landslide, pledging to sustain Social Security's income floor.

Doubts that surfaced in the 1930s about the program's solvency have amplified over the decades, as scholars in right-wing think tanks and media journalists predict that Social Security is headed toward bankruptcy. "It's time to face facts: We have lied to our kids," thundered Cato Institute. "Social Security and Medicare cannot pay for all the benefits that we have promised them—and until we admit that, we'll continue down the road toward national financial ruin."[25] *Newsweek*'s Robert J. Samuelson for three decades blamed "the cowardice of the political class" for dithering over Social Security's fiscal woes, warning that "we are passing along to our children a governmental apparatus that invest heavily in the past and shortchanges the future. Shame on us."[26]

This brings us to the second "S" of our new set of keywords—fears about "sustainability." Worries about Social Security's financial prospects nowadays arise in part from an unresolved, unsettling disconnect between rosy forecasts and grim projections. For too long, Social-Security optimists have not convincingly countered arguments by naysayers. Critics present scary stories and numbers as they sensationalize the massive infusions of Federal funds required to keep Social Security afloat. "Congress has conspicuously declined to raise taxes enough to fund Social Security's current benefit schedule."[27]

Within the decade, Social Security Trustees report, the program will not be able to pay full benefits, unless Congress acts. Over the next 75 years, financial challenges will mushroom.

Middle-range models estimate a deficit roughly 1% of the Gross Domestic Product, less than the cost of recent wars.[28] Disagreements widen as commentators assess the impact of Social-Security deficits on the health of the U.S. economy.[29]

Just as solidarity under Social Security emboldens a transgenerational approach to reframing Social Security, so too can the program's notion of "sustainability" be reworked. Some members of FDR's Committee on Economic Security (CES) wanted universal coverage:

> All workers face the contingency of dependent old age, whether employed in large factories or in small shops or offices, and only serious administrative difficulties, previous legislation, or constitutional limitations should be permitted to interfere with the provision of basic, uniform protection related to contributions.[30]

Over the objections of its chair, Secretary of Labor Frances Perkins, CES informed Congress that universal coverage could not be realized initially. Secretary of Treasury Henry Morgenthau excluded farm laborers and domestic servants. The House Ways and Means Committee exempted another group of workers—employees of charitable agencies. The 1935 Act covered only privately employed wage earners, though some workers were already protected by the 1934 federal Railroad Retirement Act. Once Social Security became law, officials proceeded to expand coverage incrementally, raising it from 24% in 1939, to 55% in 1959, and to 89% in 1977. The 1983 Social-Security amendments extended protection to federal employees, a provision long resisted by their union representatives and postal workers. Pocketbooks and public sentiment prevailed, nonetheless. "With social security in financial trouble, and only a limited range of unpleasant options available to restore solvency," argued Senator John Heinz (R-Pa), a NCSSR member. "There has been a growing public sense that continued exclusion of Federal workers from social security is a luxury the taxpayers can no longer afford."[31]

Social Security now remains sustainable, thanks to taxes paid by 94% of the U.S. work force. FICA contributors represent a voter block large enough body to uphold FDR's belief that "no damn politician can ever scrap my social security program."[32] Transgenerational links between solidarity and sustainability are a powerful lever for rectifying enduring gender biases. Experts have failed to respond to changes in women's earnings records by giving caregiver credits for their unpaid assistance to young and aged members of the community. And there are bound to be administrative difficulties in identifying fraud and adapting to societal-aging's diverse changes in household patterns. Policymakers have time and the requisite expertise to adjust the program's criteria and benefit structure for current and future stakeholders.

The real obstacle is determining whether Social Security is discriminatory toward women. Defenders of the status quo point out that women collect more than half of all Social-Security benefits but contribute less than a third of FICA payments. Far more divorced or widowed women than men receive spousal benefits. These facts are true yet rarely contextualized in light of Social Security having prioritized "adequacy" over "equity" since the passage of the 1939 amendments. Other demographic trends complicate definitions of sustainable rights: Women play vital roles as caregivers of older Americans as well as children.

Modernize Social Security by giving credits for eldercare

Women account for 75% of the roughly 40–65 million unpaid U.S. caregivers; a quarter are between ages 45 and 65. This labor force (half of whom feel unprepared and untrained for the job) on average devotes at least 25 hours per week during four-year stints. Economists estimated that, in 2013, providing for patients' health and hygiene, running errands, taking patients to doctors, and doing housework should be valued in excess of $470 billion, which approximates Walmart's sales that year, and exceeds Medicaid outlays for paid home care.[33]

Eldercare exacts an economic and physical toll. Career women lose wages (in excess of $3 trillion), health insurance, and retirement investments; 39%, who arrive tardily to work are reprimanded by human-resource managers. So many quit jobs or work part-time in order to spend time to care for loved ones.[34] Furthermore, women caregivers' health deteriorates—91% report depression, anxiety, sleep disorders, and other facets of "caregiver syndrome."

Generating Social-Security caregiver credits will not eliminate these problems, yet the system can prepare for the coming decades in which Baby Boomers will need extra support. There are precedents for counting time devoted to caregiving. Historically, spousal benefits under Title II and through credits under the Supplemental Security Income and Disability Insurance programs could reduce stringent eligibility criteria in caring for patients with ALS (amyotrophic lateral sclerosis, also known as Lou Gehrig's disease), multiple sclerosis, cerebral palsy, Parkinson's, or cancer. Current recipients in many states live in near poverty because SSA determines eligibility and documents childcare credits unlike other countries' requirements. To reduce gender gap, Americans could join Germany, Sweden, and the United Kingdom in giving credits for elder care.[35]

Just as FDR and his policy advisors adapted social-insurance principles to mesh with U.S. workplace and welfare traditions, so too we can broaden fiscal notions of "sustainability" to compensate elder-caregivers who attend to the physical and social needs of a fast-growing segment of an aging population. Adding this provision to evaluating childcare credits will not bankrupt the program. Instead it valorizes and sustains assistance that that far exceeds purely monetary cost–benefit calculations. Underwriting this service will tap Trust Funds, but it will enable Social-Security stewards to act to benefit the commonweal.

Stewardship ensures solidarity and sustainability under Social Security

"Stewardship" is more than the third leg of the tripod that anchors Americans' ties to Social Security. Trustees, who are accountable to lawmakers, reporters, and watchdogs, interconnect solidarity in supporting social insurance and the program's fiscal sustainability.[36] They are *de facto* Social-Security stewards designated to protect workers and their families from some hazards and vicissitudes of age and aging.

During their time-limited tenure Social Security Trustees assess current operations and estimate future developments; they disseminate their reports in optimistic, middle-range, and dire projections. For solidarity's sake, these stewards safeguard commitments made to FICA contributors. Failure to warn about possible shortfalls would undermine trust and confidence among generations of worker-citizens who count on Social Security being there. *Benefiting from nearly universal coverage protects age groups' solidarity-stake in the program's sustainability.* Reinforcing a sense of self-reliance and mutual responsibility moves FICA contributors beyond particularistic self-interests to embrace calls for shared unity amidst the diversities of an aging society. Solidarity, ideally, breaks down dualisms that pit young against old, majorities against minorities, and the privileged against the disenfranchised.

Responsible stewardship also buttresses generations' faith in Social Security's capacity to maintain and sustain an income floor for millions of Americans. Disparities in other transgenerational transactions have changed with societal aging, which has resulted in significant inequalities nowadays. The top 1% of the Baby Boomer cohort, forecast to leave inheritances totaling $20 trillion by 2050, mainly view Social-Security checks as an insignificant portion of their retirement portfolios. Their annual earnings in 2022 were not subject to FICA taxes beyond $147,000. Sources of wealth among the truly affluent—compared to those of most Baby Boomer women, minorities, and naturalized citizens—has magnified disparate retirement floors across and within segments of older Americans.

Social Security's impact becomes even more multifaceted among Baby Boomers in the shrinking middle quintiles. Roughly 60% anticipate Social Security to be their primary source of retirement income—a figure up from 43% among those surveyed as recently as 2010. Mergers and outsourcing downsized employer pension plans. Forty-five percent of all Baby Boomers have saved little for retirement; few had more than $25,000 in bank accounts or IRAs.

Social Security staves off the incidence of poverty for aging Baby Boomers shadowed by financial exigencies and medical catastrophes. The overall poverty rate among Social-Security checks is 8.8%; poverty rates since the 1983 amendments among older Hispanics have fallen to 15.7% in 2019; for African Americans, 22%. Pockets of old-age dependency persistently afflict the low-educated, low-skilled, and disabled. Beneficiaries over age 80 (58%) face more financial vulnerability than those between the ages of 65 and 79 (44%).

How stewardship interacts with younger workers' solidarity in sustaining Social Security

In contrast to most Baby Boomers, Millennials over the course of their lives have been saddled with market forces beyond their control. Rates of child poverty rose 37% between 1970 and 1995. Earnings for college graduates fell 10% between 1989 and 1995. Career opportunities were scant for male high-school dropouts. When only gig work is an option, entry-level employees stumble to make ends meet. The young struggle to get health insurance, much less plan for retirement. Besides tuition debts and mortgages, Millennials pay high taxes for fewer public services, as they deal with growing income differentials and wealth disparities.

Younger workers' opinions of being Social-Security stewards take a surprising turn, however. They reject calls for ending the program, and want the Federal government to shore up transgenerational safety nets. Many Millennials want to rally around boosting the program's solidarity and sustainability. They favor benefit increases for low-income retirees and those who cannot pay hospital bills or suffer life-threatening disabilities.

Gaps in the U.S.'s overlapping retirement systems complicate how various ages of stakeholders perceive the relationship between solidarity and sustainability under Social Security. On the one hand, the distinction between public- and private-sector programs diverge since lobbyists pressure Congress in regulating corporate pensions under U.S. tax codes. On the other hand, the functional status of employer pensions has changed, as funds invested to pay for workers' retirements constitute one of the greatest sources of financial power in America. The amount spent on retirement income programs represented less than 1.5% of the Gross National Product in 1950; it now exceeds 8%.

To uphold the synergistic interdependence of stewardship as related to solidarity and sustainability under Social Security should not be the task solely born by the program's Trustees. Should stakeholders of all ages engage as stewards with policy elites, this alliance seems a far cry from generational-equity debates of the 1980s, when elders and grandchildren sought pride of place. Stewards can reasonably expect those coming of age in the 21st century to modulate rivalries between Boomers and Millennials. Too young to vote but old enough to watch classmates murdered in schools, adolescents already are pivotal players in transforming debates over gun control and advocating climate change. Grade-school students know that Black and Brown Lives Matter.

The civic engagement that now brings the very young to center stage is not a new development in U.S. history. The American Youth Congress, with support from Eleanor Roosevelt, lobbied Congress to end racial discrimination during the Depression. Historians identify at least 21 different youth-centered protest movements in the 1960s and 1970s. Before the multigenerational demonstrations for racial justice that spread through urban and rural communities during the pandemic, the greatest outpouring of student activism had occurred when four million students protested the invasion of Cambodia in the spring of 1970.

Many older Americans—notably Baby Boomers who were activists in youth—can readily identify with the enthusiasm, idealism, and electrifying efforts by new generations coming into their own. My generation is wisely *leaving a legacy* that invites Millennials and younger Americans to augment the boundaries of Social Security's stewardship so that people can evaluate its interactions with other U.S. priorities. "Only when the tide goes out," billionaire octogenarian Warren Buffett observed, "do you discover who's been swimming naked."

Social Security's stewards must link the program to other U.S. retirement resources

Half of all state and local pension benefits were cut after the 2008 recession. The pandemic is further destabilizing their status. "Plans that have either taken action in the past to reduce contributions or lacked action when actuarial recommendations increased are seeing increased stress now."[37] With average public pension now only 70% funded, these retirement vehicles may fare worse if the pandemic prolongs the current economic conditions.

Corporate pensions embody more distressing disparities than exist under Social Security. Coverage is neither as uniform nor as universal. Forty percent of aged Blacks living alone depend on Social Security for 90% of their income. Well-off retirees, in contrast, supplement the program's monthly checks with savings, IRAs, delayed compensation, and inherited wealth. Employer pensions constitute a much smaller portion of the income available to other senior Americans. Depending on race, gender, and household status, savings and supplemental assets provide roughly 10–15% of the monthly income of Social-Security recipients.

"All social policy can do is provide a mechanism that allocates aggregate output in some democratically agreed-to-optimum fashion, the optimum allocation ... having a lifetime as well as a temporal dimension," observed economist Juanita Kreps instructively decades ago.[38] Social Security's stewards must ensure an adequate floor of protection for older workers and their families. Doing so will reinforce intergenerational solidarity and bolster the system's solvency. Implicit in Kreps' statement are ways that reformers' remedies must not mislead stakeholders' outlooks on Social Security. "We have never expected governments to change hearts or even to solve every social problem. We have expected governments to have an impact on culture, changing and adjusting laws," a *New York Times* editorial reminds us.[39]

New Dealers undoubtedly had values-laden thoughts that permeated Social-Security policymaking—older Americans would sit on a three-legged stool: the program's checks would be supplemented by employer pensions and private savings. And working Americans capitalized on this arrangement during and after World War II. Poverty rates fell as Congress liberalized the program's benefits, Unions demanded raising wages and obtained health benefits. The Federal government in the 1970s started to regulate corporate pensions and individual retirement accounts.

Since the passage of the 1983 Social-Security amendment, the golden age of retirement has been transformed by historical forces that have changed the retirement-relevant context in which the program has evolved. "The unequivocal message from the 1990s: Washington only cares about long-term problems that poll well."[40] Since then, unions have lost members and clout. American families that survive from paycheck to paycheck cannot set aside much for later years. Private pensions are underfunded, and some plans for state and municipal employees have gone bankrupt. It goes beyond the scope of this book to detail what remedies should be initiated across individual, private-sector plans, and age-bounded Federal relief and social-welfare programs that impinge on Social Security's status in an aging society. Suffice it to say that timely assessments and action must salvage if this institutional interplay to benefit longer-lived generations to come.

All three of these retirement resources, coupled with job retraining and eldercare credits, should guarantee older Americans more robust transgenerational standards of living. Amid the coronavirus pandemic that reportedly had a negative impact on financial situations, 73% of workers were confident that they would retire into a comfortable lifestyle. The same percentage, worried about Social Security, anticipated relying on savings.[41] These mixed survey opinions underscore limits to artful stewardship. Social Security Trustees do not regulate options beyond their mandate. Disinformation would lessen if program's stakeholders "have some degree of certainty about what they would look to get."[42]

That said, we can dare to perceive Social Security and other retirement vehicles in a broader societal context, not just in terms circumscribed by Federal mandates and institutionally based operations. If we do so, we can imagine how safeguarding stakeholders' well-being solidifies the societal foundations of the United States that bolster our nation's competitive advantages in an ever-changing global economy. According to a recent RAND study, seven characteristics have been associated historically with national dynamism and competitive positioning: (1) a cogent definition of purpose, (2) clearly under-stood stakes, (3) better organization, (4) sound foundational planning, (5) strong fundamentals, (6) benchmarks and measures, and (7) leaders with vision and a sense of teamwork.

Rethinking Social Security's value in terms of "solidarity," "sus-tainability," and "stewardship" will not eliminate partisan stalemates or media disinformation. Anger, fear, insecurity, and despair are ram-pant across the political spectrum. "This isn't helped by the fact that traditionally Social Security has been a third rail issue where people who seek public office don't have an incentive to attack this issue."[43] Disillusioning circumstances reveal our brokenness. Americans never-theless can mobilize around overdue Social-Security reforms.

With an appropriate measure of hope and trust, surely couched in anxieties and fear, worker-citizens and their elected officials can mobilize in *Safeguarding Social Security for Future Generations: Leaving a Legacy in an Aging Society*. Baby Boomers like me are willing and able to engage in interactive, transgenerational conversations that could result in collective action joined by younger stakeholders who have never witnessed significant amendments to Social Security. Unfortunately, our generation's children and grandchildren may not care to listen.

We can recover common ground through imaginative and critical thinking in generating a testament of measured hope. Generations united together can prevail as we deal with doubts, fears, another pan-demic, and culture wars. But first we have to integrate our minds and hearts in our own distinctive ways. Only then can we interact with "vital involvement," as Joan and Erik Erikson put it, balan-cing pragmatic wisdom and visceral awareness. We probably will encounter humbling mistakes and humiliating failures as we grapple with ubiquitous risks that threaten America's democracy now and in the future. Transgenerational talks and grassroots mobilizations among stewards will ensure Social Security's solidarity and sustainable likelihood of working for all of us.

Notes

1 McGovern, George. 2005. *Social Security and the Golden Age*. Golden, CO: Fulcrum Publishing, 44, 72.
2 Ibid., 76.
3 Social Security History. 2020. "Life expectancy for Social Security." Archives.
4 Achenbaum, W. Andrew. 1986. *Social Security: Visions and Revisions*. New York: Cambridge University Press.
5 Ibid.
6 McCormack, John. 1939, June 10. *Congressional Record*, 6964.
7 Perkins, Roswell B. 1968. Interview. Columbia University: Oral History Collection; Stone, Deborah A. 1984. *The Disabled State*. Philadelphia: Temple University Press.
8 Achenbaum, *Social Security*.
9 Merriam, Ida C. 1968. "Young adults and Social Security." *Social Security Bulletin*, **31**: 7–13.
10 Fontinelle, Amy. 2020. "8 types of Americans who aren't eligible to get Social Security." www.investopedia.com/retirement.
11 Witte, Edwin E. 1939, July 3. Memorandum to Wilbur J. Cohen. Record group 47,095. Washington, D.C.: National Archives.
12 de Crevecoeur, Letters from an American Farmer, reprint 2019 by New York: Oxford University Press.
13 de Tocqueville, Alexis. 1840. *Democracy in America*. 2 vols. New York: Vintage.
14 James Bryce, THE AMERICAN COMMONWEALTH, reprint 2015 by New York: Andesite Press.
15 Myrdal, Gunnar. 1944. *An American Dilemma*. New York: Harper & Brothers.
16 Chudacoff, Howard. 1992. *How Old Are You?* Princeton: Princeton University Press; Field, Corinne and Nicholas L. Syrett, Eds. 2014. *Age in America*. New York: New York University Press.
17 Roosevelt, Franklin D. 1934, June 8. "Objectives of the administration." *FDR Public Papers* **3**, 291–292.
18 Rogne, Leah and Carroll Estes, Eds. 2009. *Social Insurance and Social Justice*. New York: Springer Publishing.
19 Altman, Nancy and Eric R. Kingson. 2015. *Social Security Works!* New York: The New Press.
20 Field and Syrett, *Age in America*.
21 Bolles Richard N. 1978. *The Three Boxes of Life*. Ten Speed Press.

22 Kett, Joseph F. 1994. *The Pursuit of Knowledge under Differences.* Stanford: Stanford University Press; Dewey, John. 1897. *My Pedagogical Creed*; Knowles, Malcolm. 1950. *Informal Adult Education.* Chicago: Association Press; Meziow, Jack. 1978. *Education for Perspective Transformation.* New York: Teachers College.

23 Chen, Grace. 2019. "Changing student demographics." www.communi tycollegereview.com; Duffin, Erin. 2020a. "College enrollment—share of U.S. veterans by gender and age." www.statista.com/statistics/188182; Duffin, Erin. 2020b. "Share of full-time students enrolled in U.S. community colleges." www.statista.com/statistics/753295; Europa. 2020. "Adult learning statistics." https://ec.europa/eurostat/statistics.

24 Landon, Alf. 1936, October 1. "Landon based his attack on Social Security Act on report to group backed by Filene." *New York Times.*

25 Tanner, Michael D. 2018. "America's entitlement crisis just keeps going." *National Review.*

26 Robert J. Samuelson. 2018. The cowardice of the political class. *Washington Post.*

27 Blahous, Charles. 2019, April 26. "We're running out of time: Social Security must be saved now." *Washington Post.*

28 Romig, Kathleen, Broaddus, Matt, and Aviva Aron-Dine. 2019. "Financial challenges facing Social Security and Medicare largely unchanged from last year, except for improvement in Disability Insurance." Washington, D.C.: Center on Budget and Policy Priorities.

29 Social Security Administration. 2019. Sustainability report and implementation plan.

30 Committee on Economic Security. 1937. Alan Pifer & Lydia Bronte, eds. Our aging selves, 1986. New York: W. W. Norton.

31 Heinz, H. John. 1983. Senate Special Committee on Aging, 98 Cong., 1st sess.

32 Gulick, Luther. 1941. "Memorandum." Social Security Administration Research Note #23.

33 Achenbaum, W. Andrew. December 2002. "Preparing spiritual caregivers." In *Palliative Care*, ed. Levison, Jack & Robert Fine. University Park: Penn State University Press.

34 Family Caregiver Alliance. 2020. "Caregiver statistics: Work and caregiving." www/caregiver.org/.

35 Munnell, Alicia and Andrew D. Eschtruth. 2018. "Modernizing social security: caregiver credits." Boston College: Center for Retirement Research.

36 Moody, Harry R. and W. Andrew Achenbaum. 2014. "Solidarity, sustainability, and stewardship." *Interpretations*, 68, pp. 3–13.

37 Siedle, Edward. 2020, March 16. "Coronavirus could kill your pension." www.forbes.com/sites/; Katz, Mitchell. 2020, May 8. "Public pensions could suffer for years from pandemic losses." www.ai-cio/pub lic- pensions-suffer-years-pandemic-losses/

38 Kreps, Juanita. 1970. 159, 57. *Economics of Aging in American Behavioral Scientist*, vol. 14, pp. 81–92.
39 McCauley, Esau. 2022, June 11. "Don't blame violence on 'evil.'" *The New York Times*.
40 Shapiro, Walter. 2022. "1989–2001: America's long lost weekend." *The New Republic*.
41 Transamerica Center for Retirement Studies. 2021. "A compendium of findings about the retirement outlook of U.S. workers, 11–15.
42 Mark Hulbert, 2020. Pensions in MarketWatch.
43 Singh, Dhara. 2020, August 7. "America's Social Security crisis is getting worse amid the coronavirus pandemic." *Yahoo.Money*.

Conclusion

Introduction

I portray myself to this book's audiences primarily as a Baby-Boomer grandfather talking to kin and, to a lesser extent, as a seasoned coxswain stirring the imaginations of younger crews. Safeguarding Social Security, I argue, is a way for elders of the tribe to leave a legacy—one that recognizes varied self-interests and emboldens the commonweal. It can provoke an invaluable step-by-step process that restores confidence and trust within and across generational lines, as we adapt to unknown opportunities and pitfalls in an aging society.

There are legitimate concerns about Social Security's durability. Although the program has never failed to send out checks, younger Federal Insurance Contribution Act (FICA) contributors doubt that they will get Social-Security benefits. Stakeholders rightly and reasonably ask if the program will be there for them when they need it. But safeguarding Social Security requires us to acknowledge the full extent to which values and politics affect the program in ways that fiscal projections do not describe or explain.

Americans of all ages harbor tensions between realistic fears and measured hopes, symbiotically polarizing thoughts and expectations that go far beyond evaluating the institution's sustainability. Living in a distressing historical moment, we no longer trust that our children can safely go to school or that we can reverse climate warming. Americans have less faith in Big Government working for us. Should a host of "isms" (such as racism and exceptionalism) prevent citizens from healing political divisions and preventing insurrections, extremists and ordinary people will feel trapped in the U.S.'s decline.

American citizens have time to shore up the Social-Security program—even in the context of an aging society with frayed norms

DOI: 10.4324/9781003345985-14

and dysfunctional interactions. "Our goal needs to be a universal set of workforce and family security policies that can greatly strengthen risk protection through the life course."[1] We are resourcefully daring enough for generations to unite to expand earlier social-insurance concepts, which ensure that Social Security remains an essential institutional bulwark as millions of stakeholders revitalize America's democracy.

"Resilience of spirit (far more than brilliance of intellect) is the essential ingredient of a full life," declared former secretary of state Madeleine Albright. "No matter how smart we are, we can allow sorrows and grievances to overwhelm us, or we can respond positively to setbacks—be they caused by our own misjudgments or by … the shock of unwelcome and unexpected circumstances."[2] While millions of Americans recognize our nation's inability to fix all wrongs in the nation and world, our forebears and elders sacrificed much so that we could flourish. Generations together can yet honor "our fidelity to the values that bind us, both despite and because of our differences."[3]

As part of a larger campaign to restore trust and confidence in America entails bolstering Social Security's transgenerational compact, which affects the lives of millions of multicultural, multiracial Americans. If we do so successfully and pragmatically, we may acquire a heuristic paradigm with which to tackle other issues that are eviscerating resilient faith in our aging society. We must remember that this adaptive process may fail: "It was not granted you to complete the task," opined Rabbi Tarton millennia ago, "and yet you may not give it up."[4]

This book offers three interwoven takeaway messages.

1   It is not too late to honestly assess and restructure SocialSecurity.
2   Americans have opportunities to determine whether we want to greatly amplify the program's aims and operations for ourselves and rising generations.
3   We can decide how best to leave a legacy wherein Social Security remains central to America's time-tested norms and transgenerational aims.

It may help to put these three takeaways into a gripping context that confronts and inspires Millennials and Zoomers. Words of hope and fear uttered in 1968 illuminate my generation's crises, just as the pandemic, societal inequities, gun violence, global terrorism and warming transform their rights and duties.

Dr. King's memorable sermon

A 39-year-old African American delivered a fiery Palm Sunday sermon—"Remaining awake through a great revolution"—at the Washington National Cathedral in 1968. The preacher, the Rev. Dr. Martin Luther King, Jr. (MLK), challenged largely white congregants to rethink "the struggle for freedom and human dignity and discuss the issues involved in that struggle with friends of goodwill all over the nation." Besides weaving together Scripture and Negro spirituals to proclaim that "racial injustice is still the Black man's burden and the White man's shame,"[5] Dr. King urged worshippers to combat global poverty and end the Vietnam war.

Early in the sermon, MLK reminded congregants what Washington Irving wrote about Rip Van Winkle:

> Yes, he slept through a revolution. And one of the great liabilities of life is that all too many people find themselves living amid a great period of social change, and yet they fail to develop new attitudes, the new mental responses, that the new situation demands. They end up sleeping through a revolution.[6]

Dr. King's jeremiad paralleled Washington Irving's interpretation: "The story of Rip Van Winkle may seem incredible to many [but] I have heard many stranger stories than this … all of which were … authenticated doubt."[7]

Baby Boomers like me dare not sleep through a revolution, thereby our avoiding stark choices about Social Security. We can build on MLK's exhortation to rethink vital American institutions like Social Security that provide income floors for millions of U.S. citizens. Otherwise, we shall awake in a miasma as did Rip, "with his long grizzled beard, his rusty fowling-piece, his uncouth dress."[8]

Baby Boomers like me face tough odds in leaving a legacy that includes safeguarding Social Security for future generations. Sensational headlines attract stakeholders' attention, reinforcing uneasy perceptions of the program's sustainability.[9] Without any major reforms in four decades, people of all ages rightly wonder about whether they will collect Social-Security benefits, when they are expected and needed. Senate Minority Leader Mitch McConnell praises planks in the 2022 National Republican Senatorial Committee that would "sunset Social Security and Medicare in five years."[10] Meanwhile, proposals by Democrats (Rep. John Larson, Senators Bernie Sanders with Elizabeth

Warren, and President Biden) to expand Social Security seem unlikely to muster sufficient congressional support.[11] Yet hope remains, despite prolonged stalemates and vitriolic rhetoric. We do not have to sleep through a revolution.

Measured hope animated Dr. King's most riveting sentence in 1968: "We shall overcome because the moral arc of the universe is long but it bends toward justice."[12] Op-ed writers since then have noted MLK's affirmation of faith and confidence for re-forming a just society, one worthy of the Founding Fathers' dreams of their New Republic, *secula seculorum*.[13] President Obama was so touched by the sentence that he had it woven into his Oval Office rug. MLK's sermon still rings true, as we individually and collectively transform ourselves and prepare for engaging in transgenerational conversations and legacy-leaving Social-Security reforms.

Dr. King was paraphrasing a passage from Theodore Parker's 1853 sermon: "I do not pretend to understand the moral universe. The arc is a long one. My eye reaches but little ways. I cannot calculate the curves and complete the figure [yet] I can divine it by conscience. And from what I see it bends toward justice."[14] The abolitionist's congregation was confronting a grim future. Eyes, minds, and souls toggled between being true to their consciences and making concessions to slave owners. An impending crisis loomed.

But I wonder: Did Dr. King's rewording of Parker's sermon unintentionally lull his congregation into magical thinking in 1968? MLK presumed that his audience knew that his story began in a segregated pulpit a block away from the Alabama state capital. All appreciated the fragility of life that Palm Sunday without foreseeing King's unfinished ministry ending four days later.[15] We the people in the 2020s are enmeshed, seemingly powerless in a diverse and divided aging society. History spirals in mysterious flux; technical fixes and teleological promises tend to be misleading. The moral arc of transgenerational justice may never be fully attained. "The flag, the cross and station wagon" might not, and looking backwards, possibly should not, "be reclaimed in the fight for a better future."[16] We must own up to the certainty of uncertainties.

Such sobering realizations do not entitle us, however, to delay reckoning with strategic decisions about whether we scrap or reform the program. The three takeaways from *Safeguarding Social Security for Future Generations: Leaving a Legacy in an Aging Society* create a template for imaginative thinking about the program. It may serve as a model for engaging citizens to deal with other policies, priorities and problems.

It is not too late to reframe conversations and mobilize support for Social Security

Policy experts, idea brokers, lawmakers, media commentators, and stakeholders must resist dualistic thinking about Social Security's current financing and long-term prospects. Neither rosy forecasts nor scary scenarios have prevented logjams, stalemates, and disillusionment. There remains time for conversations based upon mutually acceptable facts to replace disinformation. Americans should act transgenerationally in the face of unexpected but inevitable turn-of-events. Equipped with a rudimentary understanding of Social Security's assets and shortcomings, the program's diverse constituency can decide to proceed together, receptive to the interplay of opinions and biases at this pivotal moment in our nation's history.

The first takeaway theme from this book seems straightforward, but not utterly sanguine. Felicitous outcomes are hardly predestined in American society's polarized political economy. Measured hope will always be counterbalanced by realistic dubiety. Yet fears ought not to dissuade current and future generations from investing in renewable social-insurance compacts that we have shared for nearly ninety years.

Soul craft feeds state craft in addressing the challenges posed by Social-Security shortfalls, thus spurring efforts to actualize "the moral arc of justice"

George Will published *Statecraft as Soulcraft* in 1983, the same year that the last major Social-Security amendments became law. Those bipartisan 1983 amendments, which reaffirmed the New-Deal program's aims as they rectified transactional shortcomings, were intended to keep Social Security in concert with population aging as well as unexpected developments that would alter the Federal agenda and the country's priorities. The National Commission on Social Security Reform (NCSSR) in 1983 reaffirmed the 1938 Social Security Advisory report, which declared that "we should not commit future generations to a burden larger than we would want to bear ourselves."[17] Planning for Baby Boomers' retirement years, NCSSR embellished Will's proposition that statecraft depends on soulcraft: "We serve good governance by acting on the assumptions that underlie our moral language."[18] President Reagan and Speaker O'Neill extolled the continuing allegiance to U.S. vaunted values and transactional norms upheld in bipartisan policymaking.

Reinterpreting the 1983 Social-Security amendments through the lens of Wills' *Soulcraft as Statecraft* clarifies what Dr. King meant when he invoked "the moral arc of justice." It animates an obligation to act fairly within and across competing generational claims. Allocating the program's resources equitably entails respecting the well-being of generations of stakeholders, encouraging contested views on Social Security, and infusing personal rights with communal obligation. In a pluralist democracy, liberals acknowledge limits to what Big Government can do. Conservatives must give up thinking that providing an income floor makes Social Security an intrusive welfare institution.[19]

Safeguarding Social Security for Future Generations: Leaving a Legacy in an Aging Society foregoes any exegesis of theories of justice. Philosophers, politicians, judges, and ordinary people for centuries have defined "justice" in myriad—and conflicting—ways. Thrasymachus, the Sophist orator in Plato's *Republic*, proclaimed that "justice is nothing but the interest of the stronger." Some modern-day sages valorize the notion of a "common good," while others proffer definitions of redistributive justice that maximize utility or freedom of choice.[20] This book opts for a restorative justice grounded in moral judgments of soulcraft in order to envelop and propel statecraft: "To argue about the purpose of a social institution is to argue about the virtues it honors and rewards," George Will observed.[21] Stakeholders are free to *recognize* this proposition or to *reject* its implications as they initiate or deny transgenerational, fluid commitments to respect the dignity of citizens who live in precarious circumstance beyond our ability to control.

Interested persons across party lines profit mightily from continuously assessing how solidarity, sustainability, and stewardship interact symbiotically in shaping Social Security's evolution. These keywords build on and amplify what terms such as risks, rights, and responsibilities implied in the interpretation that I discarded after decades of speaking and listening to students and Rotarians. Hopefully, this substitution persuades younger readers.

The summons to *solidarity* pertain to responsibilities that we owe one another. We must encompass the concatenation of disparities and inequities that penetrate the experiences and pierce the expectations of Social Security's diverse stakeholders. To ensure the program's *sustainability* invites all U.S. age groups, gripped in societal unraveling, to face how dangerously polarizing polemics and grandstanding impede transacting any meaningful transgenerational compact. Authentic *stewardship* privileges critical thinking and dynamic deliberations, rather than avoiding conversations and fueling lies and disinformation about Social Security. It is a daunting challenge, not preordained, for stewards to seek grassroots mobilizations.

A functional participatory democracy conjoins U.S. commentators and experts' attempts to explicate necessary changes to stakeholders who usually are ill-informed about how Social Security works yet responsive to doomsday scenarios. Without access to straightforward, comprehensible, and informative lines of communication, there will be no solidarity. FICA contributors and Social-Security beneficiaries—who are also the program's stewards—will submit in fright, not consent to the governed. A disconnect between idea brokers and ordinary citizens creates obstacles to progressive reforms.[22] Naysayers will continue to convince those who depend on an income floor that it is folly to preserve and sustain Social Security. Advocates meanwhile should listen to overwhelming majorities (81%) who favor raising wages subject to FICA from $147,000 to $400,000 and the over 70% of Republicans and Democrats who would raise the payroll tax from 6.2% to 6.5%.[23]

Fears that impede reforming Social Security can, with a measure of guarded hope, empower Americans faced with uncertainty to take meaningful risks as they embrace transgenerational rights and responsibilities toward the arc of justice

Evaluating Social-Security reforms helps to promote moral justice; mobilizing grassroots support can enhance chances for economic prosperity in a functioning democracy. A relentless pandemic, implosions of political rights and financial institutions, gun violence, climate warming, as well as a global awakening to the depths of structural racism may fashion red-letter dates in world history, which reinforce culture wars between "us" and "them" in the United States. Many in Washington and millions of stakeholders across the country resist problem-solving about Social Security—it's a relatively low priority—and resist honest, pragmatic talk about how safeguarding Social Security bolsters a transgenerational legacy for the common good.[24]

Personal conflicts—be they familial, policy relevant, national, or global—subconsciously feed *our collective conflicts*. "Our history to the present day is proof that people find justice hard to reach and sustain," observes Marilynne Robinson, adding that "this country was, from the outset, a tremendous leap of faith."[25] Plumbing behind perennial fears and tears, Seamus Heaney envisioned the possibility of redemption insofar as "hope and history rhyme."[26] To be keenly alert to the tragedies inherent at any moment, to elaborate the poet's verses, enables us (shielded in hope and courage) to seize the powers of transgenerational talking and action. Social Security's historical development and current effectiveness afford hope that Americans will choose to surmount fears about the program's sustainability.

A surprising number of Baby Boomers and Millennials are willing to assess a range of options already proposed by Social-Security policymakers, lawmakers, and by media outlets that propose hybrids. In the context of the national debt and defense outlays, the cost of sustaining the program is relatively small. To maintain the current pay-as-you-go financing would, according to the latest Social Security Trustees annual reports, would require the equivalent of 1% of the Gross Domestic Product (GDP).[27] Compare this to America spending 0.2% of its GDP on children under age 2; U.S. child poverty rates (21.7%) far exceed 23 other rich countries.[28] Winning World War II consumed 36% of GDP; Vietnam, 2.3%. The cost of wars in Iraq and Afghanistan has yet to be determined, but its expenditures were staggering.[29]

Misinformation about Social Security, moreover, parallels longstanding debates over women's rights and the 2nd Amendment.[30] It complements a pervasive lack of knowledge about current events. How many Americans can locate Middle East hotspots on a map? Could most of us pass citizenship tests required of immigrants? Hence the conundrum: How can we mobilize solidarity around Social Security beyond if stakeholders are distracted by other issues, which they deem to be disconnected from one another? Besides reducing communication voids that cause tone deafness, U.S. history lessons can help to fill the knowledge gap.

Baby Boomers remember that Maggie Kuhn's Gray Panthers were radicals in the 1970s who promoted "age and youth in action," forging alliances that instigated protests to extirpate ageism, racism, and sexism. Many of us want to include such a reference point in leaving a legacy. Today's youth rarely want to listen to stories about how my age group succeeded in surviving bad times in our life histories. Rising generations have different perceptions and experiences, which surprise us oldsters: while many distrust government, Millennials and younger generations already are demanding equality and "climate reparations and justice."[31]

Generational alliances can take shape by affirming and sharing a common set of values often poorly expressed in the United States. Overlapping age groups can fight cynics whose nihilistic commentaries fuel the politics of despair.[32] We "elders of the tribe" can join younger Americans to build on spontaneous, multicultural, transgenerational movements that made abortion protests, Occupy Wall Street and Black Lives Matter newsworthy. Grassroots demonstrators nonetheless must be convinced to trust that Congress will ensure that U.S. citizens of all ages benefit from building on Social Security's support of an income floor, sustainable enough to uphold its effectiveness against hazards of poverty and hopelessness. We "can't transform the economy without first transforming government."[33] We should focus on values that are often forgotten or underplayed in headlines about lies and power plays in the country's Federal system.

Social Security symbolizes a commitment and embodies a compact that depends on U.S. citizens to act responsibly as we honor and vouchsafe universal rights in an aging society. This emboldens stakeholders to engage beyond the institutional mandate that Thurman Arnold in the 1930s characterized as the program's "faceless bureaucracy." If we dare to hold transgenerational conversations, Social Security can be useful as policymakers and politicians try to create remedies as they deal with other political hot potatoes.[34]

Precisely because Social Security provides an income floor for millions of U.S. citizens, it performs an often-underplayed patriotic mission of serving Americans that surpasses any other institutional structure besides the U.S. Postal System. "Patriotism in the right spirit fosters the civic trust and solidarity that democracy needs."[35] Patriotic visions and convictions vary in a diverse population, but they can enrich partisan struggles even if they rarely transcend disillusionment or eliminate sensationalized doomsday fears. If we free ourselves to reconfigure political strategies, we can dare to be creative in dealing with the issue below.

Social Security can affect how Washington deals with student debts

Roughly 45 million Americans have to repay $1.6 trillion that they used to cover college tuitions. The median debt is $17,000; 86% of African Americans reduce their debt through salary cuts, compared to 60% of Whites who take out loans. The number of Americans over age 60 with unpaid student-loan debts quadrupled between 2005 and 2015; 2.8 million retirees and disabled individuals had offsets reducing monthly checks. "The effects are pushing people below the poverty lines."[36]

Forgiving student debts would promote transgenerational justice, but it securing legislation will be difficult. Partisan attacks and legal challenges stymie Biden's proposal. President Biden has proposed measures, such as eliminating $10,000 in student loans and forgiving the debts of those who attended public universities and historically Black colleges. This step, affecting 15 million people, would reduce the total debt by one-third.[37] It would give entry-level workers and middle-aged parents more disposable income to stimulate economic recovery; older Americans would no longer be liable for debts they had acquired decades earlier.

Alternatively, Congress might raise the amount of Pell grants by half (to nearly $10,000) or, more ambitiously, to double current levels. This would permit students to pay tuition bills and to purchase school supplies as they enroll in community colleges or public four-year colleges in their state. An emerging generation of Americans could obtain a quality education to prepare for meaningful employment without unduly burdened with debt.

Social Security has precedents with which to play a bigger role in dealing with student debt relief. Since 1965, loans for people with severe disabilities have been forgiven under the program, but the appeal process is daunting and often fails. "The problem we've been trying to solve is a problem a lot of government programs face, which is just bureaucracy and complicated paperwork." Social Security Administration records are used for verifying earnings history, but (at age 62) Social Security moves people with disabilities onto retirement rolls.[38] Congress has the power to change these criteria.

Expanding Franklin Delano Roosevelt's vision of social-insurance jibes with Abraham Lincoln's appeal to "the better angels of our nature." In confronting politics of fear, Americans have time to move ourselves toward a hopeful if elusive arc of justice. We now have an opportunity to safeguard Social Security's time-tested aims and ensuring its good-faith operations for our sakes and for those unborn. There are new possibilities for refurbishing the scope of a diversely democratic citizenship under the program. Deciding to act justly and kindly in rethinking how Social Security binds us together will not solve all crises that we face. But it constitutes a turning point, an incremental step advancing prosperity for all.[39]

Until a newer narrative and different interpretation unfolds, this book offers a bold vision for leaving a legacy in an aging society. Measured hope will not make fears evaporate, but it can persuade Americans to work together for what really matters. That is the real takeaway that a Baby-Boomer grandfather can bequeath to citizen-stakeholder generations who will outlive me.

Notes

1 Rother, John C. 2020. "Social insurance needs to be flexible going forward." In *The Future of Social Insurance*, ed. Thomas N. Bethell. Washington, DC: National Academy of Social Insurance, 40.

2 Albright, Madeleine K. 2022, March 29. "Opinion." *The Washington Post.*

3 Walker, Darren. 2022, July 4. "America is worth saving." *The New York Times.*

4 Goldberg, Michelle. 2022, February 8. "Requiem for a Liberal Giant." *The New York Times.*

5 King, Rev. Dr. Martin Luther, Jr. 1968. Ucc.org/sacred.com.

6 Ibid.

7 Irving, Washington. 1819; reprinted 2011. *Rip Van Winkle.* New York: Puffin Books.

8 Ibid.

9 Quinby, Laura and Gal Wettstein. 2021. "Does media coverage of the Social Security Trust Fund affect claiming, saving, and benefit expectations." Boston College: Center for Retirement Research.

10 Cohn, Peter. 2022. "Social Security fixes could animate post-midterms agenda." https://rollcall.com; Phelan, Michael. 2022. "Rep. John Larson." Social Security Works PAC.

11 Werschkul, Ben. 2022. "'Transformative' retirement reform package passes the House and heads to the Senate." https://finance.yahoo.com/news.

12 King, Rev. Dr. Martin Luther, Jr. 1968. Ucc.org/sacred.com.

13 Holmes, David L. 2009. *Faiths of the Founding Fathers.* New York: Oxford University Press.

14 Quoted in Haught, James. 2020. "Moral progress." Goodmenproject.com.

15 Smith, Mychal Denzel. 2018. "The truth about 'the arc of the moral universe.'" www.huffpost.com/entry/opinion-smith-king_n_5a5903e0e4b0 4fc55a252a4.

16 McKibben, Bill. 2022. *The Flag, The Cross, and the Station Wagon.* New York: Henry Holt & Company.

17 See the appendix in Brown, J. Douglas. 1977. *Essays on Social Security.* Princeton: Industrial Relations Section, 47.

18 Will, George F. 1983. *Statecraft as Soulcraft: What Government Does.* New York: Simon & Schuster, 70.

19 Smarick, Andy. 2020, June 6. "Why statecraft is still soulcraft." www. theamericanconservative.com; Review of *Statecraft as Soulcraft: What Government Does.* www.conservativebookclub.com.

20 Rawls, John. 1993. *Political Liberalism.* New York: Columbia University Press, xx.

21 Sandel, Michael J. 2009. *Justice: What's the Right Thing to Do?* New York: Farrar, Strauss and Giroux, 253–254.

22 Tilly, Charles. 1985. *War Making and State Making as Organized Crime.* New York: Cambridge University Press.

23 Wetzel, David. 2022, June 12. "New survey shows what sacrificing Americans would accept to keep Social Security from running out." Knewz.

24 Patrick Taylor Smith. 2013. "The intergenerational storm: Dilemma or domination." www.academia.edu/7411149/.

25 Robinson, Mailynne. 2020, October 11. "What does it mean to love a country?" *The New York Times.*

26 Heaney, Seamus, The cure of troy. 1991. New York: Farrar, Straus and Giroux.

27 Bieber, Christy. 2020. "A surprising number of Americans support these 4 big cuts to Social Security." www.fool.com/retirement/; Arends, Brett. 2020. "Opinion." www.marketwatch.com.

28 Isaacs, Julia B. 2009. "A comparative perspective on public spending on children." Washington, D.C.: Brookings Institution Center on Children & Families; Miller, Claire C. 2021, October 7. "Bill would aid U.S. in closing child care gap." *The New York Times.*

29 Aftergood, Steven A., Zuliski, Rosella C., Crawford, Neta C., Hentz, James and Heidi Potter. 2021. *The Cost of War.* Providence, RI: Watson Institute, Brown University.

30 Osnos, Evan. 2020. "The violent style." *The New Yorker.*

31 Sengupta, Somini. 2022. "Follow the global youth protests this week." *The New York Times.*

32 Moody-Adams, Michelle. 2022. *Making Space for Justice.* New York: Columbia University Press.

33 Klein, Ezra. 2022, May 31. "What America needs is a liberalism that builds." *The New York Times.*

34 Drutman, Lee. 2022. "Our three futures." *New America.*

35 Britten-Purdy, Jedediah. 2022, July 3. "The left must reclaim patriotism." *The New York Times.*

36 Edleson, Harriet. 2018. "Student loan debt can sink your retirement plan." www.aarp.org/money.

37 Nova, Anna. 2020. "How Biden can free Americans from student debt." *The New Yorker.*

38 Marcus, Jon. 2022, May 3. "How to get loan forgiveness if you have a disability." AARP Real Possibilities.

39 Zilmer, Paul. 2021. "Fellow Feeling." *Tidings*; Gerson, Michael. 2022. Opinion. *The Washington Post*.

Social Security 101

An overview of keywords and operations—How the U.S. program works in a global context

Differentiating social insurance from other private- and public-sector programs helps to define Social Security's aims and workings

How does Social Security, the U.S. brand of social insurance, differ from private insurance, welfare systems, income-redistribution plans, and various Federal and State programs that deal with hazards of living and/or reduce the threat of poverty by offering monetary benefits or in-kind relief?

- Social Security is not a private-sector contract. Transactions do not take place under commercially stipulated restrictions and benefit calculations—themselves to subject decisions made by the insuring agent in response to volatilities in market capitalism.
- Nor is Social Security a welfare system. The program does not determine benefits on the basis of means tests or asset ceilings.
- Social Security is America's social-insurance institution. Its primary task is to provide an income floor for participating contributors. It neither redistributes money from the wealthy to families mired in poverty, nor designates relieving victims during natural disasters, 9/11, or Covid-19.

Present-day confusion about the scope and limits of "social insurance" bewilders stakeholders. The term, which a century ago appeared regularly in the print media, now seems a foreign concept. (In 1935, in contrast, U.S. citizens were more familiar with the concept of social insurance; they saw it as a way to lift the nation out of the Great Depression.)[1] And misunderstandings about Social Security are also due to a time warp. Since there has been no major reforms of the program for 40 years, Millennials and younger stakeholders are a "lost generation." They are among the millions of Americans covered by Social Security during their lifetimes, but they have witnessed only annual cost-of-living-adjustments (COLAs). Periodic debates over current options seem academic, without mooring.

So what can serve as a working definition of social insurance to inform readers of this book? The program has "come to define our notion of social insurance: payroll contribution funding, benefits based on contributions, trust fund public accounting, and extra consideration for those with lower incomes."[2] Several corollaries should be added to this working definition:

* Social insurance protects "people against risks, small and large, predictable and unforeseen, routine and calamitous."[3]
* Coverage under Social Security in the United States, which conforms to other nations' forms of social insurance, is virtually universal nowadays. This makes Social Security one of the few institutions that binds diverse age groups together in our aging society.
* Social Security is an earned right because American workers have paid into the social-insurance system.

Social Security, like any comparable social-insurance plan, needs a firm financial base. Social Security continues to be an ongoing, viable U.S. social-insurance policy initiative. It offers "the continuity, stability, and security of the reciprocal social compact between governments and promised guaranteed earned benefits to which we contribute across our lifetimes and generations."[4] The program requires widespread political acceptability to do its job.

Even these working definitions of social insurance and Social Security are laced with values-laden policy aims and complex operational assumptions. This is why most Americans have to rely on insiders to monitor the program. We depend on seasoned experts to be responsible for maintaining equitable and efficient standard-operating procedures. The Social Security Administration (SSA) updates and continually provides verifiable statistics, memoranda, and annual forecasts about the program's projected surpluses and deficits.

Technical data and bureaucratic language are comprehended by independent analysts and routinely conveyed to members of Congress and the officers in the executive branch; to Social Security Trustees, appointees, and Federal administrators; and to men and women working in local offices around the nation. The internet and social media vary in their complete summary of developments. Commentators in some outlets distort and sensationalize news.

The SSA makes concerted efforts to keep contributors and recipients aware of changes in their personal records. SSA sends letters to stakeholders, invites face-to-face interviews in community-based agencies, and contacts with well-trained personnel on the phone or through the internet. It is beyond SSA's power, however, to oversee informal communication networks or to correct factual errors. In many instances U.S. citizens trust information from the media and advice they get over dinner tables. Disconnected stakeholders' segmented outlets have created a disturbing communication gap in safeguarding Social Security.

Putting the program's developments in the context of recent U.S. history underscores the challenge that New-Deal architects encountered in convincing disparate audiences, holding different viewpoints, that 1935 Social Security Act was fair and equitable. Subsequent amendments between 1939 and 1983 replaced terminology with new technical words and operational alterations. Recent stalemates permit information disconnects that prove overwhelming and misleading. This appendix thus tries to shore up the communication gap, to engage and empower critical thinking.

How Social Security Works: A Primer

Social Security initially was designed to provide retirement support for American workers in certain occupational categories who paid into the system when gainfully employed. The numbers of contributors and beneficiaries has been incrementally expanded over time. Social Security pools workers' mandatory contributions and pays beneficiaries out of trust funds. Virtually all U.S. workers contribute 6.2% of their wages up to $147,000 in 2022, an amount matched by their employers.

The program allocates cash benefits, indexed up to a monthly maximum of $3,345 in 2022. Besides sending checks to retirees, survivors' benefits go to spouses (as well as qualified divorced persons), dependent children (including those disabled before age 22) and financially dependent grandchildren and grandparents—if they meet existing criteria. SSA determines the actual dollar amount of average monthly checks according to benchmarks, such as the age at which persons who fit into specific criteria elect to start receiving benefits.

To be "fully" insured, all workers paying into Social Security must have contributed for "forty quarters of coverage." To compute the primary insurance amount—or "PIA," which is the basis for determining retirement and disability benefits—SSA calculates the Average Indexed Monthly Earnings with two corollaries. First, time out of the labor force (including the PIA of those engaged in years of full-time voluntary caregiving for elderly parents, friends, and neighbors) before the stipulated age of full eligibility translates into accepting smaller monthly benefits. Second, a worker's monthly disability benefits, which can be received (or disputed in courts) after reaching age 40, represent 100% of a worker's PIA.

SSA uses explicit formulae to calculate workers' retirement benefits. There is an actuarial reduction (currently 0.33% for every month) for those who wish to receive benefits earlier than the statutorily defined retirement age. (That criterion varies according to sex and year of birth. Early retirement in all cases reduces benefits). Those who delay collecting benefits receive an upwards actuarial adjustment, up to individuals choosing to retire at age 70.

The 1935 Social Security Act gave retired workers benefits in proportion to their contributions. Subsequent amendments set benefits for low-income workers and their qualified dependents that have become progressively generous. By enacting the 1939 Social-Security amendments, Congress and Franklin Delano Roosevelt (FDR) recognized that low-income workers need to replace a larger percentage of their preretirement wages—if they are to approximate the standard of living they had while gainfully employed. Furthermore, because SSA calculates benefits on the basis of career earnings, contributing workers who endured periods of unemployment typically get larger proportionate benefits as well.

Perhaps one of the most "progressive" features of Social Security are the Cost-of-Living-Adjustments (COLAs), enacted into law in 1972. COLAs ensure that Social-Security recipients can maintain their monthly checks' purchasing power. Adjusting the income floor mostly insulates individuals from recessions and inflation. COLAs also are not subject to legislators' infighting and decisions by the executive branch that occurred during Social Security's formative decades, which short-circuits candidates' appeals to voters before elections.

The amount that worker's pay into Social Security is adjusted annually. Mandated deductions (designated as FICA [Federal Insurance Contributions Act]) on gross wages is the same for all employees and the self-employed nationwide. Bending the principle of equity promulgated in the 1935 Act, low-income workers' payroll deductions fall far short of the maximum ceiling. The salaries of people who earn far higher annual salaries are only taxed up to the nationwide maximum. (This means that contributors with high-earning salaries receive monthly benefits that are larger in absolute dollars—but smaller proportionately—than beneficiaries who contributed less over the course of their working careers.)

Two other policy features often remain unspoken. First, self-employed workers make contributions equivalent to those made by employees (which is paid out of after-tax earnings) and employers (whose portion is deductible as a business expense). Second, Social Security manages to operate for multinational employees and employers, by coordinating treaties and arrangements with other nations' pension and welfare systems. That "social insurance" resonates with global economies enables readers of this book to put the U.S. version into international perspective.

The status of Social Security Trust Funds: The money collected from contributors and their employers are presently placed into two trust funds: 85% of FICA contributions go into the Old-Age and Survivors Trust Fund and the other 15% into Disability Insurance Trust Fund. The status of funds to be paid out to FICA contributors in the short-term and long-term have been a source of misunderstanding by those who view their "scientific" reporting as an accounting gimmick. Alf Landon in 1936 denounced the reserves as worthless IOUs, "a cruel hoax."

The sustainability of Social Security trust funds remains controversial to the present day. Criticisms are not likely to disappear. Social Security is undermined whenever stakeholders are presented evidence that a demographic tsunami is imminent. Are fears warranted in the face of claims that unproductive, frail Baby Boomers squander the contributions made by their children and grandchildren that support Social Security and Medicare? Is Social Security really a Ponzi scheme after all? This is why this book appropriately entertains such serious questions about the program's present fiscal stability and long-term prospects.

Relying on facts, not fantasies, is critical in evaluating Social Security's future: The two Trust Funds are usually discussed together, and those Social-Security reserves currently exceed $2.9 trillion. They are legal instruments backed by interest-bearing U.S. Treasury bonds, arguably the safest investment guaranteed by the Federal government. As such, these so-called "entitlements" do not add to the public debt even in periodic recessions and economic downturns, or during the recent pandemic.

Doomsday scenarios defy the historical record and fair-minded interpretations. Congress thus far has never failed to secure Social Security's funding. They also do not embrace simple logic—as long as workers are required to pay part of their earnings to FICA. Employee/ employers contributions constitute a dedicated revenue stream. Even in the worst-case scenario (wherein no Social-Security reforms occur in a polarized political economy), there are funds sufficient to cover most outlays anticipated in the coming decade, and there are large reserves at hand over the next 75 years. Lawmakers are bound to take actions that avert this worst-case scenario. Doing otherwise will cost votes if they renege on generational claims.

More detailed information is available beyond what is offered here. Readers of this book can google the websites of the SSA (www.ssa. gov) or the National Academy of Social Insurance (www.nasi.org). Books and updates from Social Security Works are trustworthy.

This appendix ends with underscoring six comparative primer-messages to consider

1   U.S. Social Security was enacted decades after comparable programs were adopted by Western European countries. Architects of this New-Deal legislation were able to study social-insurance models already in operation.

2   Rather than emulate aims and protocols in practice elsewhere, FDR and his experts seized on State and municipal retirement plans and corporate pensions refined in the United States. These initiatives arose in a piecemeal fashion. Domestic programs were neither interchangeable nor universal across public and private spheres. They nevertheless represented applicable experiences in administering earnings-related employer/worker financed provisions to reduce the threat of old-age dependency.

3   Cross-national comparisons reveal many similarities. Retirement ages on average fall into a 62–66-year range here and elsewhere. Every country has amended tax and benefit schedules, and liberalized, added, or reduced eligibility criteria. All advanced industrial countries are grappling with the opportunities and problems that arise from societal aging. They have an impact on financing retirement and issues such as health, material well-being for the vulnerable, and quality of life.

4   Social Security in the United States possesses certain special and distinctive features. They are evident in periodic and annual

Government reports; studies issued by independent researchers and reputable think tanks, and evidence-based media accounts: Social Security Trustees, SSA staff, and experts in relevant public-policy circles communicate pages of footnoted statistics and actuarial projections in ongoing efforts to serve the public interest. Balancing individual equity and social adequacy, they are keenly aware of the respective needs and transgenerational appeals made by diverse constituencies.

5   Social Security's agenda will always remain unfinished because it must adapt to promises and paradoxes that inhere in the dynamics of societal aging. Americans can anticipate further calls to privatize the program, which are based on doomsday scenarios that grip stakeholders in fear. Experts and faithful stewards must weigh risks, rights and responsibilities as they reinforce stakeholders' solidarity and the program's sustainability. This means that they will repeatedly be summoned to evaluate and negotiate how differences in age, race, gender, and class are items that apply in allocating family benefits, in providing credits for child support and elder care, and reconsidering rules concerning survivor benefits, divorced spouses, and unwed parents.

6   Keywords and operations under SSA are often misconstrued by media commentators or misinterpreted by Social-Security stakeholders. Phrases that make sense to my Baby-Boomer generation often trigger pushback from Millennials.[5] Three examples suffice.

- Since "safety net" connotes a sense of failure that Big Government cannot remedy, this book talks about "income floors" or Social Security as a "foundation" in the composite income flows for the program's beneficiaries.

- Rather than talking about "vulnerable" people, the preferred emphasis is on the actual risks and potential hazards all U.S. citizens face over the course of our lives in nation characterized by population and societal aging.

- "Entitlements" do not mean that cash flows only to honorable Americans. The term indicates that U.S. workers have paid for benefits through FICA taxes contributed during their careers.

Safeguarding Social Security for Future Generations: Leaving a Legacy in an Aging Society is critical to the well-being of all age groups of Americans.

Our transgenerational stake in time-tested and resilient institution is why Social Security matters to us, our parents and children, and those unborn.

Notes

1 Marmor, Theodore R. 2020. "Reimaging the future of Social Insurance in the wake of the pandemic." In *The Future of Social Insurance*, ed. Thomas N. Bethell. Washington, D.C.: The National Academy for Social Insurance, 27–28.
2 Rother, John C. 2020. "Social insurance needs to be flexible going forward." In Bethell, *The Future*, 40.
3 Munnell, Alicia. 2020. "Social insurance is the best way to save—now more than ever." In Bethell, 33.
4 Estes, Carroll L. 2020. "Social insurance: Proof of concept." In Bethell, 23.
5 Arnone, William. 2022, April 18. Private conversation about NASI's gauging of Millennials' syntax.

Four episodes in U.S. history, illustrating how we bridge hopes and fears, help to situate Social Security's opportunities and challenges in societal context

Introduction

I was a teaching assistant (TA, 1972–1976) in the Department of History during my twenties at the University of Michigan. When I returned to Ann Arbor as a professor in 1988, I regularly lectured in both halves of the American history survey and met with an honors section. The seven or eight doctoral students served concurrently as teaching assistants (TAs). Charged with instructing roughly 400 undergraduates every term, we reworked syllabi each semester. I sometimes had difficulty accepting differences in generational perspectives and melding pedagogical styles, but we managed to bridge age gaps. (Usually over TAs' objectives I insisted on giving a Social-Security lecture.) I learned much about sharing responsibility by listening to students who were decades younger than I. To reach increasingly diverse youthful student audiences, I counted on TAs being supervised with on-the-job training to add fresh topics into syllabi and display their technological skills.

I am still adapting ideas and pedagogy at age 75 while I compose this book. Making a case entails more than being forthright about my biases and preferences. I want to persuade overlapping generations of individuals who have distinctive encounters with lived history and different styles of critical thinking. This means that I must reach out to many audiences who almost are as ignorant about U.S. history as my grandchildren, now aged 12 and 10.[1]

A 2014 report by the National Assessment of Educational Progress indicated that only 18% of high-school students grasped American history. More than a third could not pinpoint the century in which the American Revolution occurred. Only a third of college graduates knew that Franklin Delano Roosevelt launched the New Deal; only 41% of those surveyed in 2018 were sure that Auschwitz was a Nazi concentration camp. More Americans knew that Michael Jackson composed "Beat It" than were certain about the connection between the Bill of Rights and the U.S. Constitution. Such ignorance creates blind spots in imagining this society's future.[2] It also distorts positions about Social Security.

What follows is a second primer that amplifies four historical turning points—the Revolutionary period, antebellum culture, Reconstruction, and the Progressive era. This book is an iterative, fluid, open-ended interpretation embedded in the context of U.S. history. The program's current status and future prospects, I believe, require a working knowledge of past events that still influence and constrain policymaking decisions about the societal context to which social insurance must "fit" if it serves Americans.

Episode one: *Our Founding Fathers hoped that nation-building would allay fears of tyranny and invasion.* Having enshrined noble principles in a Declaration of Independence, which proclaimed that "all men are created equal" (but not necessarily British soldiers, women, and certainly not slaves), Revolutionary patriots renounced tyrannical George III and won a war of independence, with help from foreign allies. Then an elite group of property-owners, many of whom were slaveholders insistent on protecting their investments, set about creating a nation that would flourish *secula seculorum*.[3] The Founding Fathers feared that tribes and empire-hungry kings of France, England, Holland, and Spain would reconquer North America. And delegates did not entirely trust one another.

Organizing a just form of governance to satisfice competing and often irreconcilable interests of 12 independent states undercut Enlightenment virtues that the Revolutionary generation wished to institute. The Articles of Confederation, drafted in 1777 but not ratified until 1781, formed a "league of friendship" among autonomous States busily disputing territorial rights with European princes and Native Americans.

The Articles established a weak central government in 1783, which had no executive agency, no power to pay off war debts or to protect shipping and manufacturing. Its major achievement—passing the Northwest Ordinance—set a pattern for forming new states, which gave slave states more representation in Congress than free states. Shays' Rebellion (1786–1787), by threatening the stability of Massachusetts government, unmasked additional shortcomings in the Articles of Confederation that could only be rectified with rethinking a system of federalism that might better serve the polity.

The men who gathered in Philadelphia in 1787 were realists, astute observers of human characters and individual frailties, tempered by their classical educations and cosmopolitan worldviews. Dreading to concentrate too much power in executive, legislative, or judicial branches of a national polity, they designed a system of checks and balances, which did not dilute states-based sovereignty. Behind closed doors in stifling summer heat, the Founding Fathers engaged in lofty conversations and contested truths, as they debated ways to ensure equitable representation for governing states, large and small, free and slave.

"No man," observed James Madison, "felt himself obliged to retain his opinions any longer than he was satisfied of their propriety and truth."[4] On the slavery issue, the discontented delegates to the Constitutional Convention wrestled with negotiating options that pitted hard-headed vested interests calculated according to sources of regional wealth. "The morality or wisdom of slavery are considerations belonging to the states themselves."[5] The Founding Fathers crafted the most representative and participatory system known at the time—and excluded Blacks, women, and men without land from exercising power.

Before the Constitution could be ratified, however, the public had to be persuaded and committed to its grand design. Revolutionary veterans, along with their children and wives, read tracts and speeches by Federalists and Anti-Federalists intended to justify contested opinions and reservations about various sections of the Constitution. A majority of states agreed to unite together, after a ten-item Bill of Rights was appended to the original document. These were necessary to secure individual rights and responsibilities amid perilous risks.

Yeoman farmers scraped by, most Blacks remained slaves, women could not vote, and elites dominated politics. Self-governance, noted Thomas Jefferson, required vigilant leaders to rethink how the Federal compact would unfold:

> Can one generation bind another and all others in succession forever? I think not. The Creator has made the earth for the living, not the dead. Rights and powers can only belong to persons, not to things, not to mere matter unendowed [sic] with will.[6]

Implications for *safeguarding Social Security for future generations*

The Founding Fathers left "in usufruct" a legacy that affected launching and amending Social Security. Franklin Delano Roosevelt

(FDR), a wealthy heir to the Revolutionary-era natural *aristoi*, forged a program that accommodated the strengths, deficiencies, and ambiguities instituted in the Constitution and Bill of Rights. To win support of southern Democrats, Social Security originally did not cover Blacks in the work force or women at home. Like Madison and Jefferson, he anticipated that radical and incremental reforms would transform the program's aims and operations after the Great Depression and World War II, and adequately deal with changes in the nation's population structure, political economy, and societal mores.

Episode two: *Jacksonian America often failed to remember hopes and fears, promises and paradoxes in the Founding Fathers' legacy.* "Those who went before are soon forgotten; of those who will come after, no one has any idea," Alexis de Tocqueville observed in *Democracy in America* (1835–1840). The nobleman, whose grandfather was executed in the French Revolution, probed aspects of how people in the new republic's antebellum decades went about their business, as he studied innovations in U.S. prisons. Echoing Jefferson in comparing America and France, he added, "Democratic nations care but little for what has been, but they are haunted by visions of what will be … [for] each new generation is a new people."[7]

Early 19th-century Americas relied on voluntary associations, declared de Tocqueville, to prevent their vaunted self-reliance from degenerating into selfishness, patriotism into parochialism, altruism into paternalism. *Individualism*, "a calm and considered feeling which disposes each citizen to isolate himself from the mass of his fellows," fueled an equality of opportunity for middle-class merchants, farmers, and working-class laborers. de Tocqueville saw culture wars in the making: around Cincinnati ("its whiteness by design"), men carried guns.[8] Insistence on self-reliance and self-serving interests did not restrain them, however, from energetically helping others when they needed assistance.[9]

de Tocqueville noted that as individuals in this new generation blazed frontiers, they subjected Cherokees to a trail of tears, debated what could be gained by extending women's suffrage, and mobilized temperance campaigns. But *Democracy in America* did not much elaborate on how greatly racism sustained the political economy or how slavery desecrated both the nation's ideals and social order. "The society of the modern world has but just come into existence, still encumbered by the remains of the world which is waning into decay," he wrote; Jacksonians clothed nationalism in exceptionalism.[10]

Americans divided loyalties to states and the Union in defending and condemning Whites who prospered in the United States by dehumanizing Blacks. Gold rushers brought struggles over slavery to California; Kansas bled as residents fought over popular sovereignty. Congress, having issued dilatory compromises in 1820 and 1850, seesawed on Indian affairs and passed the Fugitive Slave Law. The Supreme Court's 1857 Dred Scott enflamed agitators North and South, which incited war-mongering that an ineffectual President Buchanan hoped to avert.

Implications of practicing the politics of avoidance

Antebellum America presents a second, paradoxical lesson about structural reforms: There often is a price in overlooking or denying flaws in leaving legacies to successive generations. Real, unexpected problems plagued antebellum America presaging decades before the 1983 Social-Security amendments dealt with the program's fiscal crisis. Can we see parallels in pre-Civil-War politics of avoidance and today's polarizing U.S. cancel culture? Democracy, de Tocqueville warned, is not benign: An American running afoul of tyrannical opinions in both eras "returns to silence as if he felt remorse for having spoken the truth."[11]

Episode three: *Eventually, Americans waged a Civil War.* "All dreaded it, all sought to avert it," Lincoln stated in his second inaugural address; ex-slave Frederick Douglass called the speech "a sacred effort" in which the Reconciler-in-Chief sought to reaffirm common values to bring peace to a divided country. Each side was convinced that theirs was a self-righteous cause, the president knew: "Both read the same Bible, and pray to the same God," so "it may seem strange that any men should dare to ask a just God's assistance." Lincoln in 1858 anticipated how a "House divided" seemed to justify verbal and physical assaults in Congress over slavery. After the 1860 election, Southern states joined together in establishing a Confederate slavocracy. The ensuing four-year conflict pitted brother against brother, who died confident that the Lord was on their side.

The Civil War (1861–1865) resulted in a "harvest of death." Roughly 620,000 soldiers were killed—a total that approximates total fatalities in the Revolutionary War, the War of 1812, the Mexican War, the Spanish American War, World Wars I and II, and the Korean War combined.[12] After Lincoln's assassination, Radical Republican added three amendments to the U.S. Constitution: one abolished slavery, a second defined U.S. citizenship, and the third extended the right to vote to adult Black men. Between 1865 and 1877 Congress established unprecedented educational opportunities, welfare support, and land for former slaves and their children.

Reconstruction then fell apart. To secure Rutherford B. Hayes' presidency in 1876, Federal agents and military returned north. The Ku Klux Klan already was stoking a reign of terror, which insidiously culminated in peonage, discriminatory Jim Crow laws and eligibility criteria that disenfranchised Blacks.

Implications for Reforming Social Security: This third watershed in U.S. history shows how fear and carnage can forestall opportunities to sustain democracy in America. After all, Lincoln's first inaugural address envisioned citizens swelling "the chorus of the Union, when touched again, as surely they will be, by the better angels of our nature." The Civil War (1861–1865) and Reconstruction (1865–1877) demonstrated what can happen when ordinary Americans and their leaders (often demonized by opponents as extremists) succeed in putting prejudices and aims ahead of common interests.

Privatizing or bankrupting Social Security will probably not instigate a Second Civil War, though the system may be jeopardized if a minority party in power seeks to do away with Constitutional rulings and Congressional precedents. Little stops influential doomsday commentators to convey disinformation to anxious stakeholders and ill-informed younger workers. Yet according to the National Academy of Social insurance, vast majorities of U.S. stakeholders do not mind paying taxes to ensure benefits to retirees, disabled individuals, and the children and widowed spouses of deceased contributors. This finding holds across party lines. Roughly three-quarters of Americans say they support the system because of its continuing value to themselves, families, and neighbors.[13]

That said, elected officials and their constituents someday may decide that Social Security no longer serves a worthwhile national purpose. That would undoubtedly be indicative of a broader disentangling of shared values and institutional networks that have safeguarded Social Security for nearly a century. FDR launched, the Supreme Court validated, and Congress enlarged the scope of Social Security to relieve individual risks, generational suffering, and societal losses during the greatest economic downturn in American history. The program's principles and operations still work. But Social Security's future is contingent on systematic scrutiny and efforts to effect pragmatic reforms—reminiscent of the Progressive era that followed Reconstruction.

Episode four: *During the Progressive era (ca. 1890–1920), concerned citizens elected officials who made concerted efforts to create regulatory mechanisms to deal with societal problems.* Much of the reformist impulse attempted to deal with political corruption in the nation's federated governance. Idea brokers and muckrakers identified and documented wrenching disparities in the political economy inflamed by immigration, urbanization, and industrialization—the very factors that were fueling America's rise as a world power years after the Civil War.

Notable regulatory scaffolding was instituted in the Capitol, during the presidencies of Theodore Roosevelt, William Howard Taft, and Woodrow Wilson. Congress enacted The Pure Food and Drug Act. The Departments of Labor and Commerce became executive-branch cabinets. The Constitution was amended to authorize an income tax, direct election of senators, prohibition, and women's suffrage. Measures also revamped American federalism at lower levels. Some states emulated Robert LaFollette's "Wisconsin idea," which allowed voters to cast secret ballots, and lawmakers to enact workers' compensation, child-labor laws, and old-age pensions. City managers and municipal commissions oversaw public utilities and juvenile courts.

These resulting structural reforms were dazzling. Equally impressive was the way pragmatic thinkers like Charles Peirce and William James proposed paradigms for investigating social problems and advocated innovations for the public good. "There is nothing new in the enunciation of the idea that political economy cannot be separated from sociology," John Dewey declared as he praised Henry George's *Progress and Poverty*, which had argued for a single-land tax 60 years earlier: "I do not claim that George's remedy is a panacea for our ailments," but the Columbia philosopher asserted that he knew "no other writer by whom the interdependence of all aspects and phases of human relations, economic, political, cultural, moral has been so vigorously … set forth."[14]

Newspapers increased circulations by muckraking. Lincoln Steffens's *Shame of the Cities*, Ida Tarbell's *History of Standard Oil Company*, and Upton Sinclair's *The Jungle* galvanized public outrage. Experts conducted surveys and compiled statistics, which marshalled data to bolster support for correcting conditions dramatized in print media. A Columbia University professor published *Social Insurance* in 1910.[15]

Lawmakers established standards of scientific management, which foresighted industries were then utilizing. Once institutionalized, pragmatic measures were reevaluated through trial and error.

Critical and pragmatic thinking, in concert with disinterested negotiations and grassroots agitation, rectified some but not all glaring defects in the United States. Robber Barons pocketed disparities in wealth. Soldiers massacred 300 Lakota Indians at Wounded Knee (1890) as vigilantes attacked and relocated Chinese workers. Blacks were lynched. The Supreme Court ruled in *Plessy v. Ferguson* (1896) that segregation laws did not violate the Constitution as long as facilities for Blacks and White were equal in quality.

Progressive-era implications for today

The hopes and fears interwoven in the Progressive era's advances and setbacks are timely and pertinent to lawmakers and stakeholders grappling with Social-Security shortfalls in the nation's fearfully inequitable political economy and entrenched viewpoints on what matters in America. Drawing parallels between Progressive reformers and contemporary actors in an aging society underscore the necessity for candor that facilitates constructive debate and substantive interactions across generational lines. The process, bound to be experimental and messy, will transmogrify the philosophy and evidence-based best practices of articulated by William James, John Dewey, and other pragmatic reformers.

Recalling ways that past events put current challenges into an historical context does not mean that these lessons determine what happens next. Turning points in how various generations respond and adapt to lived experiences are instructive, not predictive. Taking the four episodes together, this appendix shows that the United States is neither exceptionally great nor uniquely evil. Acknowledging possible parallels and contrarieties in interpreting our nation's contours is an invaluable perquisite for safeguarding Social Security as a legacy for future Americans in an aging society.

Notes

1   Boot, Max. 2019, February 20. "Opinion: Americans' ignorance of history is a national scandal." *The Washington Post.*
2   Brownfeld, Allan C. 2018. "The danger ignorance of history poses to the future of a free society." Communities Digital News.

3 Wood, Gordon S. 1969. *The Creation of the American Republic.* Chapel Hill: University of North Carolina Press.

4 Quoted in Frost, David B. 2017. *Classified Jefferson.* North Carolina: McFarland.

5 Quoted in Lepore, Jill. 2018. *These Truths.* New York: W. W. Norton, 126. See also Ellis, Joseph J. 2021. *The American Revolution and Its Discontents.* New York: Liveright and Wood, Gordon S. 2021. *Power and Liberty.* New York: Oxford University Press.

6 Jefferson, Thomas. 1824; reprinted 1953. "The earth belongs to the living." Letter to John Cartright. In *Thomas Jefferson on Democracy*, ed. Saul Padover. Letters of Thomas Jefferson, ed. Saul Padover, New York: Oxford University Press.

7 de Tocqueville, Alexis. 1835–1840. *Democracy in America*, 2 vols. Ed, Phillips Bradley. New York: Vintage.

8 Zunz, Oliver. 2022. *The Man Who Understood Democracy.* Princeton: Princeton University Press.

9 de Tocqueville, *Democracy.*

10 Commager, Henry Steele. 1993. *Commager on Tocqueville.* Columbia: University of Missouri Press, ch. 6.

11 Bouie, Jamelle. 2022, March 12. "Cancel culture in 1832 sounded pretty fierce." *The New York Times.*

12 Faust, Drew Gilpin. 2008. *The Republic of Suffering.* New York: Vintage.

13 National Academy of Social Insurance. 2013-present. "Public Opinions on Social Security." Nasi.org/learn/social-security.

14 Dewey, John. 1941. "Introduction." *The American Journal of Economics and Sociology*, **1**, i–iii.

15 Seager, Henry Rogers. 1910. *Social Insurance: A Program of Social Reform.* New York: Macmillan.

Index

AARP 80
abolitionists 40, 140
abortion 12, 28, 97, 101, 113, 145; see also gender discrimination and women
academics 56
Achenbaum, W. Andrew 1–5, 36, 43, 60–3, 65, 72–3, 75–6, 79, 81–4, 88, 97, 98, 101, 105–7, 110–11, 159; and this book 105–8, 116–17, 119, 133, 137, 139, 140, 142, 147
actuaries 84
actions, pragmatic and transformative 62
"adequacy" vs. "equity" 52–5, 127
adolescents 130
adult(s) 26, 90–1, 121; and education 124; and ages thirty to fifty 121
advocates 32, 83, 110, 143
affluence 56, 67, 93, 98, 129
Affordable Care Act (ACA) see Patient Protection and Affordable Care Act
Afghanistan 101, 144
AFL-CIO 79
Africa 72, 129
African Americans 52, 92, 93, 129; see also Blacks; racism
age forty-five 48; and retirement 11, 119–22
age-based criteria 9, 48, 90–6, 119–24
age discrimination 49
aged's COVID risks 129
ageism 25, 49, 91, 114, 117, 123, 144

age groups 1–5, 11–13, 15, 25–7, 35, 61, 62, 114, 116, 119–20, 124, 127, 129, 145
agents of change 105–13
aging population see population aging
aging society 2–3, 32, 41, 88, 107, 132, 137, 140, 145, 156, 165
Agricultural Adjustment Act 44
AIDS 27, 89, 101, 115
Ailes, Roger 80
ailments, chronic 26, 56
Alabama 140
Albright, Madeleine 138
alliances 145
allied-health professionals see public health
almshouse 44, 49, 120
Altman, Nancy 123
Altmeyer, Arthur 51–2
Alzheimer's disease 91
America 137–47
American Civil Liberties Union 112
American Commonwealth 122
American Dream 123
American Historical Association (AHA) 98
American Medical Association 56
American Nursing Association 79
American Rescue Plan 81
"American Scholar" 10
Americans 163, 165; and Social Security ignorance 158–9
Americans for Generational Equity (AGE) 77, 130

Americas 31
amyotrophic lateral sclerosis (ALS) 128
antebellum 10, 162; see also Jacksonian
    America
Anthony, Susan B. 124
Anti-Federalists 37, 40, 160
anti-poverty 121; see also income floor
anti-semitism 123
anxiety 12, 90
applied history 36, 65, 71
Archbishop of Canterbury 30–1
Arendt, Hannah 31
Arizona 130
Armstrong, William 68
Arnold, Thurman 50–1, 145
Artful Work 72, 75
Article One, US Constitution 37
Articles of Confederation 159
Asians 123, 165
attitudes, old age 57, 112–13
Audacity of Hope 18
Auden, W. H. 14
autocrats 31, 90
avoidance, politics 12, 15, 18, 26–30,
    160–3

Baby Boomers 1–5, 9–20, 36, 61–2,
    70, 84, 100, 105, 106, 128, 129, 137,
    139, 141, 143, 147
Baker, James A. III 69
balancing Social-Security tradeoffs 18,
    53, 76
Ball, Robert M. 57, 69–70, 123
banks 46
Bannon, Steven 18
"be the change" 110
Bellamy, Edward 29
beneficiaries, Social Security 24–5, 83,
    116, 125, 129
benefits, Social Security 152
"better angels of our nature" 146, 163
Bezos, Jeff 94
biases 141
Biden, Joe 27, 30, 81, 86, 89–91, 94,
    97, 98, 139
Big Government 68, 76, 89, 109, 134,
    137
big lies 24–33, 62, 143

Bill of Rights, U.S. Constitution 37,
    159
binary divisions see demography;
    us-v-them
Bismarck, Otto von 46
Black Lives Matter 17, 97, 113, 131,
    145
Black Panthers 100
Blacks 25, 38, 47, 93, 95, 123, 131, 146,
    160, 165
bonds, transgenerational see
    transgenerational
Boomer America 16
Born to Pay 77
Boskin, Michael J. 72, 75, 79
bottom-to-top grassroots pressure 113
Bowles, Erskine 80
boxes of life see three boxes of life
Brown, J. Douglas 52–3
Brownlee, W. Eliot 72
Brown Lives Matter see Hispanics
Bryce, James 122–3
budget, Federal 114, 126, 130
Buffett, Warren 131
bureaucracy 27, 50, 124
bureaucratic markers 95, 145
Bush, George H.W. 77–9, 115
Bush, George W. 30, 79–80, 115
business, small 92

California 123, 162
cancer 91, 128
caregiver syndrome 127
caregiving 124, 125, 127–8
Carlson, Ava Dungan 88–9
Carlson, Tucker 30, 100
Carter, Jimmy 65–8, 77
caste 95; see also race
Catholic see Roman Catholic
Cato Institute 80, 125
census 124; see also U.S. Bureau of
    Census
Center for Countering Digital Hate
    31
Central and South America 31
change agents 105–6
Chautauqua Institution 10, 124
checks and balances 37

child(ren) 10, 15–16, 22, 123, 130, 144;
  and poverty 94
chronic maladies and ailments 26, 56,
  91
Cincinnati 161
citizen(s) 36, 76, 140, 143, 163
citizenship 38, 113, 163
civic virtue 38, 40, 94, 122–3
civil rights 99–101; *see also* minorities
Civil War 38, 162–4
class 12, 175
Classes of 2019 and 2020 93
climate change 24, 28, 86, 131, 137
Clinton, Bill 30, 77, 79, 80
Cohen, Wilbur J. 43, 65, 67, 68, 71,
  110, 122
colleges and graduates 91, 145
Columbia Exposition 98
commentators and media 3–6
Committee on Economic Security
  (CES) 46–8, 126
common ground 133
common sense 39, 92
commonweal 137
communication gaps 5, 7, 9, 51, 83,
  144
Communist 31
community colleges 176
compact(s) 2, 29, 76, 138, 145
complacency 39
Compromise of 1820, and 1850 162
computers 91
Conable, Barber 72
Confederates and slavocracy 38
confidence 140
conflicts, personal and collective 143
confusion, Social Security 54
Congress, U.S. 28, 67, 69, 81, 121, 145
Congressional Quarterly 70
consensus building 77
conservative(s) and media 33, 49, 65,
  69, 70, 75–86, 125
Constitution, U.S., Preamble 164
contemporaries 14
context 107; *see also* history
contingencies 163
"Contract with America" 76
contributors, Social Security 24–6,
  84, 116

conversations 33, 111, 112, 115, 140,
  141
Coronavirus Aid, Relief and
  Economic Security (CARES) 94
corporations and corporate pensions
  46
cost-of-living-adjustments (COLAs)
  26, 58, 67, 70, 94
cotton as king 38
Council of Economic Advisors 79
counter-narrative, Social Security 37
COVID-19 12, 28, 31–2, 81, 88–91,
  100; *see also* pandemic
Cox, Archibald 57
coxswain metaphor 19, 36, 41, 62
crew teams metaphor 19–20, 62
crises 38, 115
Critical Race Theory 36
critical thinking 36, 41, 63, 109, 133,
  143
critics 28
Cronkite, Walter 100
Cruz, Ted 30, 80
Cuba(n) 122
culture wars 92
cybersecurity 101

Dale, Edwin L. Jr. 66, 68
deadlocks 97
death(s) 32, 90, 91
debts, student 125, 145–6
Declaration of Independence 159
de Crevecouer, Hector St. John 122,
  123
Delayed Retirement Credit 70
democracy 63, 66, 94, 134, 161
Democracy in America 122–3, 161
Democrats 28, 67, 69, 77, 78, 98, 143
demography 3–6, 25–7, 85, 95, 108
Denmark 46
de Nemours Dupont 10
dependency, old-age 57, 119, 120
depression 90
despair 35, 91
de Tocqueville, Alexis 38, 85, 122–3,
  161, 162
Dewey, John 39, 124, 164, 165
Dewson, Mary 51
diabetes 91

digital media 11
disabilities 56, 66–7, 91, 97, 128
Disability Insurance, Social Security
  56, 65–8, 81
discourse *see* conversations
discrimination *see* ageism; gender;
  nativism; racism; sexism
disengagement 17
disillusionment 63, 83, 141
disinformation 12, 91, 112, 141, 143
disparities, economic 88, 92, 93
distrust, government 84, 144; *see also*
  trust and distrust
diversity 29, 88, 94, 98, 107, 117
divorce 70, 107, 122, 141; *see also*
  women
doctoral students 91
Dole, Robert 69
domestic workers 49
doomsday scenarios 143
double-think 72
doubts, Social Security 2–5, 16, 26, 27,
  32, 61, 67, 76, 84, 126, 132–3
Douglass, Frederick 162
Dred Scott 38, 162
drugs and prescriptions 79, 91
dualistic thinking 5
dubiety 141
Duffy, Bobby 12
Dustbowl farmers 47
duties 138; *see also* responsibilities
Dylan, Bob 105

early retirement 93, 121
earnings record 70
economy 30, 85
education 10, 124
Einstein, Albert 30
Eisenhower, Dwight D. 30, 65
eldercare 127–8, 132
Elderhostel 124
elders 105, 137, 138, 145; *see also* older
  Americans
elites 78
Emerson, Ralph Waldo 9, 124
emotionality 12
Employee Retirement Income
  Security Act (ERISA) 66
employees 70, 93

employer pensions 90, 130
England 46
entitlements, Social Security 49, 85,
  156
environment 31
epidemics 89; *see also* pandemic
E Pluribus Unum 94
Epstein, Abraham 47
equity and adequacy 52–5
Erikson, Joan and Erik 133
ethnicity 14, 15
evidence *see* facts
exceptionalism, U.S. 36, 96, 137, 161
Exit, Voice, and Loyalty 75
expenses, medical 56–7, 90
experimentation 40–1
experts 60, 110, 112, 141

facts 112, 125, 141, 154
faith 138
fake news and half-truths 36, 78
Families USA 79
family and Social Security 138
farmers 47, 49
Fauci, Anthony 93
fear and hope 18–19, 137, 143–6
fears 12, 18–19, 35, 37–9, 84–5,
  88–101, 122, 137, 141, 143, 147
federal compact *see* compact
Federal Emergency Relief
  Administration (FERA) 47
federal healthcare *see* Medicaid,
  Medicare
Federal Insurance Contributions Act
  (FICA) 2, 7, 48, 62, 67, 74, 94, 116,
  120, 127, 143
Federal Railroad Retirement System
  126
federalism 38
Federalist Papers 40, 160
Federalists 37, 160
15th Amendment 38, 163
filibusters 97
Filopovic, Jill 16
First New Deal 30
fiscal threats, Social Security *see*
  doubts, Social Security
Fisher, Roger 70, 75
Flagg, James Montgomery 65

Flemming, Arthur 65, 67
flight 93 115
flip 112
floor of protection 54; *see also* income
Florida 32, 92
Floyd, George 95
Folklore of Capitalism 51
Ford, Gerald 66–7
Ford, Henry 36
forecasts 28
Founding Fathers 37–8, 159, 160
401k 26, 90
14th Amendment 31, 113
FOX News 30, 80
Franklin, Ben 10, 51
Freedman, Marc 14
Freud, Sigmund 105
Fugitive Slave Law 162
Fuller, Ida 43
funds *see* Social Security
future, ambiguous and uncertain 88, 110–11, 116, 134

Gallup polls and pollsters 2, 30, 50, 80, 101
Gang of Five 69, 70
Gates, Bill 93
gender discrimination and inequities 14, 49, 124
gender gap 26, 93, 131
"General Welfare" 38, 49
generation(s) 11–13, 25–7, 61–3, 107, 117, 142, 147, 161, 165
Generation X 114, 116
Gen(eration) Z 41, 106, 114
generational frameworks and styles 7, 12–13, 90–6, 115, 124, 130
Generations United 14
George, Henry 164
Georgia 120
German 10, 46, 128
The Gerontologist 70
gerontologists 60
Getting to Yes 70, 75
gig jobs 17, 26, 83, 93
Gilded Age 38
Gingrich, Newt 76–7
global terrorism 32, 89
Gold Rush(ers) 162

golden age, retirement years 26
government is the problem, Reagan 68
grandchildren 60, 116, 119
grandfather(s) 1, 36, 41, 107, 119, 137, 147
grassroots pressure and protests 5, 47, 95–6, 111–13, 134, 145
gray lobby 57, 69, 80, 83
Gray Panthers 14, 144
Great Depression 24, 44–6, 101, 116, 119, 123, 160
Great Society 56, 57, 89, 100
Greatest Generation 84
"greedy geezers" 122; *see also* ageism
Green New Deal 113
Greenspan, Alan 69
Gross Domestic Product 114
Gross National Product 126, 130
guideposts 35
gun control and violence 86, 97, 101, 130

Halbertal, Moshe 12
Harper's Magazine 89
Hayes, Rutherford B. 163
hazards 52, 128
healthcare, public and professionals 89; *see also* abortion
Heaney, Seamus 143
Heinz III, H. John 70, 121
Heritage Foundation 79–80
high income *see* affluence and workers
high school students 124
higher learning 124
Hirschman, Albert O. 75
Hispanics 10, 97, 125, 129
historians 36
historical context 62, 75–6, 115, 117, 137, 165
history 33, 73, 140, 158–65; and matters 35–41
History of Standard Oil Company 164
homeless persons 91
Hoover, Herbert 30
hope(s) 12, 18–19, 35, 37–9, 41, 83, 88, 101, 137, 141, 143, 147
hope and fear 138; *see also* fears and hopes

hospitals and hospitalization 26, 32, 56–7, 82, 83, 90, 92
House of Representatives, U.S. 69, 121; *see also* Congress
households 131
humility 35–41
Hungary 31
hypertension 91

idea brokers 19, 36, 41, 47, 66, 83, 141, 143; *see also* experts
identity politics 78
ignorance of history and Social Security 12, 143
imagination 12, 61
immigrants 10, 30, 85, 101, 121, 144
In the Fullness of Time 88
income 51, 88, 123; and floors 115–16, 123, 132, 139, 145
incremental politics 55, 68, 72, 83, 108, 121, 126, 161
India 92
Indian affairs *see* Native Americans
Individual Account Plan 79
Individual Retirement Accounts (IRAs) 26, 66, 129, 131
individual rights 53; *see also* rights
individual transformations 109–13
individualism 38, 46, 52, 161–2
inequality, economic 25–6, 32, 83, 93, 128
infants and toddlers 90
information 77
insecurity 119
insiders 56
institution(s), democratic 101, 139, 142, 143, 163
intensive care units (ICUs) 92
interest rates 67
intergenerational conflicts 4–6, 14–16, 66, 71, 91, 114, 122, 125, 132
international social-insurance programs 46, 155
interpretations 36–7, 137–47
intra-generational 14–16, 83
"in usufruct" 160, 161
Iraq 30, 101, 144
Irving, Washington 139
Italy 92

Jackson, Michael 159
Jacksonian America 38, 161–2
James, William 39, 164, 165
January 6, 2021 insurrection 31
Japan 30
Jews 95
Jim Crow laws 38, 95
job(s) and retraining 124
joblessness *see* unemployment
Johnson, Lyndon Baines (LBJ) 30, 56–7, 72, 85
Johnson, Malcolm 17
journalism and journalists 29, 36, 56, 78, 82, 88, 125
Jung, Karl 105
The Jungle 164
justice 86, 97, 142–3, 146

Kansas 120, 162
Kansas-Nebraska Act 38
Kendi, Ibram 115
Kennedy, John F. 30
Kennedy, Robert F. 31
Kennedy, Robert F., Jr. 71
keywords 7, 106
King, Rev. Dr. Martin Luther, Jr. 95, 100, 139–40
Kingson, Eric 70, 123
Kloppenberg, James T. 40
knowledge 144
Knowles, Martin 124
Korean War 162
Kreps, Juanita M. 132
Kuhn, Maggie 14, 144
Ku Klux Klan (KKK) 38, 95, 123, 163

LaFollette, Robert 164
Landon, Alf 40, 49, 125, 154
lawmaker(s) 36, 141
Larson, John 81, 139
Latin Americas 123
LBJ *see* Johnson, Lyndon Baines
legacy 12, 32–3, 35, 41, 45, 76, 105, 107, 110
leisure 124
Letters to an American Farmer 122
LGBTQ rights 91, 100
liberal consensus attacked 66, 67, 69, 76, 77, 79

Liberty figure 65
Library Company of Philadelphia
    10
lies *see* big lies
life expectancies 26
life experiences 62, 138
Light, Paul 72–3, 75
Limbaugh, Rush 30
Lincoln, Abraham 38, 146, 162
Lippmann, Walter 29
literacy 10–11
loneliness 90
longevity dividend 21
Longevity Revolution 114
Longman, Phillip 77
long-term care 25
longitudinal historical comparisons
    108–9
Looking Backward 29
Looking Forward 28–9
low-income workers 10, 153
lyceum 10

McCarthyism 30
McCartney, Paul 114
McConnell, Mitch 18, 27, 30, 80, 81,
    139
McCormack, John 120
McGovern, George 119
McKinley, William 35
Madison, James 160, 161
Maddow, Rachel 100
maids 49
Maintain Benefits Plan 79
Make America Great Again (MAGA)
    30
Malcolm X 95
Manchin, Joe 81
Mannheim, Karl 13–15
market(s) 78, 133
masks 106
mayors 164
Meacham, Jon 35–6
meaning-filled legacy 9–10
means tests 150
measured hope 41, 44, 62; *see also*
    hopes
media 3–6, 29, 78, 141
Medicaid 25, 57, 121, 127

medical catastrophes 129
Medicare 25, 56–7, 80, 114, 121, 125,
    138
Medicare Catastrophic Coverage Act
    (MCCA) 79
Medicare Prescription Drug
    Improvement Act 79
melting pot 122–3
Mencken, H. L. 37
mental-health crisis 91
mentors 43, 65, 76
Merriam, Ida 121
Mexico and Mexican War 95, 162
Mezirow, Jack 124
Michigan, The University of 30
micro-macro flip 112
middle-aged Americans 4–5
middle-class Social Security
    contributors 38, 44, 92, 93, 128
Middle East 144
mill owners 38
Millennials 9–20, 82, 84, 89, 100, 106,
    114–16, 122, 130, 131, 138, 143,
    144
minorities 85, 95; *see also* African
    Americans; Blacks; Hispanics;
    Native Americans
misconceptions 11–13, 27, 93
misinformation 24–33, 62
Missouri Compromise 38
mobilizations 35, 43, 62, 109. 133, 134,
    141
models 140; and trans-theoretical
    110–11
Montaigne, Michel de 18
"moral arc of justice" 140–3, 146
More Security for Old Age 50
Morgenthau, Henry 126
mortgages 92
mothers 49
Moynihan, Daniel Patrick 69
mulatto(s) 95
multiculturalism 138, 145
multiracial 139, 145
municipal 164
Muslims 95
mutual responsibility *see*
    responsibilities
Myers, Robert J. 69, 70, 72

Myrdal, Gunnar 122–3
myths 24–33, 86

narrative line 107–8
Nation of Islam 31
National Academy of Social Insurance
    (NASI) 108–9, 155, 163
National Assessment of Educational
    Progress 158
National Center for Educational
    Statistics 124
National Commission on Fiscal
    Responsibility and Reform 80
National Commission on Social
    Security Reform (NCSSR) 68–72,
    75, 76, 111, 123, 127, 141
National Commission to Preserve
    Social Security and Medicare 79
National Industrial Act 44
National Journal 70
 National Planning Board 55
National Republican Senatorial
    Committee 139
nationalism and exceptionalism 161
Native Americans 113, 161, 165
nativism 123
Nazi(s) and concentration camps 31,
    158–9
negotiations 33, 40–1, 111, 119–34
neo-conservatives 30
Neuthaler, Paul 43
New Deal 29, 40, 44–6, 71, 83, 89,
    120, 124, 158
New Nationalism 39
The New Republic 37, 39
The New York Times 66, 70
Newton, Huey 100
New York City 65
New Zealand 46
9/11 27, 30, 101, 115
1983 Social Security amendments
    132; *see also* Social Security 1983
    amendments
1950s Social Security amendments 55
1972 Social Security amendment 58
1960s 11, 114; and 2020s 99–101, 106,
    108–9
1968 138, 139
Nixon, Richard M. 57–8

nonviolent 113
"normal" retirement age 48, 120, 121
"normalcy" 39, 97–8
normative foundations, Social Security
    46–51
norms 137, 142
North Carolina 126
North Korea 31, 122
notch babies 67
nuclear holocaust 89
nurses and nursing 92
nursing homes 91

Obama, Barack 18, 40, 80
Obamacare 30, 81
obstacles 29, 112
Office of Management and Budget 68
Ok, Boomer 16
old-age assistance and states 49–50;
    see also Medicaid; old-age poverty
old-age attitudes and images 46
Old Age in the New Land 43
old-age poverty 4, 47; *see also*
    dependency, old-age
Old Age Reserve Account 120
Old-Age, Survivors, Disability and
    Health Insurance (OASDHI) 25;
    see also Social Security
older Americans 4, 25, 26, 56–7, 131,
    132, 146
Older Americans Act 57
O'Neill, Tip 68–9, 141
opinions 11–13, 57
opportunities 137
oppositional politics 98
optimism and realism 18
options, Social Security reforms 33, 41
Origins of Totalitarianism 71
Orwell, George 28
"other persons" *see* minorities

Palm Sunday sermon, MLK 139–40
pandemic 81, 88–101, 132, 138, 143
paradigm 138
parents 10, 84, 105
Parker, Theodore 140
Parkinson's disease 128
partisan obstacles and showcasing 12,
    32, 108–9

past, guidepost 30–2; and Social Security 62; *see also* historical context
Patient Protection and Affordable Care Act (ACA) 80; *see also* Obamacare
patriotism vs parochialism 145
Pavlov, Ivan 105
pay 132
pay-as-you-go and FICA 26, 143
peers 16
Peirce, Charles Sanders 39, 160
Pell grants 146
Pelosi, Nancy 27
pensions 125, 135; and state 131–2
peonage 38
Pepper, Claude 69
Perkins, Frances 44, 46–8, 126
Personal Security Act Plan 79
Peru 92
Pew polls 30
Pierce, Franklin 49
Philadelphia 10, 62, 123
Planned Parenthood 113
plans borrowing, future retirement 160
Plessy v. Ferguson 165
pluralism *see* diversity; *E Pluribus Unum*
pogo stick 26
polarization 61, 78, 83, 97
Polarization Lab 11
policy architects 127, 140; *see also* idea brokers
Policy Institute, London 12
policymakers' options 41, 78
political economy 4, 88–101
political identities 78, 94
polls 14, 30, 50, 67, 78, 80, 81, 89, 94, 98
Ponzi scheme 26
population aging 88
post offices 57
poverty 14–15, 56, 57, 77, 92, 129, 143
pragmatism 35–41, 107, 117, 138, 143, 165
Preamble, U.S. Constitution 37
prejudice(s) *see* ageism; minorities; nativism; racism; sexism
prescriptions 79, 91
"present-mindedness" 114

Presidents, U.S. as centrists 28
price(s) 92
priorities, Social Security 140
private savings 129
privatization, Social Security 33, 79–80, 163
problem 109, 140, 162
"The Problem of Generations" 13–15
processional nature of generational succession 17
Progress and Poverty 164
progressives 33, 71
Progressive era 38, 44, 164–5
propaganda 31
property 37, 95
Protestant 39, 123
protesters 96; *see also* mobilizations; multiculturalism; multiracial
public health 95
public intellectuals 36
public opinion 73
public pensions 131–2
public schools 90, 91
public trust 56, 67, 77
Pure Food and Drug Act 164
Putin, Vladimir 90, 92

Quaker City 36, 91

race 10, 14, 15
race-based health disparities and longevity gaps 93, 95, 101, 124
racism 32, 49, 56, 86, 95–6, 88–101, 123, 137, 144, 161
Radical Republicans 34, 162–3
radicals 112
RAND 133
rationality 12
Reagan, Ronald 65, 68–71, 73, 77, 79, 115, 141
recessions 51, 80, 92, 101
Reconstruction 163
Redbook 89
reforms, no major Social Security 9, 27, 78, 88–101, 150–1
Relief, Recovery, and Reform 46, 120
Republic 142
Republicans 17, 28, 58, 65, 69, 77, 78, 97–8, 143

resilience 138
resolutions 112
"responsibilities" 65, 121, 138, 143
restaurants 92
retirement, "normal age," overlapping
    retirement systems 33, 93, 125, 129,
    141
Revolutionary era 159–61
right-wing speakers and dogma 30, 77
"rights" 45, 57, 121, 138, 143
Rip Van Winkle 139, 140
"risks" 12, 45, 59, 119, 121, 122, 143
"risks," "rights," and "responsibilities"
    as keywords 43–58, 81–2, 111, 113,
    142
Robber Barons 39
Robinson, Marilynne 144
Roe v. Wade 113
Roman Catholic 39
Roosevelt, Eleanor 131
Roosevelt, Franklin Delano (FDR)
    28–9, 40, 44–56, 72, 76, 81, 89, 119,
    123, 125, 127, 145, 158, 161
Roosevelt, James 79
Roosevelt, Theodore 35, 41n1, 46, 164
Rossant, Murray J. 72
Rubinow, I. M. 47
Russia 31, 92

Safeguarding Social Security for Future
    Generations: Leaving a Legacy in an
    Aging Society 1–5, 32–3, 156–7; and
    book take-aways 138–47
St. Louis Post-Dispatch 89
safety net 156
Samuelson, Paul A. 57
Samuelson, Robert J. 125
Sanders, Bernie 98, 139
Save Our Security 65, 67
savings 10, 131
schools 91, 95
Schopenhauer, Arthur 32
Schumer, Chuck 81
Schuylkill River 62
Seale, Bobby 100
2d amendment 97, 144
Second Bill of Rights 55
second civil war 3
Second New Deal 44

Secretaries, U.S., of Agriculture and
    Treasury 47
"secula seculorum" 159
SECURE (Setting Every Community
    Up for Retirement Enhancement
    Act) 90
"security of citizen and family" 55,
    123
self-employed 121
self interest(s) 129, 137, 160, 161
self-reliance and self-awareness 117,
    161
self transformation 107–13
semi-retirement 17
Senate, U.S. 68, 97
senior citizen(s) 79; see also older
    Americans
sexism 32, 105, 144, 161–2
sexual health 14, 97
Shame of the City 164
Shanksville, Pennsylvania 115
Simpson, Alan 80
Sinclair, Upton 47, 164
Sioux and Lakota see Native
    Americans
Skinner, B. F. 105
slaves and slaveholders 10, 38, 95, 159,
    160, 162
slums 39
Small World, Long Gone 89
social compact 2–5
social insurance 46, 47, 72, 83, 122,
    128, 141, 150–2
Social Insurance 164
social media see media
social movements 112–14
social policy 132
social reformers 39
social scientists 60
Social Security Administration (SSA)
    24, 51, 52, 66, 67, 82, 85, 116, 146,
    151–2
Social Security advisory councils 52, 79
Social Security aims, assessments, and
    myths 1–5, 7, 24–33, 43–58, 78, 80,
    101, 107, 114, 121, 138, 150–7
Social Security amendments 9, 55, 56,
    58, 66–71, 75, 76, 79, 81, 119–21,
    141

Social Security Board 51
Social Security Bulletin 70
Social Security cards 51
Social Security different other U.S.
    and international programs 52, 62,
    66–73, 88–101, 105–6, 116, 150–2,
    155
Social Security's distinctive features
    110, 121, 129, 155–6
Social Security keywords 128, 154;
    see also COLAs; FICA; OASDHI;
    Old Age Survivors Trust Fund;
    primary insurance account;
    responsibilities; risks; rights;
    solidarity; stewardship; sustainability
Social Security 1983 amendments
    65–73
Social Security 1935 Act 7, 48–51,
    120, 121
Social Security operations 24, 82, 94,
    118, 126, 152–5
Social Security options 28, 33, 62–3;
    see also policymakers' options
Social Security support 108–9, 132
Social Security Trustees reports 2, 52,
    68, 94, 126, 129, 133
Social Security 2100 81
Social Security: Visions and Revisions
    70–2, 82, 111
Social Security vulnerabilities and
    fears 15–17, 24, 26–7, 60, 66–73, 77,
    78, 80, 83, 85–8, 125, 132
Social Security Works 80, 123
social services 60
social structures 124
societal aging *see* aging societies
societal mores 32, 133, 137
sociologists 60
"solidarity" 116, 117, 123–5, 128, 142,
    144
"solidarity; sustainability, and
    stewardship" keywords 113–17,
    119–34, 142
soul craft 141–3
"soul of America" 86
South Carolina 120
South Dakota 92
Southern Christian Leadership
    Council (SCLC) 100

Southern redemption 40
Soviet Union 92
Spanish American War 162
Spanish-speaking 25, 92, 93
spouse 127
stagflation 115
stakeholders, Social Security 25–7,
    40–1, 76, 78, 82, 98, 101, 110, 113,
    124, 139, 142, 144, 147
standards of living 132
Statecraft as Soulcraft 141–2
state legislatures 95, 96
statisticians 47
Steffans, Lincoln 164
stereotypes 12–13, 17
stewardship 116, 117, 128–33, 143
Stiglitz, Joseph 92
stock market 92
storyline and stories 35–6
strokes 91
student debts 26
Student Nonviolent Coordinating
    Committee 112
Supplemental Security Income 81,
    128
Supreme Court 30, 38, 51, 78, 90
The Survey 47
survey data 39
sustainability, Social Security 116, 117,
    126–8, 137, 139, 142
Sweden 128
Symbols of Government 57

Taft, William H. 40, 164
take-aways, this book 137–47
Tarbell, Ida 164
Tarfon, Rabbi 138
taxes, Social Security 70, 153–4
teachers and teaching assistants 90, 91,
    159
Teamsters Convention 54
technical fixes, Social Security 18
Tennessee 120
Tennessee Valley Authority (TVA) 44
tensions 101, 137
Texas 25, 30, 32, 92, 97
third rail, Social Security 28, 78–81,
    133
13th amendment, 38, 163

Thomas, Clarence 27
Thrasymachus 142
3 boxes of life 124–5
three-legged stool, retirement income 26, 131–3
Till, Emmett 95
Titles 1935 Social Security Act 48–9, 51
Too Many Promises 72
top-to-bottom influences and miscommunication 31, 153
trade union pensions 46
transformation(s) 107, 109–13, 114
transgenerational bonds and conversations 3–6, 11, 14–17, 35, 88, 101, 106, 109, 111, 122, 141, 145, 165; and intergenerational wounds and intra-generational fights 14–17
Truman, Harry S 30, 56
Trump, Donald J. 18, 27, 30–1, 80–1, 90, 91, 94, 97, 98
trust and distrust 35, 106, 108–9, 111
tuitions and debts 83
Tulsa massacre 95
Turkey 31, 92
Turner, Frederick Jackson 98–9, 101
Twentieth Century Fund 50, 71, 72, 75, 79
2020s and 1960s compared 108–9
2000 29, 121

Ukraine 28, 81, 90
ultra-rich 93
Ullman, Al 68
uncertainties 123, 140
unemployment 46, 49, 67, 83, 92, 94
unions 46, 56, 69, 79
United Kingdom 30, 92, 128
U.S. Attorney General 87
U.S. Bill of Rights 160
U.S. Bureau of the Census 26, 95
U.S. cabinet secretaries 43, 65, 126, 145
U.S. citizenship 36, 113
U.S. history 1–5, 7, 30–2, 158–65
U.S. House Ways and Means committee 126
U.S. population 91
U.S. Postal Service 86, 91, 145

U.S. Treasury notes 85
unity 85, 115, 138
unmasked COVID 92
unrest, societal 112
unskilled laborers 47
urban violence 28
urbanization 98
Ury, William 70, 75
us-v-them 123, 143

vaccine, COVID 31–2, 89, 91, 145
values 63, 89, 113, 124, 141, 163
veterans 30, 81, 91
vicissitudes *see* Great Depression; recessions
Vietnam War 30, 43, 85, 91, 105, 114, 144
violence 101, 123, 131
Virginia 120
vital center 130
vocational education 124
voluntary associations 38, 161
voters 66

wage earners *see* workers
wages 67
Wall Street Journal 70
Walmart 127
War on Poverty 52
warming *see* climate change
Warren, Elizabeth 81, 98, 139
Washington Post 2, 70
Watergate 30, 101
Ways and Means committee, U.S. House 126
"We the People" 37, 125
wealth 123, 160
welfare system 150
white-collar employees 93
White House 28, 30, 67, 78
White House Conference on Aging 57
whites 10, 16, 38, 77, 95, 161
Will, George 68, 100, 141–2
Wilson, Woodrow 40, 164
"Wisconsin idea" 122, 164
Witte, Edwin 47
wives 49
women 4–5, 10, 37, 40, 70, 85, 90, 91, 97, 121, 123, 127, 128, 149, 160

worker satisfaction 124, 125, 138
workers, low income and young 4–5, 160
workplace 52, 56, 70
The World as Will and Representation 32
World War I 30, 44, 122
World War II 55, 77, 89, 160, 162
worship 139
Wyden, Ron 81

young citizens 16, 36, 60, 76, 82, 84, 89, 91, 93, 100, 106, 114, 130, 142, 144
young Republic 3
younger workers 13
youthful protests 130–2

Zangwill, Israel 122–3
Zoom 93
Zoomers 16, 138